Mentalligence

A New Psychology of Thinking

W9-CEK-192

Learn What It Takes to Be More Agile, Mindful, and Connected in Today's World

KRISTEN LEE, EdD, LICSW

Health Communications, Inc.
Deerfield Beach, Florida

www.hcibooks.com

This is a work of nonfiction that accurately conveys a multiyear teaching, learning, and qualitative research endeavor. In order to protect the privacy of those featured, certain names and identifying traits have been reconfigured and/or compressed to protect privacy, without compromising the integrity of the narrative presented.

This book is not intended to be a substitute for professional consultation, therapy, or medical advice. Neither the author nor the publisher shall be held responsible or liable for any loss or damage arising from any recommendations provided in this book.

Library of Congress Cataloging-in-Publication Data
is available through the Library of Congress

ISBN-13: 978-07573-2059-0 (Paperback)
ISBN-10: 07573-2059-7 (Paperback)
ISBN-13: 978-07573-2057-6 (ePub)
ISBN-10: 07573-2059-7 (ePub)

HCI, its logos, and marks are trademarks of Health Communications, Inc.

Publisher: Health Communications, Inc.
3201 S.W. 15th Street
Deerfield Beach, FL 33442–8190

Cover design by Jim Pollard
Interior design and formatting by Lawna Patterson Oldfield
Signature design by Alexa Nguyen
Author photo by Alexandria Mauck

To my students, of course—
for teaching me more than I could ever teach you.

For Anna Hrvatin—
for modeling the good life.

We are not
going in circles,
we are going upwards.
The path is a spiral;
we have already climbed
many steps.

—Herman Hesse

CONTENTS

mentalligence

[men-tell-a-jence]

1. A new psychology of thinking model that teaches ways to launch UPward spirals through a process of unlearning and pivoting away from social conditioning and indoctrination that damage human progress.

2. A collection of reflective, mindful, universal, and imagineering lenses to overcome blind spots and primitive instincts that lead to ignorance, mindlessness, insularity, and stagnation.

Terry is the ultimate embodiment of mentalligence—always such an agile and mindful thinker who brings social impact and can connect with anyone, anywhere.

STUCK
An Introduction

*I thought how unpleasant it is to be
locked out; and I thought how it is worse,
perhaps, to be locked in.*

—Virginia Woolf

It was 10:10 a.m. and I was in full sprint mode, running down Boylston Street, the historic site of the Boston Marathon finish.

Not that it was official race day—just my own variation: à la pencil skirt, sneakers, beat-up tote bag brimming with long to-do lists, a now-too-heavy laptop I'd wished I'd left back at the office, and remnants of half-eaten Scooby snacks for those *just-in-case* but *all-the-time* moments when there wasn't time to stop for a proper meal.

I managed to blend in with my fellow harried travelers even as I broke into a massive sweat, while internally defaulting to a slew of self-criticisms for finding myself in yet another time pickle. My plan had been to arrive a little early. Today was important.

Between my poor sense of direction and chronic propensity to pack too much in, here I was on the verge of missing my first appointment and sending my system into complete anxiety overdrive once again. Plus, I had a meeting back at work at the top of the hour and hadn't told anyone I had left or where I was going.

Heart pounding, I finally made it to the office of Lyla, my new therapist.

"So, you're here because you want to manage the pressures of your new job, right?"

Right on cue, I was totally out of breath.

Even with all the efficiency and productivity strategies I'd cobbled together, the eighty-hour workweek was putting me on the brink of adrenal overload.

I presented the sanitized story, for starters: the polished, carefully edited version to give her context so that she wouldn't think I was a total mess. The bullet points spilled out: *Age thirty-eight. Fast growth trajectory. Seasoned human behavior expert. New faculty position. Two teenagers. Book about to be released. Chronically sick mom. Crazy travel schedule. My family, students, colleagues, and patients show lots of affinity. I love them, too. I handle it all pretty well . . . most days.*

I wanted her to see my best side: that I was relatively smart and capable, that I had it together. Not that I was a lot like Dory from *Finding Nemo*—forgetting everything else I'd previously learned about not overloading my plate.

I downplayed my Dory moments and true anxiety levels. I was simply a seasoned behavioral health clinician practicing what I preach. My harried arrival into her therapy office signaled a proactive approach. Everyone should take advantage of the free EAP sessions, after all. I left out the footnotes about the constant knots in my stomach, middle-of-the-night panic jolts, endless time spent ruminating over everything, and the alienation and loneliness I often felt, even within my closest relationships.

Lyla didn't appear convinced that my workaholic ways were just for the love of the sport, or just because I'm from Boston.

"You seem to take a lot of pride in your work and family. But it seems you're stuck in constant overdrive. . . ."

It was only eleven minutes into the session.

"It sounds to me like you're a bit of a perfectionist."

I instinctively nodded and smiled politely, as only a true seasoned perfectionist can.

Inside, I fumed. *Did she miss how conscientious I am? How challenging working in a university was? How much my family and patients needed me? Isn't my session time up? Maybe this therapy thing was a huge mistake. I* need *some peanut butter cheesecake and wine,* now! My impulse was to run, so I scrambled for clever rationalizations.

Luckily, she didn't budge. She masterfully connected the dots between my gluttony for work and the extreme performance obsession embedded in my fabric. She saw I was working myself to the bone. My perpetual yes was costing me a lot. My definitions of working hard and worthiness had collided.

The anxiety I was marinating in, she felt, was evidence of me living in extreme overcompensation mode to please everyone. She saw how much I relished my identity as someone who does it all, in true heroic fashion. *Great, I'm a superhero wannabe.* Lyla knew that the ridiculous messages lambasting us at every turn were dumping gasoline on my fire.

You've got to have the Kardashian ass. Be a goal-setting machine. Start your own nonprofit by the time you're twelve. Answer every ding within milliseconds. Parent like Jolie, joke like Schumer, shake like Shakira. Don't let anyone see you sweat—unless it's to show off the insanely hard hot yoga class you managed to sneak in between all the deadlines, meetings, and time spent triaging the latest disaster.

There's even pressure to be Zen. Mindfulness has become the new kale. We're supposed to be fully present every minute of our day—from the boardroom to the bedroom, even when our brains have been violently sucked into the vortex of perpetual chaos. *We're expected to meditate like the Buddha, eat our five almonds a day, swoop down, save the day, land on our feet like ninjas, have a good hair day, and pretend it's all easy and normal, as if there are such things.*

Clearly, this wasn't working for me. My pursuit of the good life wasn't turning out so well. Like a doctor who smokes, my hypocrisy was incredibly difficult for me to admit. Here I was, the go-to person at work and home—twenty-two years under my belt in behavioral sciences, hooked into being puppeteered to act perfect, while behind the curtain I was crumbling. The words to one of my favorite Alanis Morissette songs flooded my mind:

Isn't it ironic?
Don't you think?
A little too ironic.
Yeah, I really do think. . . .

I don't blame Lyla for thinking I was a bit of a mess. My attempts
to disguise my disarray were no match for her clinical eye. My *frenetic,
always-in-my-head life* was not without cost. She was right. I had some
changing to do. And she reminded me this didn't mean peanut butter
cheesecake and wine interventions, slugging down more power smoothies,
or finding ways to barrel through my list more efficiently. I swore at myself
on the way out of her office. She must have heard me; she smiled and gave
me the proverbial therapist head nod. We exchanged knowing looks. This
was going to be a lot of work.

I would need to start thinking and behaving differently. I had fallen for
the delusions of our culture, telling me to be pretty, bootstrap, suck it up,
and calmly carry on so that I could achieve "success" in this world. If I
kept on making the textbook mistake of confusing *doing* with *being*, I was
destined for even more trouble.

This wasn't new behavior for me. And it was more than the stereotypi-
cal plight of being an overworked high achiever that was pinning me down.
My strict religious-brownie-points upbringing had trained me to hustle for
acceptance.

For a while, I stewed in resentment at the church, bitterly shutting
down my spiritual side. In many ways science rescued me, but my new
obsession with measurability wasn't bringing relief. I was living entirely in
my head, disassociating from my whole self. I didn't know who I was, what
I believed, or how to make the million-mile march from my brain to my
heart. I craved certainty, not the messy and uncomfortable state in which
I found myself. Something was missing.

The same mind that had gotten me stuck was (hopefully) the same one
that could set me free. I started to realize that indoctrination wasn't limited
to religion. It was everywhere: work, school, and society. It was time to rip
up the script, breathe deep, and reclaim a healthy definition of success

that wasn't compartmentalizing my mind, body, and soul. I needed a new organizing framework that allowed more flexibility and moral grounding—one that lets *science + emotion + spiritual* to fuse—not to bicker with each other on who's superior or, worse, dismiss the other's credibility and value.

When I arrived back at my desk, a mound of data greeted me from questions I'd asked my high-performing graduate students, gathered over years of teaching. Here in front of me were the stories of hundreds of incredible people, with their own ups and downs. As graduate students of all ages, they were the classic heady, overachieving, cape-always-on types who wanted to bring impact, and sometimes got a little stuck hustling for brownie points. They were weary, too.

> **Rethinking what you've been taught is the greatest gift you can give to yourself.**

I wanted to know what was happening behind the scenes for them. Were they reeling from the forms of indoctrination they underwent? What types of strategies were they drawing upon to avoid compartmentalizing? What helped them find their way, without losing their way?

The analysis seemed daunting, but just a few minutes in, I couldn't put it down. I could see they also were struggling with disintegration. They had their own wounds from being prescribed a formula for life that just didn't serve them well. But they'd also found ways to wriggle their way out of it. Soon, the discoveries would help me unlock important truths. I'd been given a major gift, as I began to realize my students were just as much my teachers as I was theirs.

A few months later, I had broken new ground and developed a framework that allows us to build mental agility, so that we can work to not only accelerate progress for ourselves but for all—the real good life that we all want.

The mentalligence (mental intelligence) model—born out of my grounded theory research, the latest behavioral science, and all my years as a clinician, educator, and parent—isn't a magic wand or linear process. It has limits, too. We should be skeptical of any advice that makes big promises or overgeneralizes life's complexity to a simple 1-2-3 solution. There's no quick-fix, one-size-fits-all formula to crack life's code.

But Mentalligence is an inclusive framework, grounded in new neuro-science, that consciously integrates the many sides of human essence while embodying our global context. Mentalligence guides us to become agile thinkers who:

- Rethink and unlearn behaviors that leave us stuck.
- Refuse to be held hostage by prescriptive, socially indoctrinated norms and rules.
- Prioritize human progress and collective success.
- Open the mind, integrate, and spiral upward toward social impact.

Or, put Twitter style: Rethink. Unlearn. Sleepwalking through life is dangerous. #SpiralUP #Agility #MI #Learn4eva #Consciousness #Onlywe #GoodLife.

After months of immersion in the data, and all the moments of pains-taking learning, unlearning, and relearning, I couldn't wait to share my new mentalligence model with Lyla, my students across the world, and especially now with you.

Dr. Kris

Boston, Massachusetts
February 6, 2018

PART I

The Waking UP Sessions

Find Your Reflective Lens

Rethink the 5 Forms of Indoctrination That Lead to Unconsciousness:

→ From Fake It 'til You Make It to Agile Thinking

→ From Me, Myself, and I to Do-It-Together Thinking

→ From Performance to Meta-Awareness Thinking

→ From Hiding to Healing Thinking

→ From False Truth to Evidence-Based Thinking

The Waking UP Sessions will help you unlearn five forms of indoctrination that lead to unconscious behavior. You will pivot to become more expansive in your thinking, stay woke, and learn how to develop five thinking practices to find and strengthen your reflective lens. The sessions will help you stay alert, not lulled to sleep by the lies of our culture. They help combat inauthenticity, insecurity, unhealthy behaviors, avoidance, and wrong conclusions. This is our new psychology of thinking: becoming an agile twenty-first-century citizen. *Sounds good right about now, doesn't it?*

agility

noun | [e'jilide]

1. The power of moving quickly and easily; nimbleness.
2. The ability to think and adapt; intellectual acuity.

Hayden works hard to be the embodiment of agility—always on toes and ready to make needed shifts to avoid being rigid or being subject to society's many forms of indoctrination.

indoctrination

noun | [in͵däktrə'nāSHən]

1. The process of teaching (someone) to fully accept the ideas, opinions, and beliefs of a particular group and not consider those of other persuasions.
2. To imbue with a usually partisan or sectarian opinion, point of view, or principle.

Camelia works hard to make sure students don't accept an entire set of beliefs uncritically, without a second blink.

The Physics of Mental Intelligence

Objective:
Unlearn fake-it-'til-you-make-it indoctrination
that breeds inauthenticity.
Pivot toward agility.

*The quality of your life depends on
the quality of your thinking.*

—Richard Paul and Linda Elder

W hen you're a human behavior analyst, you're like a people watcher on steroids. In the twenty-two years I've been doing this work, I've seen it all. Human beings act in mysterious and interesting ways. There's never a shortage of material—from toxic to bizarre—proving that fact is, indeed, often stranger than fiction.

You have your own material, too. Personality quirks. Family drama. Relationships. Hard-to-shake habits. Emotional baggage. Unexpected twists. The seasons of life. Plus, someone at work is bound to be simultaneously entertaining and annoying. And if you're stuck in a cube, *Fuggedaboudit.*

When first asked to teach a new graduate class to help students make their way through all of this, I was excited. Then it started to smell bad. The name hit a nerve—Personal Branding. *Am I going to have the students develop their very own creepy all-about-me sales pitch so that they can climb the ladder? Not into that. No thanks.*

My colleague Barry convinced me otherwise. He gave me license to approach it creatively—code for he was too busy to contribute. I immediately interjected the word *authentic* into the title. In a culture that primps and primes us to show up as airbrushed, caricatured versions of ourselves, authentic was becoming elusive. I wanted my students to stop drooling over society's narrow prescriptions for success and start living more agilely, mindfully, and purposively.

Before the teaching assignment, I'd been thinking about authenticity for a long time. As a therapist, I've seen a lot of airbrushing tendencies. We expend a lot of time and energy covering up because the worry about what people think is so ingrained in us. *No, no, no. I'm not a hot mess. Everything's fine, really.* This can only take us so far.

My patients, students, and colleagues were telling me how hard *authentic* was. They were afraid to really be themselves. Ditto for friends and family. Everywhere—at work, home, church—it was easier to fake it 'til you made it.

As great as is the desire to be yourself, the pressures to conform and perform are also intense. Even play-by-play social media displays reveal just how paradoxical this situation is. We put it all out there, while saying little beyond the superficial. *Did we really need to know you just got flipped off on your way to the market, or that you just found your very best selfie angle?*

Watch Out for the ASSIE Trap

If we're not careful, authenticity becomes rhetoric. It's a popular buzzword, permeating our work and home conversations: authentic leadership, authentic parenting, authentic living. Its overuse can make it start to feel trite and inauthentic in its own way.

One of the biggest roadblocks to authenticity is rigidity about who we think we're supposed to be. I refer to this trap as Asinine Societal and

Self-Imposed Expectations (ASSIEs). The term may not seem very scientific, but it captures the consistent theme running through my research, teaching, clinical work, and own self-flagellating moments.

We're afraid to cry uncle and say what everyone else is thinking. Like characters in the Andersen tale, we're caught in a culture of emperors, salivating for success and scrambling for status, to the point we're not willing to admit there's a foolish naked guy in the room.

Being real is the power skill of the century, but we're taught to be otherwise in the places that should hold it most sacred: our families, schools, workplaces, communities, houses of worship, and governments.

Our legacy can be so much more. In the grand scheme of the universe, we won't be remembered by how fast we responded to emails or how many letters we have after our names. Most people aren't going to sit at our funeral and carry on about the length of our resume, the car we drove, or how well we took a photo.

ASSIEs metastasize into an airbrushed you, and although kinda cute, the real you is waaaay better. When our emperors go unchallenged, we're held hostage, forgoing the mental agility to rethink what we've first been sold and break free.

Like millions of people, we simultaneously buy into and resent the ideas of our culture. Instead of calling the absurdity out on the carpet, we force a smile and nod politely because we're afraid people will shun us if we go against the grain. We cover up, rehearse, and isolate. We get so caught up in our own agendas that we miss chances to bring our full presence and impact to our roles and relationships. It's a *nice-knowin'-ya* form of authenticity.

A lot of books teach ways to neatly resolve the whole authenticity dilemma. Most of them present a prescriptive path with a certain number of easy steps based on a set-in-stone organizing framework that's supposed to help you instantly find deep purpose and work your magic. I've read dozens of such books,

"I no longer look for the good in people. I search for the real . . . because while good is often dressed in fake clothing, real is naked and proud no matter the scars."

—Chishala Lishomwc

Show up as the real you. The airbrushed you isn't sustainable, or even half as awesome.

and maybe you have, too. And like Bono, you still haven't found what you're looking for.

ASSIEs are rooted within a deeper issue most of us know all too well: self-serving perfectionism. If you're the kind of person who is sick of ASSIEs and want to escape them—along with the many ridiculous traps society sets for us—prepare to unlearn most of what you've been taught and pivot toward a new direction. It's time to accept the airbrushed you's resignation before the cancer spreads.

What Is Mentalligence, and How Can It Help Me?

Mentalligence (pronounced "MEN-tell-a-jence") is a new psychology of thinking model that launches us into UPward spirals through a process of Unlearning and Pivoting away from indoctrination that damages human progress. We then become more agile, mindful, and connected thinkers who bring social impact. Mentalligence helps us rethink our way to the *real* good life, not the one that's being sold writ large.

You've probably already noticed that mentalligence is a fusion of the words *mental* and *intelligence*. It might remind you of the term *emotional intelligence*, coined by Daniel Goleman. As you'll soon see, many popular terms and theories need some rethinking.

Mentalligence helps you rethink your way to the good life. It's a pretty tall order, but worth the investment. Throughout this book, you will learn how to unlearn and pivot, or "spiral UP," through four sets of sessions that teach how to use specific lenses to help undo damaging indoctrination. You'll get the backstory of how these lenses emerged from my research findings, clinical practice, and the latest neuroscience.

Certain key words and concepts can change the way you engage with the world: *agile, mentally intelligent, forever learner, ethics of reciprocity mind-set, impact-driven living, imposter syndrome,* and *collective efficacy.* Academic and more common definitions throughout will help you put your learning into action. For now, here's the short list of the driving principles behind Mentalligence.

Agile beats strong.

Since the beginning of time, being strong has been hyped up. Despite the overemphasis on mental strength, IQ, and bootstrapping, agility is what really matters. With change as life's only constant, it isn't brute force, will, or sheer genius, but the ability to pivot and adapt to life's twists that make us mentally intelligent.

Everything is learning, learning is everything.

The desire to be right can trip us up. None of us have all the answers; everything has contradictions. When we commit to becoming *forever learners*, we seek opportunities for constant growth and discovery, not alleged certainty or fake truth. We unleash creativity and curiosity, finding out just how many lenses are available to help us see better. The true marker of learning is turning up more questions than answers.

Sleepwalking through life is a waste.

We can't afford to snuggle up with blind comfort and compliance. We need a dose of smelling salts to awaken us to the possibility of finding the path to the good life as conscious, reflective thinkers who refuse to approach life with eyes closed. None of us want to experience regret, but a lack of thinking and the resulting behaviors can leave us stewing in it, if we don't pay attention. *Ethics of reciprocity mind-sets*, those focused on the Golden Rule, can help us upgrade individual purpose to *impact-driven* living.

It's okay to be messy.

Check your pretenses. "Control" and "neat" are illusions. None of us can hold it together every second. We're always spiraling up and down. Chaos and homeostasis are always at odds. Life isn't linear; it might be a little boring if it were. Spirals are everywhere in nature—sunflowers, galaxies, our fingerprints, ears, thoughts, and even our behavioral patterns. Your wrinkles, bumps, and bruises show the world you are truly a force of nature. Messy is authentic—and orderly in its own unique way.

Being judgmental leads to trouble.

When we're our own worst critics, we bind up and fall prey to *imposter syndrome*. Perfectionistic thoughts hold us hostage and are the birthplace of self-loathing. We salivate at the thought of becoming a better version of ourselves but don't stop to celebrate who we are now. The airbrushed you always wants to make a return. We downgrade ourselves, thinking we're imposters about to be exposed. Self-compassion needs to be a daily practice to fight off ASSIE tendencies, so that we can have an integrated view of ourselves based on our mindful presence, not a performance.

Unlearning has to happen.

The greatest gift we can give to ourselves and one another is to be open to rethinking and unlearning what we first believed. Some call this flip-flopping; my research shows that mental flexibility is a key to progress. When we avoid succumbing to blind spots that impede our ability to see beyond primitive instincts, indoctrination, hierarchies, and social pressures, we can strip down and rebuild in ways beyond our imagination.

Fusion takes the cake.

We don't have to subscribe to myopic ways of seeing the world. Centric beliefs and behaviors hinder progress. We need to stop bickering about who's the boss and instead find spaces for all voices to contribute. When we unbind ourselves from prescriptive formulas and egocentric tendencies, we find intersections where we can break new ground to accelerate progress. Cliques, silos, and the ignorance they breed bring us all down. Fusion is the gateway to *collective efficacy*, one of the key findings from my research: the idea that we do well when we all do well.

* * * *

These guiding principles of mentalligence help us avoid the four most common mindless behavioral traps: shutting down, numbing out, binding up, and staying stuck. These traps, caused by sleepwalking, perfectionism, groupthink, and stagnation blind spots, don't have to trip us up indefinitely. There's a way to see beyond them.

The Sessions

Through a process of behavioral change, mentalligence teaches you to drive your brain through a series of waking up, tuning in, breaking out, and going beyond sessions. You will develop reflective, mindful, universal, and imagineering lenses to overcome blind spots caused by indoctrination and primitive instincts, and you will learn to Spiral UP (unlearn and pivot).

When we approach life with this new psychology of thinking, we awaken to endless possibilities for growth and progress. We build meta-awareness, the capacity to *think about thinking*. This helps us deliberately refine behavior, moving toward better cognitive habits, skills, and mind-sets that support individual and collective success.

Knowing that you are capable of seeing with greater clarity is the start of something beautiful: behavior change that helps dismantle blind spots sabotaging human progress.

Mentalligence helps us overcome rigid mental inertia. It helps us become more conscious, focused, connected, and resilient. Without it, we become trapped in the devices of the downward spiral—oblivion, frenetic energy, ignorance, and stale chronic behavior patterns. With mentalligence, we move from being

- Sleepwalkers to reflectors—those who are meta-aware and able to actively improve life for themselves and others.
- Perfectionists to mindful thinkers—those who are self-compassionate and value presence over performance.
- Centrists to conscious contributors—those who work toward the good life by connecting and contributing as universal, global citizens.
- Stagnates to imagineers—those who defy convention and beat the odds by imaginatively engineering a path for better living.

Mentalligence helps us use new lenses to reduce blind spots based on raw, fear-based emotions, groupthink, bias, and the breakneck speed we contend with. We learn to be open, agile thinkers, and ultimately wield our greatest resource—our capacity to use our minds purposively to contribute as awake, tuned in, connected, imaginative citizens.

The true marker of learning is turning up with more questions than answers.

These sessions didn't appear in the air out of sheer magic. They emerged from over twenty-two years of working with thousands of patients and students who were trying to undo their own types of indoctrination. As the book unfolds, I'll share their stories with you to help you rethink your own.

WAKING UP is our strength.
TUNING IN is our way back to center.
BREAKING OUT is our birthright.
GOING BEYOND is our dance.

Session One Worksheet:
The Physics of Mentalligence

Unlearn fake-it-'til-you-make indoctrination
that breeds inauthenticity.
Pivot toward agility.

Rethink Your ASSIEs

Societal norms are so engrained in us; it can be difficult to get to a place of true authenticity. We're afraid of exposure, so we dress according to society's one-size-fits-all standards. As with fashion trends, we need to recognize what works for us and what doesn't. Instead of being forced to layer up based on someone's definition of "acceptable," we need to evaluate our wardrobe and make sure it's the right fit. When we strip down to find our own signature style, the one that we're truly comfortable with, proud to display, and that reflects the real us, it helps us worry less about being judged, and we work toward a place of full presence, connection, and social impact—the *real* good life we want to have.

Authenticity Check

- Is the image I portray consistent with my true self?
- What's the one word or phrase I want people to use to describe me?
- Would people be surprised to know my true thoughts and feelings?
- Do I tend to go along just to get along?
- How many people know the "real me"?
- Do my values align with the things I do every day?
- How often do I compare myself with others, or even try to be more like them?
- Am I holding back from doing things I really want to do or say out of fear of being judged?
- Is my image or personal agenda interfering with my ability to bring impact within my circles or on a broader level?
- What is my current definition of the good life?

Action Step: Assess Your Mental Agility and Potential for Getting to the Good Life

Test yourself. Visit *www.kristenlee.com* to take a mentalligence quiz. Throughout the book, you'll have a chance to build off your strengths and work on areas you want to keep developing that will help you become more agile and able to bring your potential for impact to scale.

Changing Directions

Objective:
Unlearn me-myself-and-I indoctrination that breeds insecurity.
Pivot toward do-it-together living.

*The way you live your days is the
way you live your life.*

—Annie Dillard

"It's kinda not really about you. It's more than that."

Clearly, this wasn't one of my most eloquent teaching moments, but I was trying to deliver the truth as plainly as possible. My nerves were a little frayed after a trying conversation with one of my students, and it was all I could muster up.

Usually, things go smoother with my graduate students. You should see them on the first night of class. Straight out of the gate, they hit the ground running, eager to start overachieving.

To break the ice, some guy asks whether I know where the professor is. Where *he* is, to be precise. It's *me. She.* The room gets noticeably quiet. He blushes. Apologies fly. *Well, you just made first impressions a little easier on the rest of us, no? Have a seat, please.*

That wasn't what flustered me. It would take time for me to unravel. We were off to a good start overall. Besides the where's-the-professor guy, everyone else put their best foot forward. They were in classic thirsty-for-points-mode, fighting to hold their "Will work for *A*" signs highest.

Grad students are their own breed. They come early, stay late, and make sport of answering questions. And on the first night, there's always a full-fledged make-the-best-impression competition that unfolds before my very eyes. It's slightly entertaining, but mostly concerning.

One student thought our opening introductions, intended to be simple bios and proverbial hellos, offered the right moment to test out his very own elevator pitch. Even what was supposed to be a little blurb in the online group board revealed he had revised his anthology over seventy times. *Can't wait to see his papers. He's gonna be one that takes constructive criticism really well.*

Unsurprisingly, he turned out to be the ultimate humble bragger, minus the humble. In every class, he peppered us with details from his resume like we were a panel of judges during his audition for CEO of the universe. His classmates rolled their eyes but still took the bait, chirping back with their own five-star comebacks.

Why are you trying to make Ryan Seacrest seem lazy, Mother Teresa selfish, and Bill Nye the Science Guy look stupid? Enough already. Nobody cares about all the companies you've started or the trophies you've amassed. We know you're smart. That's why you're here. We like you already. But the incessant self-patting isn't pretty. Just stop. Nobody's that friggin' perfect. Except Beyoncé, but we can't all be a boss like that. Your inflated ego is just a decoy. Let's work to repair this together, please.

As the weeks unfold, behaviors intensify. The students egg each other on, upping the ante at every turn. Grades and money do this to us. The moment that either factors into a situation, people start going a little cray-cray. You know this already if you've ever tried to divide a dinner bill with a group. There's always *that person* who eats and drinks like it's their last day on earth, then goes on to suggest the even split to "make it easier." *Yeah, those four mai tais you guzzled made life sooo much easier on all of us. Really?*

After many attempts to bring the collective anxiety down, we seemed to be making some progress. This was until one of my 4.0 diehards called me from her hospital bed. She was riding her bike; the driver was texting, disaster struck. As she relayed the sequence, I found myself side-eyeing the phone. *Why me?* You'd think she would've called her priest, sister, life coach, significant other—or even her cute little dog first. I think at that point, she had all her professors on speed dial.

Her biggest worry after her near brush with death was that it'd jeopardize all the points she'd chocked up. I tried to assure her that arrangements could be made, since she'd officially cleared the bar the syllabus set for "extenuating circumstance" and "emergency situation."

Despite my pinky swear she wouldn't be penalized, she signed herself out of the hospital, going both *AMA and APA—Against Medical Advice and Against Professor's Advice.* She even arrived early as usual to class, this time concussed, black-eyed, and limping toward her holy grail. I scanned the classroom for hidden cameras. *Is this a* What Would You Do *spoof? Why bother listening to mere doctors when there's an* A *to earn?*

You'd think she would've been glad to be breathing. She was miffed when I suggested she was getting carried away. Last I'd checked, being run over by a car constituted at least a few hours in bed. Beyond the shock of the condition in which she showed up, I was worried about the underlying insecurities behind her behavior. I was starting to feel more like a weird mix of *Survivor* meets *Wheel of Fortune* game-show host, not graduate professor.

She wasn't the only one. Many of my students had been on the losing side of the game throughout their educational careers. They'd felt the painful sting of being voted off the island. The drill-and-kill academic treadmill had left them mentally drained and emotionally bankrupt. To them, it was redemption time.

It's okay to be messy. Like sunflowers, galaxies, and fingerprints, your life is an intricately designed spiral. Your wrinkles, bumps, and bruises show the world you are a force of nature. Forget linear. When you embrace chaos, it brings its own kind of order.

Find a New Point

As I worked with my students, I worried that, despite good intentions, they were missing the whole point. Learning can help us become conscious citizens who connect to live out an impact-driven life—one that moves beyond me-myself-and-I indoctrination. It helps us get to what positive psychologists define as the *good life*—one marked by wholeness, well-being, and deeper levels of satisfaction than the typical superficial "good life" that's equated with making money and chalking up letters after our names. Hence, my "kinda not really about you" remark at the beginning of the session. I admit I needed to find a better way to put this. My mind swirled with questions:

- What if "fake it 'til we make it" behaviors are creating a big mess for everyone?
- How can we replace desperate "Will work for *A*" mind-sets with something more constructive?
- What's the point of having personal success if it's not doing any good for anyone else?
- What does it mean to find the good life?

Perfect is annoying, boring, and impossible to sustain. Knowing how to translate conscientiousness into something beyond the fleeting satisfaction of "me" toward a "we" mind-set is the best move you can make.

The gravity of the situation wasn't lost on me. I knew we'd have to get to the root of the behavior to understand how it could be changed for the better. If my experience had taught me anything, it's that unless you get to the underlying reasons behind behavior, you end up going in circles, with no real improvement. We need to find the point of what we're even after.

Move Beyond Wit and Grit

When school, the place that's supposed to help us flourish, becomes a source of dread and despair, you know something is wrong. Ideally, education should teach us how to be positive, contributing members of society.

Instead, schools cheer students on to individual achievement and looking good rather than doing good.

This is why educational expert Howard Gardner, the father of the theory of multiple intelligences, advocates that we move "beyond wit and grit." He and his colleagues at Harvard's Project Zero's Good Project want everyone to know that when we emphasize "goodness" in students—qualities that spur on engaged citizenry—it leads to positive social impact. This isn't just touchy-feely stuff: they've found over decades of research that excellence, engagement, and ethics are the keys to helping learners become good citizens, those who contribute to the overall well-being of society.

Know the Science and Roots Behind the Good Life

Positive psychology is the scientific study of what makes life worth living. The late Christopher Peterson, University of Michigan professor, one of the founders of the discipline, explains that psychological science and practice call us to rethink our typical ways of framing life. It calls us to zoom in on strengths and demonstrate interest in building the best things in life, rather than focusing on weakness or pursuits that bring fleeting pleasure.

Because positive psychology is a science, it requires checking theories against evidence, and should not be confused with untested self-help or affirmations that make us feel good. He emphasizes that the good life is genuine—it doesn't deny there are problems. Decades of research are now demonstrating that despite the street fight that life can be, there is hope. The science reveals that

- Most people are happy and resilient.
- People satisfied with life are able to build momentum toward desirable outcomes at school and work, and in relationships.
- Happiness, strengths of character, and positive social relationships all serve as vital buffers against effects of setbacks and disappointment.
- Money isn't what contributes to well-being—except when it is spent on other people.

- Our hearts matter: Unconditional caring is a vital skill to be taught alongside critical thinking skills. Both can be taught.
- Our best days when we shine the brightest involve feelings of autonomy, competency, and connection.

Martin Seligman, the father of positive psychology explains that rather than simplifying human well-being as "happiness," that "eudaimonia" or "human flourishing" can be fostered through habits that bring us to the highest human good.

Eudaimonia translates as "good spirit," originating from Aristotelian ethics emphasizing being virtuous and loved, and having good friends. Daimons were seen as guardian spirits that point us toward a positive and divine state of humanity. Scholars like Paul Woodruff and Luc Ferry call the good life a "rational and practical humanism with an appreciation of transcendence." Gary Chapman from the University of Texas calls it "living the change you want." He emphasizes the good life is not antitechnological or antispiritual but allows for those who hope for a better world to find a shared vision for it; one that is flexible enough for "innumerable individual circumstances, but comprehensive enough to unite people in optimism, and deliberate progressive social change."

Unfortunately, this type of conscious citizenry gets drowned out in the face of school climates that push for individual and institutional advancement. That we overemphasize personal success, rather than working for the greater good, may be one of the saddest realities of modern-day society.

Luckily, not all my students were humble bragging, breaking out of their hospital beds, or salivating for letters after their names. They had found ways to break away from me-myself-and-I indoctrination, the kind that teaches us to be hyperindividualized and self-absorbed. Yes, they were goal driven and hungry to accomplish, but their interest in doing so was for deeper reasons. While they cared about excellence, they were less obsessed with performance than they were with bringing impact. As Vanessa, an aspiring CEO, put it:

I hate the "he who dies with the most toys" mind-set of today. I think we're missing the point when we selfishly focus on ourselves and we don't see our true responsibility to one another. I'm not saying it's easy for me—sometimes I can barely keep my own head above water. But when I catch myself putting my "what" over my "why," then I know I'm going in the wrong direction.

Ben, a first-generation student, explained how he could shift his thinking from what to why:

My family never looked out for me, so I've had to do a lot on my own since I was a kid. They worked against me, not for me—they are the most critical and narcissistic people I know. I've always had a huge chip on my shoulder because of it. I had to grow up fast, and was bitter for a long time. I eventually started to rethink my situation and realized that maybe everything happened so I could be more motivated to help people who've gone through the same kind of stuff. I used to be so embarrassed and held on to a lot of rage. But with the help of a lot of people, I've worked hard to let go and take the good that came out of it. I realized it wasn't all about me and the pain, and there was a bigger world to influence. I think what helped me the most was seeing that even negative experiences can turn into positive energy.

This type of rethinking exerted by many of my students was multifaceted. It wasn't that there wasn't, or hadn't been, plenty of drama unfolding in their lives. More often, the students who demonstrated the most concern for bringing impact were the ones who had experienced a powerful combination of deep pain, along with the intervention of someone helping them find their way through it.

Storms do not automatically equal ruin. Disruption brings you down a whole new path toward delicious adventure.

With this help, and even in the face of chaos, the students took the energy that was generated through their struggles and used it as forward momentum. The lessons learned anchored them in a deep desire to give back. Even when ongoing setbacks happened, they could see them as chances to learn something that would eventually drive progress. It wasn't that they gave up their own personal interests, but such pursuits were no longer the center of their existence. Along the way, they increased their ability to be more self-compassionate, which translated into greater empathy toward their fellow human beings.

The momentum was so powerful; I started to call their behaviors "upward spirals." It became an official research code that would eventually fill notebooks with remarkable patterns. My students were harnessing the energy generated from even tough circumstances to pivot toward a positive direction. Documenting their journeys was powerful, leading me into my own process of spiraling to make sense of what I was learning and unlearning right along with them.

At first I started to think that social psychologist Albert Bandura's theory of self-efficacy was the bull's-eye explanation for what they were revealing. He asserts that our beliefs in our abilities to reach goals dictate behavior. Basically, if we believe we can reach a goal, we are more likely to set it and reach it. This is called a "sense of agency" or "self-efficacy." It seemed like he'd nailed a commonsense way of explaining the determination, grit, and resulting practices of my students.

It also seemed like the rock-story theory of our time. Emotional intelligence (EI), popularized by Daniel Goleman, was another bull's-eye. Most people in leadership, business, and behavioral science fields can recite the short list of skills EI teaches: self-awareness, self-regulation, motivation, empathy, and social skills.

We were talking a lot about EI in class, but it just wasn't sitting right, especially with my international students and those who identified themselves as globally conscious. Many of my students saw what a lot of critics have also questioned about the theory: that it's too me-focused and doesn't resonate across cultures, especially those that are collectivist.

My introverts didn't love it either. They squirmed since they thought that they'd have to manufacture a whole lot of charisma to compete with their extravert counterparts. We worried together that EI had the potential to teach us to hide emotions or use them to manipulate people, instead of being genuine.

My students weren't only interested in their own ability to set and reach goals, or to present themselves better. They were more focused on how greater self-awareness would translate into their being able to bring clear impact. Time after time, my students told me that their shift from "me" to "we" enabled them to upgrade their sense of self-efficacy to get to the good life.

Like any solid research method, this led to more questions, some answers, and again, more questions. Eventually, my theory of mentalligence was emerging, starting with a concept I began calling "collective efficacy." My students didn't think that all the emotional intelligence, or success in the world, would make them happy if they weren't applying it to make a difference. As Dawn put it:

> "It seems to me that the good life is not any fixed state. It is not, in my estimation, a state of virtue, or contentment, or nirvana, or happiness. It is not a condition in which the individual is adjusted, fulfilled, or actualized. . . . The good life is a process, not a state of being. . . . It is a direction, not a destination. The direction . . . is that which is selected by the total organism, when there is psychological freedom to move in any direction."
>
> —Carl Rogers

"I wouldn't dream of doing all this work if I thought it was just about me. I think too many times we are encouraged to be jealous, and all about ourselves. I'm happiest when I see people succeed. I hate to see suffering, and if I can do anything about it, I do. I think that's what we're here for."

While Bandura's theory of self-efficacy helps us set and reach goals, and Goleman's theory of emotional intelligence helps us develop needed skills, we knew we needed to take it further. Collective efficacy helped us fill in another corner of the human behavior puzzle. It helped us take our thinking to the next level, to translate purposeful goals into actual impact.

Move from Me to We

Collective efficacy embodies social and emotional consciousness. Inherently, it recognizes that an injury to one is an injury to all. It allows us to see that human struggle negatively affects all of us—not just those directly on the receiving end. It boils down to the idea that we do well when we all do well. *When you hurt, I hurt, and when you are on top of the world, then just call me Karen Carpenter, too.*

Collective Efficacy

Academic Definition

A belief system that holds advancement of the human condition, through conscious solidarity, empathy, curiosity, and unconditional regard for one another, as its primary objective. It espouses confidence in human potential and works to leverage it through a deliberate process of ethical reciprocity—a moral code that spurs us to treat one other well.

Street Definition

When you believe that the only way out of this big mess is to get out of your own head and become obsessed with making a difference. It's about loving your neighbor, even when they don't look like or agree with you. If you have privilege, don't be a prick about it. Use it for good. Work together. It's all we have time for. #onlywe #impact

---

Collective efficacy emphasizes mutuality, solidarity, and pluralism as avenues for human progress. It rejects insularity, bias, and centric behaviors. It widens the lens of "success" often propagated in individualistic frameworks. It views progress as transcending beyond an individual or specific group outcome. Collective efficacy can help translate me into we, working to get *everyone* to the good life. Collective efficacy relies on keeping an open mind instead of wasting time hating on everyone. It helps us avoid othering people and to see through the BS of social constructions that teach us to focus on ourselves to the point we don't realize our potential for impact.

This way of living shouldn't be that difficult, given that these teachings are embedded across every moral and religious code out there. There's no shortage of "ethics of reciprocity" rules—ones that nudge us to think about how something would feel to us—to regulate our own behavior. Most of us can recite the Golden Rule on cue. *Or, if you're creative like Confucius, you call it a silver rule: do not do to others what you do not want them to do to you.* Gold or silver, these teachings all generate momentum toward empathy, a cornerstone of collective efficacy.

Know the Difference Between Empathy and Sympathy

It's easy to confuse empathy and sympathy—since they sound and seem so alike. Most commonly, sympathy is defined as involving feeling a sense of sadness or pity for someone going through hard times. Empathy is explained as the ability to put oneself in the shoes of someone else. Empathy requires shared perspective or emotions that serve as a pathway to compassion. It often calls us to suspend our own positions of privilege to every extent possible to imagine someone's plight and point of view.

Collective efficacy also helps us pivot away from thinking traps and blind spots that keep us hungry for validation and embroiled in an unhealthy level of competition with ourselves, and each other. It helps us balk at individual perfection for the sake of success, or crushing our opponents, and instead adopt an approach focused on the greater good that prioritizes making life better for all.

My students told me time and time again that their way out of the downward spiraling associated with me-myself-and-I thinking started when they began to reject modern notions of self and success that teach us to step on anyone who gets in our way, or to gorge ourselves with the earth's treasures without stopping to give a care whether people are barely surviving. It didn't feel right in their guts, and they knew there was a better way.

An interesting plot twist to collective efficacy started to unfold. I and we didn't have to be an either/or proposition; it was both/and. When we advance ourselves, we become better equipped to advance one another, and vice versa. You don't have to go completely me, myself, and I to end up happy. Tremendous energy comes from both processes. Reciprocity was in full force.

DIY (do-it-yourself) life hacks can only take us so far. A DIT (do-it-together) life brings you to a whole new level of awesomeness.

Ethics of Reciprocity

Academic Definition

Reciprocity involves a cooperative exchange of privileges with the
implication of mutual benefit. It allows us to see ourselves in a state of
relationship with all living beings, not that our actions and influence
are entirely independent of one another. Ethics are moral principles
that govern behavior, based on virtues.

Street Definition

You look out for people. When you have something beneficial, you
don't hoard it, and you expect the same courtesy to be returned.
Be generous. Do the right thing. What goes around comes around.
Be the domino that tips positive reactions. #goldenrule #karma

Ethics of reciprocity rules are principles for treating people according
to how you'd want to be treated. These principles are found across many
moral frameworks and religious and cultural traditions. An ethics of reciprocity helps us become more willing to give and receive in abundance. It
gives empathy traction. Because you get what it feels like to have bad done
to you, you don't do it to someone else.

For my students, the less me-focused they became, the better they could
enjoy the fruits of their hard work. They didn't have to give up their dreams
and goals to be forces for good. They also didn't have to have picture-perfect
stories. Sometimes, chaos fueled them with the most potent energy that
catapulted them in a positive direction.

The upward spirals I was observing across my students were so novel
and impressive, I launched an institutional review board (IRB) application,
the permission needed to conduct human research. Too many important
discoveries were unfolding to keep them a secret.

Spiral Up

This whole upward spiral–collective efficacy thing had me at hello.
Grounded theory research helps yield what researchers like to call *thick
data*, which allows us to get well beyond what seems obvious at the surface,

to understand behavior. Unlike quantitative research, it's less about crunching numbers and more about painting a picture of behavioral nuances, otherwise known as human phenomena—or why people do certain stuff.

This type of research is rich, in that it provides a path to explore underlying reasons behind our actions. The paradoxes at hand were a researcher's dream. My students wrestled with their definitions of themselves and how to bring impact. They wanted it to be organic, but it was often awkward and bumpy. To be agile, moving along the upward spiral path, there was no time for rigid, me thinking. They needed to resist the trappings of their egos, keep open minds, and remember that reciprocity would lead to the good life—the whole point of what they valued most.

After coding all the data—which means chunking it into broad themes—and then sorting it into more discrete categories, four clear patterns of thinking emerged behind their processes of upward spiraling that would serve as a springboard for my ongoing inquiry:

Research Codes That Explain Thinking That Contributes Toward Upward Spiraling

1. **We all feel wobbly.** To be human is to experience *weeble moments*— those inevitable times when doubt and unsteadiness rent all the space in our heads. We can feel entirely grounded one second, and the next, a total mess. This is far more universal than we can imagine. We can help each other through this. My students became less "judgy" and less apt to "other" someone else when they acknowledged the paradox of human vulnerability and strength. Once my students owned their uncertainty, they gained traction toward their upward spirals, becoming better equipped to help both themselves and their fellow human beings.

2. **Hiding doesn't serve us well.** The biggest lie we're sold is that we're the *only ones* who struggle. Success isn't about having a perfect path. There is no such thing. When we hide truths, we resort to maladaptive ways of coping with them. And it sure doesn't help the person next to us, with the same types of questions and doubts. My students showed

that coming out of hiding was *the* turning point in their progress toward building the mental agility needed to break out of their downward spiral tendencies. Being honest and open accelerates collective efficacy, allowing us to act to further human progress, together in community.

3. **Integration is key.** While it's tempting to present our neatly airbrushed, sanitized version, every human being has messes underneath the surface. When we integrate the bright and dark sides of our stories, we become more open minded and agile. Integration helps us embrace a multiple-lens way of seeing the world that fuses the best of what we know from science, culture, art, and spiritual realms. My students recognized that tying this together was the best way to help them stay curious, creative, and engaged in their relationships and roles. They felt less fragmented and more whole when they strived for greater integration. Showing up as the real you is vital to avoid a slow and painful soul death, or to help resurrect one that has already been snuffed out.

4. **It's about us.** For far too long, across history and cultures, paradigms have existed that interfere with human progress and potential, teaching dominance over and othering instead of unconditional positive regard and benevolence. When people are oppressed for any reason—whether because of race, class, gender, sexual orientation, gender identity, age, ability, religion, or otherwise—it's damaging to all. Schools and societies oust people according to alleged differences and deficits rather than similarities and strengths. Building collective efficacy can help us advance the human condition through empathy, solidarity, and pluralism. Even with systemic large-scale issues to contend with, our own effort toward this can go a long way. Human progress is always possible—and more likely when we abandon antiquated paradigms that harm us all, and instead maintain genuine and consistent regard for one another.

Breaking free from the bonds of me-myself-and-I thinking and moving toward reciprocity and collective efficacy take effort. But as my students demonstrated, it is truly freeing when you recognize that moving from me to we helps bring us all to a place of tangible impact.

When I arrived at this part of my research process, I couldn't help but reflect on the tragedy of my humble bragger. After graduating, he applied for a job at my institution. When my boss checked his references, it turned out his long list of accolades were big, fat lies. Total fabrications. Not a word was true. The sad part was that he'd wasted so much time protecting his own interests when he could've harnessed his talents to make a real difference.

It's kinda not really about you, after all.

Session Two Worksheet:
Changing Directions

Objective:
Unlearn me-myself-and-I indoctrination that breeds insecurity.
Pivot toward do-it-together living.

Rethink It: Move from Me to We

Society teaches us to focus on personal success, sometimes to the point where we overlook opportunities for social impact. We are often taught to worry more about looking good than doing good. This blocks us from getting to the good life. An ethics of reciprocity often falls low on our priority lists, and we struggle to find empathy when so much of our attention is focused on self-protection. This calls us to reflect on our values and whether they are aligned with our actions. Often, the first step involves checking our day-to-day activities and seeing whether there's room to tweak our behaviors and beef up our efforts toward impact.

Collective Efficacy and Ethics
of Reciprocity Check

- Do I regularly try to imagine myself in someone else's shoes?
- How do I define my "why," the reasons behind what I do?
- What do I want my legacy to be?
- Is there a way to reorganize my schedule to reduce wasted time and increase impact-driven activities?
- Have I been able to share my backstory openly?
- What are the most salient lessons in the challenges I've faced?
- Am I actively harnessing even chaotic energy to spiral toward improving life for myself and those in my reach?

Action Steps: Identify Your
Signature Brand to Bring Impact

Who do you want to be? To understand one another better, we first need to raise our self-awareness and clarify our own goals and values. Once we've done so, we are better positioned to live the good life that emphasizes do-it-together living versus superficial selfish gains.

1. **Pinpoint your values.** Take fifteen minutes to complete a Values in Action (VIA) Inventory via *www.viacharacter.org*. This tool, designed by leading authorities in positive psychology, is scientifically validated (and free) and provides an analysis of your character strengths.

2. **Get a second opinion.** Enlist the support of an established mentor or look for one to discuss your VIA findings and how they align with your actions and pursuits.

3. **Map your life.** Jot down a brief overview of the major influences in your life. Highlight at least three key people who impacted or inspired you. Pick the format that works the best for you: a short story, timeline, bullet points, and so on.

4. **Define your brand.** Write out a short statement defining your unique personal brand. It should reflect your true essence—the things that best describe your strengths, values, roles, and personal goals, and your desire to bring impact.

5. **Make a quick list.** Sketch out three do-it-together life hacks that you could start now that reflect your VIA findings. For example, if you are creative, can you make something for someone? Or can you start something positive at work or in your community that would bring impact? If you have a strong love of learning, can you join forces in a book club or think tank or make sure you're in regular conversation with interesting people? Are there needs that you see around you that you feel compelled to address? Small things can make a big difference. Start somewhere and keep building.

CONNECTION is our way out
of the **SELF-PROTECTION** anthem of
our **ME-MYSELF-AND-I WORLD.**
Ironically, the scrambling, competing, and
clawing to find our way gets us quite **LOST.**
We salivate at the idea that we can
HACK our fears by **ISOLATING** or
RUNNING away from them.
Hiding almost **NEVER** turns out to be
the behavior that sets us toward
individual or collective **PROGRESS.**
The way **FORWARD** is to
PAY IT FORWARD.

SESSION THREE

Cutting Strings

Objective:
Unlearn performance indoctrination
that breeds unhealthy behaviors.
Pivot toward meta-awareness.

*The illiterate of the twenty-first century
will not be those who cannot read and write,
but those who cannot learn,
unlearn, and relearn.*

—Alvin Toffler

I t's August 2010. A user identifying himself as sociallyinferior[1] posted his plight, "my life is taking a downward spiral" on a forum on Social AnxietySupport.com:

> sociallyinferior: *I recently never paid any mind to how my life was heading but now that I take a closer look at it, it seems I am going nowhere in life. I have yet to finish college and I am 23 years old, my brother on the other hand is going to graduate next year and he is only 20 years of age. He wants to move out which I think is going to be hard on me. . . . I feel like I*

---

1 Note: Original spelling has been polished up a bit, but the grammar is mostly untouched to keep the full feel and flavor intact.

*really am alone and hopeless and nowhere to go. I feel like I will be a fail-
ure in life. I have a job but that doesn't pay enough for me to move out. . . .*

*I don't want to end up like a loser, I want to have a career and a life.
I just don't know where to start. I've lost most of my younger years doing
nothing but working trying to pay off a car that seems like forever. And
not even paying attention to my studies. And now is when I am actually
giving more thought to my future.*

Within eighteen minutes, his screen lights up with lots of advice:

littlemisshy: *I'm sorry it's not going well for you. But don't think life
is not going to go anywhere for you. With life you really do need to "take
it by the horns" (so to speak). I know you probably don't want to listen
to someone as old as I am . . . but personally speaking, I left home at 16
years with nothing (no money, no family support) and just had to push
myself to finish school, get a job etc. It has paid off at the end, though
I've been to hell and back on the way here.*

kos: *You can start by doing the best you can in school. . . . You should
be looking forward to this stage in your life. It can be very exciting.*

pinkpurplepink: *sounds so quarter life crisis. that is something we
have to go through, i guess. try to embrace it and embrace life.*

spaceghost: *Your life looks good. 23 is young. Forget about the past
and your mistakes. You are now conscious of your life and where it's
heading. Now you can focus on building your life, career and relationships. Focus on discovering what you want. Then you can determine
what you need to do to make a plan.*

Such slumps aren't just the concerns of millennials. We all want to get
to the good life, but sometimes we get stuck along the way. People who
find themselves in this type of funk are what psychologist Harriet Lerner
would call *underfunctioners*, which is no fun for anyone.

This infamous I'm-a-loser downward spiral is a toxic mix of regret,
self-flagellation, and hopelessness: *I haven't gotten very far. I'm done. I
suck. Never mind helping someone else. I can barely survive myself.*

Chances are if you are the classic, brain-never-shuts-down person
who picks up a book called *Mentalligence*, those slump days are vague

memories. The thought of even missing one day of work or school makes your eyes pop. You barely stay asleep all night, you're so juiced up. Your spiral is totally different.

But any *overfunctioner* knows that the I'm-out-of-control, sprinting-through-marathons spiral is not without its own anxieties: *I'm too busy. Crazy busy. Maybe I'm crazy. I'm too busy to tell. Is there a difference?*

There's no time to be bored, digress, or play. There aren't any margins in your schedule for it. People count on you to deliver, so you push as hard as you can.

And even with all you're doing, your view of yourself is skewed. After hitting it out of the park, you still stew in self-criticism. Instead of celebrating success along the way, you fall for the bait of our never-enough culture, with strings pulled in a thousand directions by your phones, bosses, partners, parents, and children.

It would be easy to chalk sociallyinferior's plight up to pure laziness or even a lack of conscientiousness. He seems to have shut down even before getting out of the gate. But in the face of our revved-up culture, the he's-a-loser explanation is an oversimplification. Today, many of us are scared off by the intimidating expectation of being college-ready by seventh grade.

The sad reality is you don't have to be living in your parents' basement indefinitely, or stuck in a dead-end job, to be beating yourself up royally. In a culture that blares messages of *doing* and not *being*, even super-achievers can end up with the same level of doubt as someone who hasn't quite gotten off the ground yet.

We have so many tabs open in our brains that we stumble around in a state of constant vertigo. Whether we're in a mode of under- or overfunctioning, these downward spirals have the following effects:

- **They catch us by surprise.** We don't see the cumulative effect of our action and inaction. We ignore important cues nudging us toward change and suddenly find ourselves on turf where we'd rather not be. The wake-up call is alarming. *(Am I really this behind the eight ball? I'll never be good enough. Why didn't I realize sooner?)*

- **They disorient us.** Life is change. It serves up whopping heapings of pain and out-of-nowhere disasters. We're catapulted into chaos, with developmental milestones and circumstances to try and figure out. (*I wasn't expecting this. I'm totally confused. My life is confetti.*)
- **They send us catastrophizing.** Our brains become gold medalists in mental gymnastics. We obsess, ruminate, and question whether we're good enough and if progress will ever be made. (*I'll never recover. This always happens to me. I'm on a highway to hell.*)
- **They shut us down.** Our lack of progress paralyzes us. We numb out and struggle to see the big picture. We let worry rent all the space in our heads instead of leveraging our minds to create new possibilities. (*I don't want to face this. Leave me alone. Get me out of here. I'm done.*)

In his groundbreaking work, psychologist Daniel Kahneman illustrates the dangers of jumping to conclusions in the middle of our negative thought spirals. Errors in judgment known as *confirmation bias* lead us to only pay attention to evidence that support theories we erroneously develop out of raw emotions. The amygdala, a small structure in the brain that regulates fear responses, takes over, instead of giving way to the frontal lobe, where reasoning happens.

Drive Your Brain

Kahneman relates much of our levels of awareness to brain functions he calls System 1 and System 2. (Dr. Seuss would be proud.)

System 1 travels highway style, unconsciously relying on the automated limbic system, which allows us to make snap decisions for survival. It steers behavior intuitively, no questions asked. System 1 is all about the shortcut.

Thinking shortcuts can be very useful. If we weren't agile enough to think quickly, we'd find ourselves in harm's way. Our primitive instincts and reflexes serve us well in many situations. But when we constantly cut corners, we become more vulnerable to dangerous blind spots. Shortcuts aren't always the best route to take.

System 2, the more back-roadsy, conscious, rule-based side, likes to take its time. With the frontal lobe in full force, it paves the way for logical,

controlled thinking. It relies on heuristics, the general rules and methods that we tend to follow to
make decisions. System 2 is like a careful over-the-

**Your consciousness
will lead you home.**

shoulder check to catch what our rearview mirrors miss. It helps us notice
blind spots more readily, avoid potential crashes, and redirect ourselves.
It helps us navigate through even the thickest of traffic in our busy brains.
Move over, Waze.

System 2 allows us to draw upon an amazing process that only human
beings are capable of, known as *metacognition*, or thinking about thinking. *Meta* means beyond. Metacognition helps us engage in complex self-
reflection to take us past basic, limiting ways of seeing to become more
meta-aware.

> ## *Metacognition*
>
> ### Academic Definition
> *Metacognition*, the ability to think about thinking, is an amazing
> feature of the brain unique to the human species. It helps us to avoid
> falling prey to blind spots that jeopardize our engagement in an active
> process of conscious cognitive behavioral monitoring and refinement.
>
> ### Street Definition
> Metacognition gives us needed reality checks. We are the only crea-
> tures on the planet cool enough to be able to think about our thinking.
> Metacognition helps us find missing pieces to the puzzle. It gives us
> the right tools for the job so that we don't get yanked around. #think-
> aboutthinking #sowoke

Use Metacognition to Avoid
Downward-Spiral Thinking Types

Since our minds can quickly spin out of control and we can acciden-
tally mistake puppet strings as necessary tools to keep us in check, we first
need to understand the common types that send us into disarray:[2]

---

2 If you identify with several, you are like most people. These common traps showed up in my study, in my therapy
room, and across the scientific literature.

Downward-Spiral Thinking Types

The Preemptive 911 Caller. Something happens, and you see it as a total emergency. When your amygdala is in full force, it's likely you are only able to see red and hear alarm bells going off. You spin into a place where you see reality as being nothing but a full-out crisis. Panic sets in, and everything gets blown way out of proportion.

The Saboteur. Difficulty strikes, and you automatically engage in self-sabotage, taking everything personally and blaming yourself for occurrence of events, even those over which you have no control. Your thoughts interfere with reasoning, and instead you beat yourself up incessantly, diminishing your sense of value and worth.

The Zero-Shades-of-Gray Thinker. When looking at a situation, you only see extremes or absolutes. You define things in black-and-white, all-or-nothing terms. Your view is that something is either this way or that, and it's hard to see the possibility that it could also be a both/and situation.

The Labeler. You look at behavior and label it in negative terms. Even though hard to deal with, you believe it is a universal defining trait versus a behavior or situation that needs modification. This trap can lead to self-labeling as well as judging other people.

The Tunnel Visioner. When evaluating what's at hand, you only zoom in on the negative details, ignoring anything that is positive and worth appreciating. When something goes wrong, you have trouble identifying the things that have also gone right. Downward-spiraling tunnel vision focuses on deficits and injuries rather than lessons and strengths.

The Broad Brusher. You paint a very broad picture, make loose connections between past or present instances, and make sweeping overgeneralizations to describe what's at hand. You use phrases like "I never," "This always," and "Everyone" to make big assertions of what you see happening.

The Superhero. Your cape is always on, working hard to never let anyone down. You pride yourself on doing all and being all, at all costs. You "should" and "must" yourself to the nth degree, but when something goes wrong, you come crashing down and your self-esteem goes plummeting. When you can't save the world, you experience extreme disappointment.

The Imposter. Because you constantly engage in social comparison, you magnify the positives you see in everyone else, but downplay your own strengths and talents. You think you're going to be found out, and that you really don't belong at the level where you find yourself. You worry that people will soon see through your façade and come to their senses on the trust they've placed in you.

Metacognition provides us with the tools to counteract these very human downward-spiral tendencies. It helps us plan, check, and evaluate our thinking and behavioral patterns, allowing us to:

- Identify creative, adaptive strategies to challenges.
- Grab hold of opportunities for growth and advancement.
- Move beyond basic and limiting explanations.

Be fearless with your questions. Don't be afraid to get a little muddy. Keep your feet nimble and eyes open for new paths and perspectives. Ready yourself to be moved.

Of course, when we're trying to become epic thinkers, we can overdo it. If we don't have the proper tools that metacognition provides, we can take a detour and end up anxiously and obsessively overanalyzing every detail of our lives, which is known as *rumination*. We become unproductively fixated, oblivious to context, and lost in our own heads.

Know the Difference Between Metacognition and Rumination

Metacognition is solutions focused, paving the path to behavioral change through a specific and structured process designed to help us pinpoint opportunities toward improvement. It's like a sander that helps buff and polish thinking practices.

Rumination, on the other hand, is a power drill that probes too deeply, haphazardly hitting delicate optic nerves, leaving us blinded from seeing positive and productive courses of action. Rumination is like a bad roommate who never stops nagging but fails to deliver possible remedies.

Metacognition helps us progress along our upward-spiral course, while rumination propels us downward, breaking down our fabric and capacity for forward momentum. Metacognition allows us to realize that one fixed lens won't help us see everything we need to. It helps us avoid rumination detours and stay on a path that keeps us moving upward.

Kahneman says we must come to terms with the flaws of our thinking to truly make progress. We have our work cut out for us to pry ourselves away from destructive traps of the mind that send us spiraling downward. There's plenty of room for unlearning. Thankfully, our brains are capable of changing throughout life because of what's known as *neuroplasticity*. Through experience, we can learn to drive our brains away from unhelpful behavior traps.

Let Go of the Puppet Myth

Our distorted thinking patterns and resulting downward spirals are in part caused by what my research revealed as the *puppet myth*, the belief that *what we do is who we are*.

Whether we are like Gloppy from Candyland, caught in a swamp of inaction, or an EF5-level tornado, emanating chaos, our spirals are heavily influenced by the *puppet myth*, thinking we have to perform our way through life. *Get it right. Don't be such a crybaby. Try a little harder. What's wrong with you? You're gonna miss the boat.*

From an early age, we're given a script to follow. Our puppeteers—our parents, teachers, coaches, siblings, and friends—egg us on. They cheer

"Responsibility to yourself means refusing to let others do your thinking, talking, and naming for you; it means learning to respect and use your own brains and instincts; hence, grappling with hard work."

—Adrienne Rich

wildly and applaud when we comply with their string pulling. The attention is addictive.

Then there's the radio silence when we go our own way. We quickly learn that compliance win friends. Groupthink sweeps us up. We go along to get along, and we're left with *contingent self-esteem*, waiting for our validation fix to calm our nerves and set us free, even if for a fleeting moment. Our worth is always based on the applause from our last trick, which is inevitably drowned out in today's noisy arenas.

This transactional way of performing for acceptance is something we all deal with—across time, space, and culture. This puppet myth—that we can do it all, singing and dancing our way to so-called success, without falter—leaves us hustling for approval, living in the extremes of being either too exhausted to think about anyone but ourselves or so consumed with everyone else that we neglect to consider our own needs.

Angelo, one of my students, told me he's sick of trying to live up to these ridiculous expectations. He says, "It's not living." When the lights go out, he told me, he feels cheapened and alone. There's so much more to Angelo than what's being celebrated in our culture.

This way of living is dangerous since it leaves the door wide open for *imposter syndrome* to strike, the feeling that we're not good enough and someone's going to find us out—that we're not as competent, talented, or grounded as people first think. *I don't deserve to be at this table. I better work my tail off. Pretend I know everything. Never admit a mistake. I hope no one catches on to me.*

> **You are not an imposter. What's behind you is behind you. Embrace your granularity.**

Historically marginalized groups—like women, people of color, first-generation college students, and those known as *straddlers*, those of us brought up with humble beginnings, who've worked their way up to high-stakes roles and arenas—are more prone to imposter syndrome than those with more privilege from the get-go.

Imposter Syndrome

Academic Definition

A form of intellectual self-doubt in which a high-achieving person struggles to internalize accomplishments, marked by a persistent fear of being exposed as a "fraud." The person often suffers in silence, questioning not only their abilities but whether they belong or not.

Street Definition

When you feel like you're a big phony and that it's a matter of time before people catch onto you. You hesitate to speak up, because you don't want to expose your greatest worry—that you're a fraud. #imposter

Ironically, most of us are born with plastic spoons in our mouths, not silver spoons, but when you're a straddler, someone with feet in both worlds, it's not uncommon to think everyone around you has a leg up, igniting insecurity and driving energies to the never-ending auditions we've lined up for so that we won't blow our cover.

It's one thing to have strings orchestrated when we're kids. We can't do much about that. But why do so many of us dutifully hand our strings over to our bosses, marketers, social media feeds, partners, parents, and even our own kids?

We suck up to ideals of being rock stars from the delivery room to the boardroom to the bedroom. We marinate in guilt and shame against the tyranny of the highly romanticized versions of success swarming us, which seem to be celebrating hard work but really are infecting us with images of perfect that are well beyond our reach—unless we're part of the elite, with our very own concierge, masseuse, makeup artists, and entourage. Well-meaning words like *work-life balance* dominate our business and social vocabularies, but *balance* is really code for *we're expected to excel at everything*.

Our compulsiveness fires up. The pressure overwhelms our thresholds for coping, and we become more apt to make rash, fear-based decisions, instead of accessing our wisdom. Cutting our strings from these unhelpful ideas takes skill. They've become painfully lodged into our identities. If we yank them too quickly, we might unravel.

Life has become a giant audition where our part is never secure: we overwork, super-parent, scramble to score our roles, and pull off our gigs. Then we're met with harsh criticism from the peanut galleries and judges' tables, and the gnawing doubts in the bowels of our own brains, nudging us to compare ourselves obsessively to a gold standard that doesn't even exist.

Being a puppet is overrated. Cut your strings. We are human beings, not doings. Knowing life is about impact, not performance, is the most badass kind of clarity you can have.

Cut Your Strings

Most of us are walking around in desperate need of soul surgery. Careful pruning is needed so that we can rescue our inner voice without cutting off our air. *We're not shaving down to apathy, folks—just a little more sanity, please.*

I think we hold onto our strings and jump through hoops because we're scared. *What will people think? What if I let someone down? What if I'm ostracized from a community of which I really want to be a part? What if I'm left behind? What if I'm not enough? What if I'm too much?*

We wonder why we're the most obese, addicted, medicated group in history. Our salaries, hips, and lips are never big enough. (Thank you, Kim and Kylie K.) Keeping up with this never enough lifestyle costs us a lot. A report from the World Health Organization warns that, by 2030, the pressures will be so intense that most of us simply won't be able to cope with the demands of life.

One of my favorite movies, *Admissions*, illustrates the puppet myth perfectly.

I nestled in to watch it with my daughter, Tori, when she was a senior in high school. Everyone said we had to watch it. Who can say no to Tina Fey? It was the perfect cap-off to the whirlwind two-year journey we'd completed stomping across several states and at least a dozen college campuses. Tori had finally finished her final application to reach, mid-line, and safety schools. It was a far cry from my admissions process of the early

1990s. The institution I attended didn't even require an admissions essay or charge a fee.

Throughout the movie, colleges reject candidates left and right, despite being champion gymnasts, chess players, and prodigies with 4.0 GPAs and perfect scores. We laughed out loud while we squirmed inside, knowing that this level of competition is today's reality.

The pressure doesn't stop once the admission letters arrive. Across our schools, workplaces, and homes, stress is at an all-time high, and our day is even being called the Age of Anxiety. Our strings can eventually start to choke us. Cutting them first requires metacognition—catching ourselves in the act of being puppeteered, then bravely letting go and driving our own brains and lives.

Strings aren't our only problem. Besides the rampant performance mind-sets flooding our consciousness, there's more to contend with. Unfortunately, one extreme often leads to another. We must watch out for bubble wrap and trophies, too, as I explain in the next session.

Session Three Worksheet:
Cutting Strings

Objective:
Unlearn performance indoctrination that
breeds unhealthy behaviors.
Pivot toward meta-awareness.

Rethink It:
Loosen Your Strings

The buzz we get from attention is temporary. When we constantly perform, it seems to be never enough. Over time, the more we put up a front, the greater risk we run of becoming fragmented and disingenuous. Our underlying insecurities and resulting cognitive distortions can ramp up our need for validation. We need to be sure that our behaviors aren't dictated by performance anxiety, to avoid being stifled by the too-tight strings that choke us. We can use metacognition to help us drive our brain to setting needed boundaries.

Behind-the-Scenes Check

- What "parts" have I been cast in within my family, at work, or in my personal life?
- In what ways do the expectations surrounding these roles impact me?
- What is my level of enthusiasm around these expectations?
- If I could change something about my current roles, what would it be?
- If I could be cast in an entirely new role, one that kept impact and collective efficacy front and center, what would it consist of?
- Who's controlling my strings? Does this need to change?

Action Steps:
Use Metacognition to Refine Behavior

1. **Measure your plate.** Grab a paper plate and write down a list of all the roles you play at work, home, and school, and in your friend groups and networks. If possible, grab a friend or colleague and show them how full your plate is. Is it overloaded? If so, what can you take off it, or at least tackle in more reasonable ways?

2. **Explore the pros and cons of your roles.** Reflect upon your favorite and the most burdensome aspects of these roles. What do you stand to gain or lose from maintaining them?

3. **Prioritize and refine.** Rate those roles according to the level of priority in your life. Is there anything you've taken on that doesn't jive with your

values and desires? Is overcommitment impeding your ability to bring impact? If so, is there a way to delegate responsibilities or relinquish your role, even for a short time? What's negotiable on your list?

4. **Target a behavior to tweak.** Pick at least one key role that you want to work on changing. How will you go about communicating this, and setting new boundaries with yourself or for others involved? Can you enlist someone to help you be strategic? What specifically needs to change? What types of thoughts or emotions might interfere—guilt, for example—and what will you do about it? How will you know when you've reached success with your goal?

5. **Work toward transfer.** We can often take prior learning experiences and transfer them to help us problem solve. Think back to a time you were stuck in a downward spiral and needed to make a behavioral change. Write out at least three actions you took to help you get back on track. In what ways do they apply or transfer to any similar situations that drain your energy today?

6. **Assess your thinking style.** Using the downward-spiraling thinking types on page 36, notice any trends you may have and whether they contribute to behaviors you want to change. In the next session, you will apply your insights to consciously change your thinking and resulting behaviors.

As people **COMMITTED** to conscious living, we won't hand our strings over and **ACT** as **PUPPETS** while making our way through life. Even though we hate **DISAPPOINTING** people, we are careful not to constantly let ourselves down, either. We know that life isn't one **NONSTOP AUDITION** for our next part. **JUDGES** aren't the ones who count. We refuse to let all the **PRESSURES** of performing send us into perpetual mental gymnastics. We feel **MOST PRESENT** with uncut strings. We are done **HUSTLING** for **APPROVAL.** We dance to our **OWN** beat, even if that sometimes means stepping **ON TOES** or **FALLING DOWN.**

Popping Bubbles

Objective:
Unlearn hiding indoctrination that breeds avoidance.
Pivot toward healing.

These pains you feel are messengers.
Listen to them.

—Rumi

The banter isn't very forgiving. *It's the generation of coddling. We're bubble-wrapping our children. Everyone gets a trophy. These kids have no backbone. They're being babied. They're made of tissue paper and allergy medicine.* Parents, teachers, and even airlines refusing to serve peanuts are being pointed at as sources of our softening, everyone-wins, bubble-wrapped Generation Z—those born from 1995 on. Allegedly, they're not just lactose intolerant—they seem to be life intolerant.

Our lives are like scenes from the movie *Parental Guidance*, where the parents track their kids with video surveillance, hold a funeral for the imaginary friend, spend endless hours in group therapy to build self-esteem, and never let their finicky child's component food items touch each other.

We offer seven choices of cereal, remove scratchy tags from all the clothes, and line up sock to toe with mathematical precision. There's no kick the can, playing in the woods, or "Are we there yet?" emerging from the backseat, clad with its own multimedia entertainment center. It's organized activities galore, starting with Baby Beethoven in utero, swimming before they walk, soccer before potty training, college choices nailed down by third grade, road trips with all the luxury of a five-star hotel, and National Guard searches when the beloved blankie or binky goes missing.[1]

How we went from generations past—who told us babies came from storks, smacked us on the butt, and sent us to bed without supper if we didn't show full appreciation for the sodium-filled casserole and red-dye punch that made us bounce off the walls and would have sent most kids of today on Ritalin—to obsessively picking the seeds of our kid's gluten-free buns topping their artisan ketchup–smeared nitrite-free meats is a matter of great public interest and, of course, finger pointing.

Gone are the authoritarian ways of yesteryear, when we'd never heard of sensory issues, and "Because I said so" brought order. Never have parents been more vilified and subjected to more parenting styles and advice. *Cut the cord. Go free-range—but not to the point your kid gets picked off by a gorilla. Douse yourself in hand sanitizer, but don't kill the good bacteria. Don't dare smear that toxic sun lotion all over your child—you'll give them a different kind of cancer. Let them go down the slide alone, but if they get concussed, you're an idiot. Don't be a helicopter, be a submarine. No, wait—there's a new trend emerging. OMG.*

Our feeds are brimming with how to embody what sociologists Susan Douglas and Meredith Michaels call the "new momism," a set of ideals negatively affecting moms, dads, and kids alike. It's the kind of pressure that keeps us up to 2:30 a.m. baking cupcakes and cutting out of work so that we, like all the other good parents, don't miss the game.

We end up with a lot of what Brigid Schulte, award-winning *Washington Post* reporter and New America Fellow, calls "stupid days," where everything seems to go wrong and we're practically imploding as we race to beat the clock and still not let anyone down.

---

1 This kind of "good life" is the head fake for the real good life. Not everyone has these luxuries, which is why collective efficacy is needed to ensure that excess for a few doesn't come at the expense of most.

Feel and Heal

Whether you've been raised this way or are in the throes of choreographing your own complicated parenting dance, understanding the *bubble-wrap surplus* is an important step to building mental agility that helps us move toward real impact.

The puppet strings and bubble wrap send us on a detour from building the agility that we and those we love desperately need.

We end up tossed around in some pretty nasty downward spirals. We get banged around, then shut down. We numb. We bind up and self-protect. We stay stuck and rigid.

We can't simply pivot with all those uncut puppet strings and thick layers of bubble wrap tripping us up. And when we do fall, we're too bulky to get back up, preventing us from building up the muscles we need and stopping the very bloodflow that allows us to *feel* and *heal*, two critical components of growth.

Feeling pain is not something we necessarily welcome with excitement. Except for Lieutenant Dan in *Forrest Gump*, in his epic pre–shrimp harvest showdown with the heavens, I haven't met a human that says to life, "Bring it on! Give me what you've got! Hammer me hard. The bigger the struggle, the better. I love to suffer!" But in my research, people who defined themselves as resilient said that pain had been one of their most powerful teachers. Getting to that point of appreciating the lessons it brought didn't happen overnight—or without support.

Acknowledging pain was a consistent theme throughout my students' stories. They said at first they went to great lengths to hide it, until they started to realize that the pain was preventing them from moving forward. As Evan put it,

> *I came from a military family and then went on to serve—so pretty much every setting I've ever been in has been about being strong . . . hiding my inner world. I think strength has its place, but once you get to thinking about it, you realize that you should be proud of the pain you go through, not embarrassed of it. The older I get, the more open I become, because anytime I've hidden it, it just makes me feel even worse and gets me nowhere.*

Healing from pain is complex and cannot be oversimplified to a three-step process. Our wounds are deep, and even with all the resilience conversation swirling across our leadership, parenting, and business spheres, we seem to be skipping over the honest and messy parts we'd rather not acknowledge. Instead, we jump to words like *bouncing back* and *stronger than ever*, making it all seem so glamorous and magical.

Just keep your ears perked up. Even at funerals you hear this type of bleached rhetoric that minimizes our human responses to pain. People offer a lot of trite advice and epithets. You never hear anyone say stuff like, "This really sucks. You're going to be in pain forever. Your life will never be the same." Instead we say things like, "Oh, he's in a better place," or "Wow, she looks good over there in that casket. Go, Sephora."

This is what social scientist Dr. Brené Brown calls *gold-plating grit*, or glossing over the pain we experience. She explains that we often minimize how difficult a process of recovery really is, and that we don't simply bounce back from everything that comes our way. Instead, it's often a "street fight" with our dark emotions, especially vulnerability, that eventually helps us progress.

Maybe our first stop is to call foul and swipe left all the messaging screaming at us that life can be solved if we drive the right car, have on-fleek eyebrows, follow some cute acronym—or that if we just try a little harder, everything will be just fine. *Keep that "Suck It Up" T-shirt on. Stay shiny. Smile. You don't want anyone to think bad of you.*

Feeling and *healing* don't represent a big Kumbaya fest or the touchy-feely stuff that most of us thinkers run from as soon as there's a whiff of it in the air. In fact, science shows quite the opposite.

Psychologist Lisa Feldman Barrett, author of *How Emotions Are Made: The Secrets of the Brain*, defines this as *emotional granularity*, the ability to adaptively put feelings into specific words. Her research shows how language affects coping. The more precise we become at naming what we are experiencing cognitively and emotionally, the better we become at taking the steps we need to maneuver through murky situations. For example, you've had an argument with your partner. If you say you feel "mad" about what happened, it's easy to feel like not much can be done.

But if you express being "completely offended," you're more likely to sit down and talk about how to make things better. Of course, this usually works better after a cooling-off period!

Know the Science Behind Feeling and Healing

Dr. Matthew D. Lieberman and his team of UCLA researchers discovered the precise science behind our abilities to name our pain and other emotions.

Their study found that when we name our emotions, even painful ones, the amygdala—the brain's usual site of a lot of anxious activity—becomes less active, while the ventrolateral prefrontal cortex, located behind the forehead and eyes, ramps up. He and his team believe this might have something important for us to consider.

They tested a total of eighteen women and twelve men between the ages of eighteen and thirty-six using functional magnetic resonance imaging to study brain activity while being shown pictures of faces and the terms "angry" and "fearful." Some participants were shown names like "Harry" or "Sally" and chose the name they felt matched. Those participants who verbalized the word "angry" calmed the amygdala, while the name Harry didn't have any influence.

This research suggests that by putting our feelings into specific words, we might be able to move beyond our raw emotional responses, helping us to feel less *angry* or *sad*, or shall I say *especially perturbed* or *excruciatingly depressed*? Not a bad deal.

Seeing that our pain can be a catalyst for our healing process helps us to avoid sugar-coating our experiences and to acknowledge the true wear and tear of life. When we skip over this part—insulating

Do you want to be shiny—or do you want to be free?

ourselves instead of letting our wounds air out—we end up becoming more rigid and less agile thinkers, creating maladaptive behaviors that limit our potential for personal growth that lead us to social impact and the good life.

Within every generation's earnest attempts to undo the past, there are unintended negative consequences. As we try to skirt around past dysfunction, we create new kinds of problems. This enduring cycle that generations engage with becomes one big avoidance swap-off. Dodging one bullet leads us to tripping into a different sinkhole. Avoidance of pain can often in its own way create more of it.

When we look at our resilience through a generational lens, we can see that every generation inherits a set of problems, goes on to correct some of them, and then makes new messes of their own. The pendulum takes violent swings in one direction, requiring us to stay alert that we don't get knocked over when it comes flying back in the other direction.

Turning Out Okay

When you're the eulogy person in your family, you learn a lot of unknown family trivia when someone dies. As I sat with my family at our local book café to gather stories to memorialize my nana, I learned something about the bubble-wrap deficit of her days—better known as the Depression era.

My nana, Teddy Lee, born in 1920, was a tough old-timer who exemplified grit. Bubble wrap was a scarce commodity through her whole life. When she was five, her mother, Agnes, died, and back in the day, that meant she and her four siblings were shipped away to a very strict orphanage—no questions asked, no therapists in sight.

The nuns were incredibly abusive. My nana and great-uncles and aunt were hit and pushed aside, and you can bet their cereal longings were not atop the priority list. When my great-grandfather met his second wife, Catherine, they were relieved to be sent back home to start their new life as a family. Then, when Catherine took sick and died, my great-grandfather's children were sent back to the orphanage for round two until their eventual rescue when my great-grandfather married Marie, his third wife.

You can imagine that my nana was a tough woman after all she'd been through. She was known for her biting humor and defensiveness. She even kept what she herself called a "shit list," and if you were on it, you wanted to get off it quick.

My grandpa, Bob Lee, wasn't without his share of burdens. A World War II veteran, he was later injured in a work accident, losing half of his left arm. At that time, PTSD wasn't recognized, and his bottle was his medicine.

Of course, all this pain spilled over onto my dad's generation. They moved several times, on the run from bill collectors. As my dad and his siblings unpacked their stories, I couldn't help but see the contrasts and progression from the Depression generation to their baby boom generation to my own Generation X, and then for my own millennial–Generation Z children, born in the mid- and late nineties.

The suffering my dad and his family had to do was heavy. They fended for themselves—no helicoptering or coddling, no trips to pediatric orthodontists serving up warm cookies with Xboxes to improve wait times, no full-out clinical-quality counseling sessions when they lost a game or got left out; no refereed recesses, helmets, and knee pads, or cartoon character Band-Aids every time there was a scratch.

They didn't worry about getting into their school of their choice—there was no choice. They moved out, went to work, and didn't blink. Only a few from their entire town actually went on to college—the ones their parents called the *smart ones*, unafraid it would bruise the egos of the ones they called *knuckleheads, dumbasses,* and *fuckups*.

It wasn't about the latest upgrade or having to contend with FOMO (Fear Of Missing Out). It was sink-or-swim, and they were content with their citizens band (CB) radios and card games with huge canisters of pennies.

They still had their share of puppeteers—but instead of overzealous teachers, parents, and coaches, they had bill collectors, drunken rages, and unfiltered adults who told them they'd be flipping burgers if they didn't shape up. The stuff they now joked about was the kind of material that would get a teacher fired, or we would file a 51-A report to child protective services about it.

My dad and his sibs laughed it off, asserting they were perfectly fine. The we-turned-out-okay mantra they kept repeating seemed to be a front, some sort of a self-convincing shield against what they had endured in their own rite. Sure, they weren't yanked in and out of a tormented orphanage, or clobbered with the ASSIEs of today, but their road wasn't without its bumps.

It wasn't until later that day when I was reviewing my pages of notes that I realized that *we turned out okay* was code for *we're incredibly wounded, too*. Suddenly, a lot of their behaviors started to make sense. *We have our own scars, but they're not as bad as our parents'. That's why we tried to protect you. That's why we butted heads and got stuff wrong sometimes. That's why my vein popped out of my forehead when you didn't show gratitude for what we've done for you. We were lucky to have food on the table. There's no way I was gonna let you slide when you complained about not having enough new clothes.*

In the wake of my nana's passing, I made some incredible discoveries that were paralleling the exact themes running through my work with my students who came from all over the world, with their own stories of tensions—all incredibly important pieces to provide context and perspective in a world where some people now throw down more money for a birthday party than we used to for a down payment on a house.

Even when we don't call our kids to the table in a pitch-perfect voice, and the dinner is *just* spaghetti, not some sort of gourmet, organic, brain-boosting dinner, we haven't damaged them. If we lose our cool with our students late on a Friday, we don't need to resign ourselves to being the world's worst teacher. And if our own parents don't run to rescue us at every beckoning call, the world isn't going to fall off its axis.

We're all survivors, just trying to break cycles and do a little better to make life a little better for the next generation. We can learn a lot from our mistakes, and our parents, grandparents, and great-grandparents provide us with endless lessons. It seems like no matter how hard a generation tries to undo the troubles of the past, mistakes will be made. It's unavoidable. And it turns out, that *is* okay.

> "If your mind carries a heavy burden of the past, you will experience more of the same. The past perpetuates itself through lack of presence. The quality of your consciousness at this moment is what shapes the future."
>
> —Eckhart Tolle

The Best Advice for sociallyinferior?

Some people would see sociallyinferior from the last session as the poster child of the bubble-wrap generation. It's easy to beat up on him with all those layers around him. My nana would have given him some tough love, for sure. But underneath it, I wonder if maybe sociallyinferior was so overwhelmed by the choices before him, and so sick of auditioning, he opted to keep his supersize bundle of bubble wrap tightly strapped to him.

The truth is, we're all scared, especially when we're in the throes of trying to feel and heal, with people yanking our strings and telling us how to think and behave, instead of letting us name what's going on and taking the action we need.

The advice from his forum mates, littlemisshy, kos, and pinkpurplepink, is fairly predictable, but not without some helpful messaging:

- Take life by the horns.
- We've all been to hell and back along the way.
- Phone home.
- Be optimistic.
- Quarter-life crisis is a real thing.
- Embrace life.
- Forget the past.

But Spaceghost nailed it:

You are now conscious. . . .
You can now focus.

Waking up is hard to do—but, as Julie Andrews sang, a very good place to start. Even when life delivers its punches, sending us from stage to stage to prove ourselves worthy, or in retreat mode, bundled up so dramatically we can't even step out our door because we're so tightly wrapped, a downward spiral doesn't have to be our default. Too many lessons are available in the mess, and there are always steps to take to lean in to feel and heal.

For far too long, the downward spiral has dominated our psyches and obstructed our view. We can't see beyond the immediate and are blinded by the trappings of our culture. Unfortunately, like sociallyinferior, most of us wait until the smelling salt of a crisis to thrust us into action. That's because we've never been introduced to an alternative way of thinking that helps us overcome the puppet myth and bubble-wrap surplus to become more agile. Until now.

Session Four Worksheet:
Popping Bubbles

Objective:
Unlearn hiding indoctrination that breeds avoidance.
Pivot toward healing.

Rethink It:
Pop Your Bubbles

Life can deliver its share of bumps and bruises. The tendency to want to wrap up and self-protect, or to insulate those we care about, is strong. After a few hard falls, we want to retreat to a place of safety and comfort. So much of life happens outside the range of our control. Instead of focusing on padding ourselves to the point we can no longer feel or move around freely without fear, it's important to try and work on skills that help us to adapt and remain nimble, even in the face of challenges. We need to look at how we think about pain, working to reframe it as a catalyst for growth.

Underneath the Bubbles Check

- What "falls" have I taken that have been particularly challenging?
- What types of situations, people, or events tend to trigger downward-spiral thinking in me?
- In my upbringing, what kinds of messages have I received about being strong and tough?
- Are there people in my life who have wrapped me too tightly, not allowing me to problem solve and develop my own ways of coping?
- What are my coping skills and thresholds for pain like? Do I readily see obstacles as paths to building mental muscle and agility?

Action Steps:
Use Words to Heal and Progress

1. **Create a shadow resume or CV.** Pull out your resume or CV, and within the comments section, make notes on all the "failures" or obstacles you experienced along the way to your "successes." Consider the blood, sweat, and tears invested in your education and within each of your work and volunteer experiences. Think of how many jobs you had to interview for, and how many rejections you faced before scoring. Note how those difficulties were common human experience, and reflect on how they shaped your development. Think about how the no's translated into resolve to find eventual yeses.

2. **Feel and heal.** Pick three words or phrases to describe two or three bothersome experiences. Give them each a descriptive name. For example, if you grew up with a narcissistic parent, you might call it "the all-about-them childhood that frustrates me hard-core," or if you have a toxic boss you might say, "It's a highly anxiety-provoking situation that brings me to my knees," or she "aggravates me to the marrow of my bones." Don't be afraid to pinpoint the behavior and the strong surrounding emotions. The more descriptive, colorful, and creative, the better.

3. **Identify your trends.** Revisit your identified trends from the list of down-ward-spiral thinking styles on page 36. Can you find any direct links to life events and circumstances that are fueling your spiral? What are they?

4. **Aim to reduce negative thinking behaviors.** Pick one that you want to target for a designated time frame (one week is a good starting point).

5. **Develop rebuttal mantras.** Pick three mantras or key phrases you want to use as a rebuttal to your experiences. For example, on childhood, "It had to happen that way for me to be who I am today," or on your aggravating boss: "I'm not gonna let her rent space in my head." Pick a simple word, phrase, or short slogan that's memorable and easy to remember. "Live and let live," "This too shall pass," and "No fear" are some of my favorite rebuttal mantras.

6. **Take off your thick padding.** Embrace experiences that make you want to hide. John Dewey said, "We can learn more from reflecting on our experiences than the actual experiences themselves." What kind of experiences usually make you cringe? Try to rethink your experience as learning, and pinpoint what steps you can take to begin healing.

When we **BURY OUR PAIN,**
it only manifests in **NEW** and
potentially **MORE DESTRUCTIVE**
ways than if we confronted
it in the first place.
GIVING VOICE TO STRUGGLE
can be counterintuitive but is the
birthplace of **HEALING** and
RESILIENCE.

Waking the Sleepwalker

Objective:
Unlearn false truth indoctrination that
breeds wrong conclusions.
Pivot toward evidence-based thinking.

*Consciousness is only possible through change;
change is only possible through movement.*

—Aldous Huxley

Mike Birbiglia unzips his sleeping bag. He's not camping, just starting his Sunday morning ritual inside his posh New York Upper West Side apartment: coffee, brunch, joke writing, and some much-needed rest. In a few hours, he'll be back on stage again.

Birbiglia, thirty-nine, is an award-winning comedian, actor, and producer. You might know him from his role on *Orange Is the New Black*, Jimmy Fallon and Conan O'Brien appearances, or his 100-city tour. Between his self-deprecating transparency and highly relatable obsession with pizza, he's become one of the hottest in the business. He's that funny.

His rise to fame also has a lot to do with his sleeping bag—or to be more precise, the reason behind it, which isn't so funny. On the road trying to launch his career, he jumped from the second-floor window of his hotel room in Walla Walla, Washington. It wasn't a *Jackass*-style stunt or a suicide attempt; he wasn't even conscious at the time. Birbiglia has a condition known as rapid eye movement (REM) behavior disorder, an intense version of sleepwalking.

Before this all went down, Birbiglia had no-showed for the sleep study his neurologist father arranged. He yes-manned every gig that came his way. Pizza and beer were his staples. His screens blared right up until the second he fell asleep. His behaviors were all on the "don't" side of the REM behavior disorder checklist. He was the poster child for overstimulation and sleep deprivation.

At night, he fended off creatures, jumped from podiums, and fought off bad guys. By day, he'd emerge bloody and bruised, dismissing the red flags, much to the chagrin of his worried family. They used every strategy humanly possible to get him to wake up to the fact he needed help: scare tactics, sleep tips, brain books, bribes, ultimatums, jumping up and down. As is with life, the disaster finally woke him.

While doctors pulled the chunks of glass out of his leg, they told him he'd just missed his femoral artery and was more than a little lucky to be alive. Thirty-three stitches and a *hella story* later, Birbiglia finally underwent the highly anticipated sleep study, which revealed his rare disorder —one that causes him to act out his dreams in full force, ninja style.

Walla Walla couldn't have been more of a literal wake-up call. It became the catalyst that spurred Birbiglia into lasting behavioral changes so he'd be less apt to sleepwalk himself into harm's way. The new protocol wasn't rocket science. Lay off the pizza and beer nightcaps. Don't screen leech right before bed. Get enough sleep. Zip up that sleeping bag, so you'll stay put.

Waking up allows us to find as many lenses as possible to widen our view of the world, and to broadcast them as far as humanly possible.

Stay Woke

If you think about it, most of us have a little Birbiglia in us. We humans don't have the best track record when it comes to being consistently attentive or following the best course. We might not thrash in our sleep or Evel Knievel out of hotel windows, but we all have foggy moments that get us lost.

This type of unconscious behavior doesn't happen because we skip our Wheaties or forget our V8. It's not a moral failing or sign of low IQ. It doesn't necessarily mean we have the latest disorder du jour, either.

An awakened mind and heart will serve you well. Rigidity stalls upward progress. Be as expansive as you can. Even when you think you've reached your limit, there's more to unlearn and relearn.

Consciousness is a state of being characterized by thought, sensation, and volition—the process of deciding on and committing to a specific course of action. It can be experienced individually and within a group with shared interests. One of the most common myths about sleepwalking is that we shouldn't wake the sleepwalker. In reality, it has to happen if we want to get to the good life.

Consciousness

Academic Definition

Consciousness is the quality or state of being awake and aware, allowing for active engagement in the world that's within and around you. It gives us access to specific knowledge about issues and phenomena. It allows us to reflect deep awareness of self and regard for contributing positively in our behavior.

Street Definition

Consciousness helps us stay woke. Instead of falling asleep behind the wheel of life, it's like a jolt of caffeine that keeps us on point. All kinds of lightbulbs go off that help us get what's really going on and what we can do about it. Consciousness is like a huge spotlight that startles us in a good way. #intentional #sowoke

Staying woke is one of my favorite terms of today. It means we stay on guard against alternative truths and falsehoods perpetuated by media, politicians, and social institutions. It spurs us on to be more socially conscious, seeing through rhetoric and refusing to assume our so-called place to those in power. Staying woke helps us guard against bullies who try to fearmonger and oppress the masses.

Realizing this helps us wake the sleepwalker and stay woke. Instead of being blindly comforted, we're ready to see beyond illusions of absolute truth. When we train ourselves to rethink what we've been sold, everything changes. We learn to productively resist whatever blocks our vision for leveraging human potential.

When we begin to shift our perspective, we become more conscious—not just for our own sake, but for the greater good. We stop stumbling in the darkness of old-school ways that squash our potential. We no longer accept simple explanations for complexity. We refuse to comply and make ourselves small. We stay on the hunt for solutions instead of lamenting about everything that's wrong.

False truths keep us from realizing we're even sleepwalking. Daytime sleepwalking, or unconsciousness, is the exact behavior my students told me got them into hot water. There were lost opportunities. Close calls. Unhealthy behaviors. Isolation. Regression. And it wasn't because of a lack of thinking. They were simply misguided.

As sapient beings, we possess a high capacity for thinking skills. This is one of our most underrated capacities, and arguably one of our untapped resources. In a world where we can find an alleged answer in a fraction of a second, we are easily distracted from being conscious and expansive. Most days we're lucky if we've grabbed five minutes of quiet. On better days, our sapience can bring us far, though.

As sentient beings, we can experience a wide range of sensations and emotions. These attributes combine to allow us to process pain and suffering in ways that spur on empathy and greater compassion toward ourselves and one another. We are capable of taking our consciousness to new levels. *Hello, good life!*

Hang Up the Telephone Game

Doug Bernstein clears his throat. I've just peppered him with a few too many tangential questions. It was hard to contain myself. A few months before our phone interview, I was inspired by a talk he gave at the

Vancouver International Conference on the Teaching of Psychology. I'm hanging on his every word. He answers me with predictable ease and brilliance. And like any good conversation, I end up with more questions at the end of it. *Mission accomplished.*

Bernstein, seventy-four years old and a professor emeritus at the University of Illinois Urbana-Champaign, has a bio like a book. That's because he's spent his life writing psychology books,[1] teaching, and trying to slow down sugary pop psychology myth contagion. After a lifetime of campaigning for better public understanding of psychology, he's just as determined as ever to help us load up on the peanut butter side of our Fluffernutter sandwiches.

> Stay woke. Jump out of bed, even if it makes you dizzy. Listen to your voice, even if it startles you. Breathe in the smelling salt, even if it stings you. Stare into the light of the reality before you, even if it burns. If you get weary, ask for help—whatever it takes to keep your eyes open. Bask in the glow of conscious living. You are awake. This is when change happens.

As we spoke, I flashed back to his presentation. There were hundreds of us behavioral science evangelists salivating for some peanut butter to bring back to our students. We all knew how spreadable fluff was. Like the childhood telephone game that starts with an original statement that ends up twisted as it's relayed around the circle, there's an abundance of sticky misinformation being passed around.

In our global game of telephone, the bulk and speed of skewed information being whispered and shouted are clouding our vision. The fluff that's being constantly waved in front of our noses and shoved down our throats is doing nothing to nourish us. But sugar is very addictive.

When you can get a roomful of academics to stay put in an air-conditioned room so cold that our lips turn blue, with dingy yellow 1970s wallpaper and no windows on a spectacular July day in Vancouver, you know you've done your job.

One of his first slides read "Introductory Psychology: Putting Students to Sleep Since 1879,"

> We want to crack the code to life, but we're using the wrong numbers.

1 If you've taken a psychology class, there's a good chance he wrote your book. For decades, he's delivered a whole lot of protein from psychological science to try and stave our mental sweet tooth.

which drew a solid nervous half laugh out of us. He was basically telling us to rip up our curriculum. After he told us our students would pretty much forget *everything* we taught them, you'd think a mass exodus to the park and gyros place around the corner would be a given—but we're that kind of quirky breed that likes these kinds of challenges.

He flashed a bunch of black-and-green slides up that read, "Myths and Illusions About Human Behavior in Everyday Life," as a guidepost. You could hear a pin drop as we scanned the list to make sure we weren't smearing any fluff around:

Myth #1: It's better to stick to your first impulse than to go back and change test answers. *Uh-oh. I just told my son that last week.*

Myth #2: Opposites attract. *My closest inner circle is stacked with introverts. C'mon, are you sure?*

Myth #3: We are in touch with reality. *Jeez, I thought I was in the moment here.*

Myth #4: We make our own decisions. *This is getting a little unnerving.*

Myth #5: We only use 10 percent of our brainpower. *Whew, I knew this one was outdated. One for five.*

Myth #6: Eyewitness testimony is the best kind of evidence. *Oops again.*

Myth #7: Subliminal messages have powerful effects on behavior. *Is he trying to send a subliminal message now?*

Myth #8: There are effective hangover cures. *Good thing I'm more of a kale juice drinker.*

Myth #9: Drug education programs (e.g., DARE) are effective in deterring teen drug use. *Is that why 90 percent of my high school classmates sported mullets (equal amounts of girls and guys) and always had the munchies?*

Myth #10. We taste sweet, sour, salty, and bitter on specific areas of the tongue. *You're making me hungry.*

Bernstein reminded us that despite the massive research that proves otherwise in each of his examples, we're still very likely to believe falsehoods. *That fluff is like tree pitch. Hard to wash off.* Even in the subzero AC, the room felt heavy. All of us had made it our life's work to stop the misinformation epidemic. We knew the telephone game was dangerous. What if it wasn't enough? What if people were prone to believe what was easy, not valid? What if they don't know or even care? What if truth isn't even a thing?

As leaders in our field, we took these questions seriously. In lockstep with the American Psychological Association, Bernstein emphasized how vigilant we need to be to make sure scientific inquiry, critical thinking, and ethical and social responsibility in a diverse world remain our absolute priorities.

That's what drew us to his talk in the first place. As head of the Behavioral Science Department at my university, the majority of my time is spent making sure we're disrupting, not perpetuating, fluffy thinking.

There are barriers to overcome. White papers are filled with esoteric jargon, making it hard to translate into everyday life. *It's like psychobabble. Esoteric means intended or likely to be understood only by a small number of people with a specialized knowledge or interest. See how annoying that is?* Our appetite for understanding human behavior sends us skimming off the top from research findings, getting a quick fix, but missing the sustenance we desperately need. When we apply with a broad brush our morsels of surface learning to everybody and everything, we engage in what's known as *overgeneralizing*, a big no-no in interpreting scientific research.

Know the Difference Between Self-Help Fads and Scientific Evidence

Self-help fads are enticing, with their "groundbreaking" and "astonishing" findings that rake in a half billion dollars a year. Fads are easy to confuse with evidence-based practice, especially since we tend to be biased toward what we think already.

Self-help books can be written by anyone. Even famous authors and TV personalities don't always have the credibility to support their claims. The principles are not supported by scientific research, and it's not a guarantee that they actually improve lives. In some cases, the oversimplifications are harmful.

> Evidence-based theories come with a solid measure of quality control, helping us work to bypass our biases and override preconceptions. They require application of scientific methods to produce findings that are well grounded. Solid research and practice that are built on evidence, not fads, will always include disclaimers so as not to overgeneralize. It will pose new questions needing to be explored to help us base what we do on something more stable than the latest five-step method that completely broad-brushes the complexity of human experience, behavior, and phenomena.

All research has limitations, even protein-filled, evidence-based psychology. Human bias, error, subjectivity, and even who's funding studies all play a role in credibility. If you look at the end of any peer-reviewed study, the researchers offer a disclaimer recognizing its limitations. But that's not the part that gets blasted across the news. Instead, results are shared as absolute truth, as if they apply 24/7 to every human being across the entire plant.

There's a big global telephone game at play. Every day, we have to listen carefully to what is being shared because chances are it's not the full story. Consider who starts the chain of information and who spreads it—and why. Don't close yourself off to one channel of communication. You'll never find honest answers that way.

At the time of my phone interview with Bernstein, my mentalligence model had already emerged from my teaching and grounded theory research, and I'd been on my own version of a fluff purge for a while. My students from around the world were showing me we couldn't keep buying into overinterpreted findings being passed around writ large.

Move Beyond WEIRD

The telephone game isn't the only problem. Most research that dictates clinical and teaching practice has been deemed *WEIRD*, meaning that it comes from a primarily *Western-Educated Industrialized Rich Democratic* bent, rather than a global perspective that represents the vast spectrum of people populating planet Earth.

The behavioral science research landscape displays only about 12 percent of the world's population. Picture standing in a room full of 100 people, and then only a dozen people are picked to speak on behalf of everyone else—and if you're not a college student, chances are only 50/50 that you'll get asked. That's because half of all behavioral studies rely on college students as subjects. Forget about understanding life across age and life stages. Instead, like mainstream television, the data only represent select slices of the human experience.

What if the theories in psychology that dominate our mainstream culture are flawed, rather than the people they diagnose? That we close our eyes to modern brain science and global context and pigeonhole human beings as "normal" or "abnormal" is one of the biggest shams of the century.

Even one of the most popular theories of our time, emotional intelligence, has WEIRD elements. Daniel Goleman popularized Peter Salovey and John Mayer's seminal article on emotional intelligence (EI) with his book of the same name. Goleman went on to sell over 5 million copies, including translations in forty languages, becoming sainted in the world of work and education.

Salovey and Mayer didn't intend for their paper to travel that far, especially when their theories hadn't been tested and measured properly. It's not that Goleman's work isn't solid. A lot of noble attributes, like empathy, are taught within the EI framework. It's the way that Goleman packaged it that makes some scientists shake their heads. The claims that EI determines real-world success are unproven, and brain research doesn't support the construct. It's not fatally flawed. It just needs to be less WEIRD.

One criticism of EI is that it doesn't translate well across cultures and varied populations. This was a hot topic in my classroom and research study. My students from collectivist cultures didn't get how EI was beneficial. They were like, *"Whaaat?* Abandon my roots and start making the rounds, to make friends and influence people?" It went against their instincts and values. It felt manipulative to them. Many of them also felt like it was encouraging stifled emotions rather than authentic expression.

Emotional intelligence has cult appeal across the business, social science, and educational sectors, informing the way we do work, school, and relationships. We love theories like this—where we can hack the system by becoming emotional ninjas. We're inclined to believe what is comforting, and many aspects of EI are useful, *for sure.*

Most people wouldn't suspect that such an accepted framework from a Harvard graduate that is built on a peer-reviewed article has holes in it. It doesn't need to be blown up, but it also shouldn't be propagated as a universal template for behavior.

We're not just subjected to this problem in popular psychology realms. Myth contagion has many launchpads—professional disciplines, religion, and breaking news, among other platforms. They all have their slant. And when word gets out on the street, it gets convoluted fast. Between the conference and my telephone interview with Bernstein, I was more determined than ever to stop sticky illusions from spreading. Myths are the last things we need to stay woke. When we hung up, I knew it was time to try to hang up from the global telephone game, too.

Session Five Worksheet:
Waking the Sleepwalker

Objective:
Unlearn false truth indoctrination that breeds wrong conclusions.
Pivot toward evidence-based thinking.

Rethink It:
Move from Sleepwalking to Consciousness

Sleepwalking is often a natural reaction to a chaotic environment. With all that comes at us, changing from long-held beliefs to new ways of seeing requires us to shift in ways that are often unsettling. We are flooded with sugary, sensational information that does little to build our intellectual muscle. Most of us wouldn't make a diet on Oreos, *even though they are allegedly addictive as crack*, because we know our bodies would be depraved of essential nutrients. Over time, if we binge on sugar and don't keep up with the mental exercises of rethinking and unlearning, we can atrophy. The resulting brain rot keeps us from reaching new heights in our awareness. We need to find and use our reflective lens to see how we engage with false truths to avoid wrong conclusions and to pivot toward conscious thinking. When we avoid the childish telephone game of misinformation that is passed around writ large, we decrease our susceptibility to myth contagion. We have newfound alertness and clarity. We avoid the tremendous waste of sleepwalking through life.

Consciousness Check

- What types of things do I believe about human behavior and psychology?
- When and where did I learn them?
- Have I tested them out over time?
- What do I need to unlearn and relearn?
- How could not having accurate information be affecting my quest for the good life?

Action Steps:
Clean Up Your Fluff

To wash off pesky fluff, we must come to understand that much of what we've learned lacks substance, or only comes from a narrow view. To find more protein, we need to be on the hunt for varied and credible sources. We need to get out of bed and try on some new shoes to get traction:

1. **Cut the bootstraps.** Don't let pride trip you up. You don't have to have absolute answers to tough life out. Ask yourself what you don't know.

Be fearless with your questions. Don't worry about being right. Gather as much information as you can from as many credible sources as you can find.

2. **Get your feet muddy.** We don't expand our thinking without getting lost first. As Harvard professor Frederick Mostelle first put it, we will inevitably have "muddy points" when we're trying to learn. When things aren't clear for us, we feel stuck. Staying clean within a muddy landscape is unrealistic. Don't be afraid to get a little dirty as you trudge through it all. Resist the urge to see things in neat, linear categories.

3. **Throw on your flip-flops.** Things are often not what they seem. Allow your positions to change. Embrace ambiguity and disruption. When we start paying attention, we see just how complicated life is, and how many lenses are available to us to try to understand the world. Don't settle for one set way of seeing things. Look for deeper meaning that allows you to update your thinking and amass an amazing collection of lenses that will not only benefit you but be brought to scale for wider impact.

4. **Take a trip somewhere else.** Take a trip to the library and ask about how to find peer-reviewed sources. Visit Google Scholar to check out articles that are frequently cited, an indicator that the source isn't just the latest pop psychology contagion. Chat with the librarian about which stacks and sites to visit to make sure you are working from solid literature.

Our brains are in a constant, weird, **PARADOXICAL STATE** of **OVERSTIMULATION.** On one hand we are gorged with information and yet we are simultaneously anorexic, hungry for **SUBSTANCE,** for **SOMETHING REAL.**

We are **STARVING** for **INTELLECTUAL PROTEIN.**

No matter how sticky and **TEMPTING** fluff is, we must remain averse to it. We keep our hands clean of the **SUPERFICIAL** and stay on the hunt to **FEED** not only our **MINDS** but our **SOULS.**

PART II

The Tuning-In Sessions

Find Your Mindful Lens

Rethink the 5 forms of indoctrination that lead to mindlessness:

→ From Deficit to Strengths Thinking

→ From One-and-Done to Resilient Thinking

→ From Sky-Is-Falling to Critical Thinking

→ From Consumeristic to Gratitude Thinking

→ From Happy Talk to Mindful Thinking

The Tuning-In Sessions help you unlearn five forms of indoctrination that lead to mindless behavior. You will pivot to become more focused in your thinking, stop being judgmental toward yourself and everyone else, and tell perfectionism to kiss off so that you can find your way back to center to a mindful lens. The sessions will help you cope with complexity, not get lost in it. They help combat instability, fear, disconnection, waste, and mindlessness. This is our new psychology of thinking: becoming mindful twenty-first-century citizens. This could be the start of something beautiful, yes?

SESSION SIX

Flipping Couches

Objective:
Unlearn deficit indoctrination that breeds labeling.
Pivot toward strengths thinking.

A "normal" person is the sort of person that might be designed by a committee. Each person puts in a pretty color and it comes out gray.

—Alan Sherman

lose your eyes. Picture the word *psychology*. What comes to mind? A brain? Diagnosis? A couch? Sigmund Freud? Your therapist's *I know you're feeding me a line of bullshit* glance? Inkblots?

If inkblots danced across your mind, that's because they are *the* most known mainstream images associated with psychology. Swiss psychologist Hermann Rorschach, a bit of a Brad Pitt lookalike, made them famous in 1921.

Rorschach was into klecksography, the art of making images from ink-blots. He wasn't just artsy or obsessed with the sensory experience of making them, but he was trying to test his theory, one that was in lockstep with the main juxtaposition of psychology: that *something's wrong with you and needs to be fixed.*

He thought that if he analyzed how his patients recognized patterns, it would reveal whether they were mentally stable. He hadn't exactly accounted for his own subjectivity or its inconsistency in predicting behavior. He didn't factor in social context, or the countless other variables that affect perception. And he never got the chance to tease it out properly.

Rorschach died at the age of thirty-seven, while his test methods were still immature. But the domino had already been tipped. His sticky idea spread, and then some. You can see why something as intriguing as the inkblot test had such a run. And it's not dead yet. Even nearly a century later—despite scientific evidence deeming the test unreliable and invalid—psychologists and websites still use them.

Like the popular inkblot test, the *something's wrong with you* position has stood the test of time. When an entire field is built on this premise, some time is needed to wash away the imprint. Since beliefs become behaviors, we need to start scrubbing the ink off our collective consciousness. Where's Mr. Clean when you need him?

You'd think we'd have magically erased it away by now. We certainly have the tools to do so. Between breaking news in brain science and all the data we have on social context, it seems like we'd have retired old diagnostic and treatment methods by now.

We've done so in medicine. In 1992 and then again in 2002, I had my ACL repaired. The second surgery went a lot smoother that the first. Smaller scars, less invasive, better recovery time. When your surgeon fixes New England Patriots and Boston Celtics players, you know you're in good hands. Mine had all the latest tools to get me back to my eclectic adventures. When we default to outdated methods of framing human behavior, not factoring in all we now know about brain science and social context, it's as absurd as me saying to my surgeon, "Oh, you wanna use that same technique from back in the '90s? Sure, put away your arthroscope, dust off your old scalpel, and get to work. I don't mind triple the recovery time and a massive scar."

That we're using old-school sit-on-the-couch-and-tell-me-your-problems methods in behavioral science realms, even though we have new learning that could revolutionize our lives, is one of our great modern shames. You'd think those old couches would be out on the curb by now, but they're heavy to move.

The misinformation spills into our communities, schools, and homes—places where we need the best of brain science to inform us. We label, shun, stigmatize, and imprison people because of it. Our classrooms, therapy

When we continuously snuggle up to antiquated ideas, we shut our eyes against the light of our potential.

rooms, boardrooms, and living rooms are stuck in the 1950s. Blame and shame techniques from yesteryear have been proven to do more harm than good, but they live on as go-to tactics for too many teachers, therapists, leaders, and parents.

We have data that should have flipped Freud and his couch over long ago.[1] But we're hard-to-budge couch potatoes, binge watching old episodes of *Freud and His Bros* telling us how pathological we are. *Who gets to decide what normal is?*

Flip the Couch

After the first few weeks of my clinical training, I wasn't only ready to flip the couch. I wanted to flip off my supervisor, Mary. Right from the outset, I noticed a lot of contradictions.

When you take master's in social work (MSW) classes, there's a lot of hype about a *strengths-based perspective*. It's ethical, evidence-based, and humane. *Three for three. Sold.*

Then, when you start clinical rounds, that perspective goes missing. There's something about how those mental health diagnostic examinations are worded. They fish for everything but something's-*right*-with-you clues. Besides the one token strengths question tacked on at the end, everything else was hard-core what's-a-matter-fa-you material.

I needed a 1-800-strengths finder hotline to help me out. "If you'd like people to understand they are wired for change, press 1. If you believe they can turn their challenges into momentum, press 2. If you worry people are blinded by their problems and stigmatized by their labels instead of

---

1 Freud made incredible contributions to the discipline. The hyperfocus on diagnosis and labeling without looking for strengths is the part of the couch that needs replacing.

appreciating their awesomeness, press 3. If you wish society would realize that the *problem is the problem, not the person*, press 4. If you think shaming people sucks, press 5. *And for all of the above?*

Of course, there was no hotline. Mary's only available options were, "If you think people will never change, press 1. If you think people are lazy, crazy, and stupid, press 2. If you think every minute of every session should be spent talking about negative stuff, press 3. If you think people are 100 percent to blame for everything that happens to them, and *deserve exactly what they get*, because they *just love being victims*, press 4. If you like to rub people's noses in their own shit, press 5."

Mary was the ultimate people hater, which wouldn't matter as much if she were an accountant. But here she was, in a field dedicated to helping people, hating on everybody like they were spotted puppies and she was Cruella de Vil.

You've seen it before: the screaming teacher who seems to despise kids or the obese doctor who smokes and won't exercise. It's confusing, right? *C'mon, didn't you read* What Color Is Your Parachute? Life is full of strange contradictions like this. I was running out of options, but I knew I wasn't going to accept Mary's abysmal way of treating people.

Sometimes you gotta take matters into your own rebel-with-a-cause hands. I'd been reading about solutions-focused, strength-based techniques, so I decided to try my own experiment.

Besides asking, "How long has your depression lasted?" or "How many panic attacks have you experienced?" or "How long has your husband driven you batshit crazy?" I decided to get creative. I started asking things like, "What's going well in your life?" "What lights you up?" "When things went off the rails, what got you back on track again?" "You know your name is 'John,' not 'bipolar,' right?"

You'd think my patients would have loved my underground intervention. At first, they seemed a little spooked. Many of them had seen a lot of different therapists, but I was the first to ask them these types of questions. It took them a little time to warm up to what they saw as a radically different form of treatment, but the approach was working.

Once my patients made a conscious effort to stop defaulting to their self-loathing recitations, everything changed. The sparkle in their eyes returned. The shame hangover lessened. They were finally free from beating themselves up.

I didn't know at that early point in my training how religiously I would cling to the strengths-based approach beyond my clinical work. It became my go-to within my own therapy process, parenting, teaching, workout strategies, and even dreaded postelection Thanksgiving dinners when the only temporary tension-breaker is pumpkin pie.

Bake Your Strengths

It wasn't just the intake forms, my crusty supervisor, or my tentative patients that were having trouble shifting. It's taken over a century to get our teeth around a different approach.

A strengths-based perspective, a social work practice theory founded by Bertha Capen Reynolds in the early 1900s, warned against the traditional psychoanalytic approach. She asserted that people are resourceful and resilient, not broken and helpless. Today, Reynolds is seen as a hero in the field, but back then she wasn't exactly the hit of the party. You can imagine just how likely people were apt to listen to her ideas at a time when women didn't have basic rights, like voting.

Years later, in 1999, when then president of the American Psychological Association, Dr. Martin Seligman, pointed to the merits of strengths-based thinking, people were warming up to the idea. He warned that "the most important thing that we learned was that psychology is half-baked. We've baked the part about mental illness, about repair damage. The other side's unbaked, the side of strength, the side of what we're good at."

The baking metaphor was sticky. He probably could have gotten carried away with it if he wanted, since the cousin theory to a strengths-based perspective is known as Person In Environment (PIE), which is worth Googling. Luckily, Seligman wasn't that cheesy and instead created his own acronym, PERMA, standing for Positive emotions, Engagement, positive Relationships, Meaning, and Accomplishment. Seligman's work emphasizes that we can no longer accept half-baked information—that we are capable of better methods.

Seligman has been named the father of positive psychology, which, like professional social work, holds central the belief that change occurs when we come out of the gate looking for what's *working well*, versus what's *not*. The starting point frames the entire change effort. He says that the goal of positive psychology isn't just to increase human happiness, but to promote eudaimonia, or human flourishing.

This perspective is not rainbows and butterflies, and it doesn't try to shove life into a childhood story template with a perfect arc and happy ending. Baking our strengths doesn't mean we won't experience pain or difficulty. It helps us work toward a more holistic approach to understanding ourselves and one another.

Our old methods of excavating for problems leaves us with more problems. Everything rides on changing the positions we hold, the questions we ask, and the answers we're willing to accept. When we only mine for weaknesses, that's exactly what we'll find.

Another positive psychologist, University of Michigan's Barbara Frederickson, is working hard to help people warm up to the idea of getting their strengths into the oven. In her broaden-and-build theory of positive emotions, she explains how negative emotions narrow *thought-action repertoires* that trigger fight-or-flight behaviors. Positive emotions, on the other hand, help broaden these repertoires, thus spurring on novel thought and action.

Frederickson's research has manifested an important discovery: deficit doesn't have to be our natural default. We can widen our attention and cognition. Frederickson says this expansion helps us initiate upward spirals.

Baking strengths can be messy and tedious work. Many of us hadn't even set foot into the kitchen until well into our adult lives. We might not think we have the equipment to get us started, or that our efforts will measure up, given our challenges.

But once we get going, we realize that our minds are capable of generating upward momentum, and things start to gel. Frederickson's theory repudiates conventional downward-spiral, something's-wrong mind-sets, and gets us asking the kinds of questions that spur on new thinking and behavior.

Save Your Normal

Dr. Allen Frances has worked hard to get us moving in a new direction. After holding prestigious chairperson roles at Duke University's School of Medicine and the *Diagnostic and Statistical Manual* (*DSM-IV*) task force, he blew the whistle on psychiatry. After years as an insider, he called malarkey on what he calls "diagnostic inflation," or the tendency to gather any hints of struggle into a full-blown diagnosis.

After some successful online stalking on my part, Dr. Frances agreed to a phone interview with me. He started by telling me that when his wife died, he felt sad—but it wasn't "major depressive disorder"; it was a natural response to losing her. He explained that using an exclusively biological paradigm without scientific justification is bad practice. To his point, a study published by the American Psychological Association reported that only one-third of patients receiving antidepressants were engaging in evidence-based interventions such as cognitive behavioral therapy.

This matter is delicate and complicated. It's not that medicine is the enemy. Medicine can be an effective and lifesaving tool in treating mental health issues. Throwing the baby out with the bathwater would be foolish. But when it's the only approach being used without factoring in psychosocial components, we're at risk of medicalizing normal. Frances is concerned that growing practices to categorize human emotions as automatic grounds for diagnosis could be distracting us from helping people who need it most.

Frances emphasized that we need accountability and more grounded, ethical policies to mitigate overprescribing, and to help us get the comprehensive help we need. A 2015 Centers

> "Normal is nothing more than a cycle on a washing machine."
>
> —Whoopi Goldberg

for Disease Control and Prevention report revealed that of the 2.8 billion drugs ordered, antidepressants were in the most frequently prescribed category. Ethical leaders need to take a stand and not let the voices of integrity get drowned out by those with their own interests in mind.

As with his book *Saving Normal: An Insider's Revolt Against Out-of-Control Psychiatric Diagnosis, DSM-5, Big Pharma, and the Medicalization of Ordinary Life*, Frances told me that "overtreatment" of the "worried well" was becoming out of control. Not only are we erring when we flag emotions like sadness, anxiety, and grief as inevitable signs of mental illness, but drug companies and physicians are making some serious funds off these framings.

Big Pharma, which has been called "America's New Mafia," pumps out a lot of commercials reminding us just how sick we are—$3 billion worth, to be exact. The catchy prelude plays. Cartoon Mom enters the scene. She looks a little gloomy. The announcer says she has "hard-to-treat depression." *Oh, she must need Abilify.*

Viewer: What about those side effects? They seem intense.

Big Pharma: What's a little drooling, a few extra pounds, dizziness, paralyzed jaw, constipation, or risk of death to deal with anyway? Plus, it can work as fast as two weeks. You can trust us.

Viewer: Will it work?

Big Pharma: Don't worry about the studies from the doctors we couldn't pay off to suppress their findings. Sure, they've shown placebos 80 percent as effective as the most popularly prescribed medicines—Prozac, Paxil, Zoloft, Celexa, Serzone, and Effexor— but none have come out against Abilify. Oh, that muffled sound coming from my trunk? Definitely not a whistleblowing doctor. It's just my stash of Abilify mugs, pens, T-shirts, and donuts to try to win a few more docs over.

Viewer: Are there other options?

Big Pharma: Lifestyle medicine—getting proper sleep, nutrition, and exercise—or evidence-based cognitive behavioral treatment have a lot of research to back them up, but you should talk to doctors we spend $1.4 billion on to verify our claims. They're totally impartial and have no conflicts of interest.

Viewer: Hasn't Abilify always been used to treat psychosis?

Big Pharma: Yes, that's always been the case, but we found some doctors who could vouch for it, plus with this new "hard-to-treat depression" that seems to be the case for so many women, one of our fastest-growing customers. . . . I mean patient groups, why not give it a try?

Viewer: Do these commercials run across the world? Is all the medicine healthy for us?

Big Pharma: Only the United States and New Zealand are lucky enough to get this kind of information regularly presented to them. Seventy percent of Americans are on prescriptive drugs, and the United States has worse health outcomes than other industrialized countries, but don't worry. Just keep on kissing our ring and we'll have your back. Did we mention we have pills for bad backs, too?

This all seems like a scene from *The Fugitive Meets The Godfather*, except Harrison Ford and Al Pacino are nowhere in sight. Commercials aren't the only problem. Drug companies have a lot of power. Big Pharma has cast a wide net for experts and patients alike.

Years ago, when I was working in a psychiatric practice, we had regular visits from drug reps equipped with donuts and every kind of office supply branded with their logo for our clinical team. They also had plenty of drug samples to get our patients on their merry way. It always seemed a little suspect to me, and you'd think they would've at least picked a healthier snack for a team of doctors, but stranger things have happened.

I once had a go-round with Drug Rep Guy, as we not-so-creatively referred to him. At the time, Depakote was the rising-star med for bipolar disorder, and he was determined to sell it to our clinic. I had some beefs with it, mainly because a lot of my patients were gaining weight right before my eyes.

The effects from the honey-glazed donuts he'd swooned us with had worn off, so I started drilling him with questions. Drug Rep Guy insisted that the drug didn't cause weight gain, even though the evidence showed otherwise.

I brought up the studies I'd read and the patient examples, but his eyes were glazing over. He kept repeating his script: While the drug hasn't been *proven* to cause weight gain, *it does* cause an increase in appetite, and special cravings for chocolate and fatty food. *Oh, alright, now it makes total sense to me. Increased cravings for Hershey's and Awesome Blossoms have zero relationship to weight gain. Sometimes I get caught up in semantics. Thank you for this important clarification.*

With the pharmaceutical industry in bed with some academic physicians, the resulting conflicts of interest bring hard-core consequences. Dr. Marcia Angell, the former editor-in-chief of the *New England Journal of Medicine*, has had plenty of her own go-rounds with Big Pharma, so much so that she warns not to "rely on the judgment of trusted physicians or authoritative medical guidelines." Now what?

In the meantime, we need evidenced-based treatment solutions that do more than push pills. A 2012 World Health Organization report calls depression a "global crisis," estimating its effect on 350 million people worldwide. Cartoon Mom has a lot of friends.

What if there's a backstory to Cartoon Mom's and Friends' hard-to-treat depression? Could it be that she's exhausted from her eighteen-plus-hour days, and then the perpetual game of musical beds with her kids by night? What if she can barely sneak in thirty minutes of walking during the intermission of her son's soccer game while she answers the ridiculous amounts of email she left behind to dash there?

Could being upset reflect a natural response to the fact she'd arrived to the game late, greeted by Good Mom who showed up fifteen minutes early with Pinterest cupcakes for all the kids, telling her that she'd *literally just missed* her son's first goal of the season? What if she's like most parents who wrestle with constant guilt that they're not spending enough time with their children,[2] even though today's parents spend more time with their kids than previous generations?

What if Cartoon Mom is tired of being vilified for her choices? What if she just needs to stop being a fembot for five minutes and grab some fresh air and solitude? Maybe she just needs one Saturday morning of uninterrupted sleep, or for someone to stop thinking her life is so easy just because she "has it all"?

---

2 All the guilt might be wasted energy. A first-of-its-kind longitudinal study reported that quantity of time spent is not a factor in how children turn out. It's quality, plus a whole boatload of other variables.

Might Cartoon Mom's hard-to-treat, atypical depression shift if her creepy boss started listening to her ideas instead of looking at her ass? What if she just needs the robotic smiles and good-for-you pats to stop when she tells someone she's a high-powered lawyer, as if she's a special-case, token successful woman? What if she's sick of everyone telling her husband how *great* he is because he so graciously shares the responsibilities everyone thinks were hers to begin with? *She's soooo lucky. He babysits their own kids. He even grocery shops.*

What if we're looking at the inkblot all wrong? What if hard-to-treat Cartoon Mom or any of her anxious and depressed friends aren't the ones with the problem? What if the interpretation of symptoms is skipping over the part about hard-to-treat social ills? What if the data we're basing everything on are flawed, not her?

And what if Cartoon Mom and her friends could see the bigger picture —that while clinically significant mental health issues are serious, sometimes we need to turn off the commercials to save normal and get us off the couch once and for all.[3]

Psychology has at least gotten us awake and out of bed, but we can no longer stay glued to our couches. We've got to flip them over, to find out

> Sometimes we need to tune out before we can tune in.

what else is underneath. In our global twenty-first century, we need to save normal. There is no good reason to be held hostage by Big Pharma, or in pseudoscience inkblot and WEIRD modes. We can think bigger and broader, using the best of evidence-based brain science and a strengths-based perspective to move us upward.

---

3 Oversimplifying mental health issues is dangerous. Treatment can save a life, and utmost care must be given to protect mental health and ensure proper evidence-based treatment. Biopsychosocial factors must be understood to determine best approaches for anyone suffering with anxiety, depression, or other symptoms. Medication can be a lifesaver but should not be the only method of intervention. The best thing to do is to see a licensed, reputable practitioner who can spend the time to evaluate all facets and make solid recommendations.

Session Six Worksheet:
Flipping Couches Worksheet

Objective:
Unlearn deficit indoctrination that breeds labeling.
Pivot toward strengths thinking.

Rethink It:
Move from Deficits to Strengths

Sometimes we've shut our ovens off before we had a chance to bake our strengths to full maturity. Like inaccurate inkblot tests, we can be sent into cycles of thinking that we are entirely flawed. When we fixate on deficits without considering strengths, we stay stuck in downward-spiral modes, instead of seeing the bigger picture of our worth and potential.

Strengths Check

- What three strengths am I most proud of?
- Are there any labels people have given me that are half baked?
- What kinds of explanations do I rely on to understand myself?
- What do people who know me well say about my strengths?

Action Steps:
Recognize Your Strengths

We're taught from an early age to be problem-focused, not solution-focused. To save our normal, we must flip the couch and see what's underneath it. Too many WEIRD framings in psychology are outdated and don't capture all the sides of life.

1. **Get off the couch.** Remove yourself from the pathologizing couch and go on a strengths-finding expedition. Go back and review your Values in Action Inventory results from session two.

2. **You can also take a SWOT analysis online to help pinpoint strengths.** Tuning in requires discovering strengths that serve as springboards for growth and development.

3. **Bake your strengths.** We all have strengths to keep developing. Pick one that you really want to work on—whether it's more confidence, public speaking skills, empathy, creativity, or otherwise. Select one that you want to focus on. Ask a trusted friend to brainstorm ways to develop it further. Keep it in the oven for at least three weeks—in other words, practice the skill diligently for that set period. When the timer

goes off, take a look at your progress and see what else you can do to keep on baking.

4. **Save your normal.** Take a close look at your whole health. Be proactive about protecting it. Consider chatting with a licensed therapist or coach to look at you in totality—your strengths and struggles—to determine the best types of support to help you cope with life's stressors and be proactive in maintaining optimal health.

spiral

noun | [spīrəl]

1. show a continuous and dramatic increase.
2. decrease or deteriorate continuously.

Joni worked hard to embrace the different directions of her life spiral.

Embracing Your Spiral

Objective:
Unlearn one-and-done indoctrination
that breeds instability.
Pivot toward resilience.

*One must still have chaos in oneself to be
able to give birth to a dancing star.*

—Friedrich Nietzsche

The inner workings of the human mind are a source of great fascination and debate from social science laboratories to coffee shops. We are in hot pursuit to figure ourselves and each other out. A lot of forces dictate behavior, and endless theories try to explain why we do what we do. It's exciting and a bit overwhelming. Just when you think you've got it figured out, you find a new contingency or contradiction. Like young Jedis, we have our work cut out for us.

Resilience has become the hot topic of today. You can barely enter a parenting, business, or school conversation without hearing about it. Some resilience researchers worry that we're asking narrow questions about individual behavior and overlooking social context. They're working to elevate the conversation to include systems analysis. Mindless banter about resilience can reinforce one-and-done framings.

Using social network analysis theory, an interdisciplinary research team comprising Jessica Shaw, Kate McLean, Bruce Taylor, Kevin Swartout, and Katie Querna point out that most of our stories of resilience are conjured up through the lens of highly romanticized, individualistic, against-the-odds ideals. We can't get enough of rags-to-riches and setback-to-comeback stories, but we rarely stop and look at why they were necessary at all.

The authors make the point that hyping displays of hardiness and intelligence while pretending the social context creating the need for these traits to begin with are irrelevant reinforces something's-wrong-with-you thinking. This approach fits with the popular one-and-done theory about trauma, performance, and relationships: If you haven't followed a straight and narrow academic or job path, you're bound to fail. If this happens to you, you're done. If you don't do well in school early in life, you're screwed. If you've had a string of bad relationships, you'll never find love. If you've messed up, it's because you're an idiot. We're not trained to look at the chaos around us to understand its push and pull on our lives. We think that *we're* unstable, not the forces themselves.

Factor in the Forces

So many factors influence our growth and development. Everything that happens to us and around us can alter the course of our lives. We try desperately to function seamlessly within a predictably unpredictable environment. We set out to find balance, only to be chewed up and spit out by life. Homeostasis comes and goes, and if we blink, we often miss it.

The deeper we peer into the black hole of human analysis, the more we realize how many forces are at hand. It's tempting to hail one explanation as the be-all and end-all. Even though taking one precise position might help us chill out temporarily,

Much is known; even more is unknown. That is the beauty and peril of our existence. Disarray is the birthplace of inquiry and discovery. Don't shy away from it. Lean in, wondrous being, and bask in the glorious ambiguity that wants to teach you.

doing so can limit our capacity for growth. Ambiguity is hard to sit with. But when we tune into the forces at hand, we open up to letting disarray serve as our teacher, not our enemy. As Greek mythology put forth, "Chaos was the first to exist."

Early-twentieth-century physicist Henri Poincare called this *dynamical instability*. His chaos theory suggests that no matter how out of sorts things might seem, they rely on an underlying order. Unpredictability is more predictable than you'd first think. Chaos isn't random. Everything happens for a reason, but as much as our minds are on constant meaning-making missions, feeling settled within chaotic conditions is still incredibly tricky.

In 1963, MIT meteorology professor Edward Lorenz revealed discoveries about the universal forces of predictable unpredictability. Much to the delight of the science community, he helped overturn prior notions of the universe as linear and deterministically sequenced. His "butterfly effect" theory explains how the timing of the flap of a butterfly's wings in one region can set off a tornado in another.

Stop subscribing to loose associations and broadbrush inferences that do absolutely nothing to bring us closer to engaging with complexity in healthy ways. Be on guard against oversimplified explanations and anecdotal tales that move us viscerally but do nothing to help our rational sides.

Lorenz's weather-pattern simulations showed how the tiniest shifts lead to big-time consequences. His work illustrates just how much we need to factor into life's equation. A lot of unseen butterfly flaps in our lives affect our resilience.

Given how complex life is, you'd think that the last urge we'd give into would be locking down on oversimplified answers to complexity, but we do it all the time. That's because we haven't been taught how to interpret all the forces at hand.

Force #1: Universal Chaos

We pine for order, but life is not orderly. Across time and space, and within every community that's ever existed, complexity and chaos are mainstays, part of

Do you want to be right, or do you want to know better?

nature. As a civilization, we've advanced significantly, but there's still problems to address. Disarray becomes the birthplace of inquiry. Disorder nudges us to ask questions and work to figure out what's going on.

Our quest for meaning-making has led to a lot of revelations, and even more debate. Every side searches for absolutes. All groups and affiliations —whether social identity, scientific, religious, cultural, or otherwise— claim to have the secrets for a successful life (and even their version of the afterlife). When we cling to one lens alone, we shut out additional possibilities for holistic thinking. Much is known, but even more is unknown. No single organizing framework gives us all the answers. There are always contradictions. But we still tend to gravitate toward cookie-cutter theories instead of embracing ambiguity. When this happens, we miss being able to adopt an integrated view of resilience that would account for chaos and help spur on greater agility.

> "The wound is the place where the Light enters you."
>
> —Rumi

Force #2: Primitive Instincts

Territory is at the heart of all conflict. As creatures wired for survival, our animalistic tendencies to self-protect and preserve are powerful forces of nature. They dictate our entire repertoire of actions. We're constantly on the hunt to satisfy our desires for food and sex, and to guard our tribe and turf. When something threatens any of these domains, we don't take it lightly.

Primitive instincts drive behavior. They all trace to self-protection. National wars. Class wars. Racial divides. Isms. Family feuds. Conflicts of all sorts. *Do it my way or else. Don't step over the line. Don't get up in my grill. Keep your hands offa her.* Our sociopolitical pissing contest is another case in point. All conflicts relate to protection of the primitive: My country. My identity. My way. My body. My guns. My house. My yard. My rights. My freedom. *My peanut butter cup.* Excessive self-protection can be harmful to individual as well as collective resilience.

Force #3: Social Conditioning and Generational Norms

Social constructions beckon us. From day one, we're handed off a code of behavior from prior generations. Our gender, social class, race, and family of origin's belief systems script precise parameters for how we're supposed to maneuver life. Humans are not acknowledged as the multidimensional beings we are. Then it gets confusing because so-called norms change by the second, and we end up straddling the fence between what we're expected to be and who we really are.

The rapid changes in society have huge implications on us. We experience identity crises and role conflicts, with epic tugs of war

Our progressive minds often run up against our weak stomachs for living our truths in their entirety. The push and pull between honoring tradition and progressivism is an epic tug-of-war. Tensions rise as the environment calls us to adapt, but we're holding onto lenses we used when the world seemed to be a radically different place, even though some of the differences across eras tend to get exaggerated because things used to be less wear-it-on-your-sleeve.

between our constructed and actual selves. At the time of this writing, it's a bit confusing since the pendulum has swung so dramatically toward monumental shifts in norms with relationships, work, communication, sexual liberation, and everything in between.

Role Conflict

Academic Definition

A perspective within the disciplines of sociology and social psychology suggesting that people act out roles that are socially defined. A person who is expected to simultaneously carry out multiple contradictory roles experiences role conflict.

Street Definition

When you're expected to be a certain way, but you feel like you're damned if you do, damned if you don't. #contradiction

---

There are more ways of communicating, work options, gender identities, relationship arrangements, and family structures than there are

Dunkin' Donuts in Boston. Expectations are often cobbled from a mix of the past and present, leading to friction and confusion over "right" versus "wrong" ways of doing things. We struggle through identity crises and role conflicts as we work to free ourselves from tradition and maintain it at the same time. The choices are exciting and disruptive.

Force #4: Developmental Perspective

Going through life's stages is like an epic game of whack-a-mole. You manage to take care of one problem; another pops up. The moles taunting you in your twenties are different from the ones from your teens, as well as the ones who will pay you a visit later down the road. Each season of life brings its own patterns, which simultaneously tax us and deliver unique opportunities. Age and stage have huge effects on our resilience.

We can be highly mature and evolved in some senses, and then feel regressed and infantile in others. This is known as asynchronous development, meaning we can be *rock* stars in some regards and feel like hot messes in others. Our brains are sometimes ahead of our emotions and vice versa.

Crises don't just happen at one chronological age, such as midlife. We are apt to hit many crises along the way as we shed skins and take on new identities as we age and evolve. These disruptions of trying to negotiate who we are and what we want from life happen continually throughout our life span.

In the face of trials, we can be spun around and sent back to face moles we thought we had whacked. It might feel like you're back to square one, but that would discount all the learning and new skills you've acquired along the way that help you meet present challenges with new resolve.

Life is unpredictable in many senses, but we can always count on change as a mainstay. We're constantly required to adapt. Each phase of adaption presents us with unique developmental tasks that pop up and grab our attention. Some of the moles we face at certain junctures are relatively predictable. Others may startle us. We weren't expecting how hard it would be to take on a new job, endure the loss of a loved one, end a relationship, move to a new area, or start a new venture.

Development is a continual process throughout our life span. Moles are always on the prowl. We can't eliminate them, so we have to decide how to outmaneuver them.

Embrace Your Spiral

From an early age, we're taught that life moves in a linear fashion, that A + B = C, and that if we do X, then Y will naturally result. We soon realize that life is anything but formulaic, and we need a new way of thinking about movement.

Mentalligence encourages us to spiral up. An ancient symbol of forward progress, the spiral itself is emblematic of agility.[1] Spirals inspire us to focus on the potential for progress, even while we're spinning and it seems like all hell is breaking loose. Spirals by their very nature demonstrate momentum, power, and hopefulness, even within chaotic conditions. They help us move from mindless reactivity to mindful presence with the forces of life.

Spirals reveal the possibilities for growth, even smack in the middle of life's simultaneous chaos and order. Since *waaay back*, as in pre-smartphones, pre-internet, pre–running water, and pre–paved roads, spirals have represented the journey of life. Attributes such as progress, evolution, initiation, centering, expansion, awareness, connecting, and development are all associated with them. Maybe spirals strike a chord because they're part of our very essence. Check out your fingerprints. *Spirals.* The sunflowers in your garden. *Spirals.* Look inside your midday apple: *spiral.* Even the galaxy we live in is a *spiral.*

If you want to get past the myth of balance, let disruption and order coexist.

In many cultures, spirals are associated with the divine feminine, the womb, and goddesses. Check out primitive rock carvings, Celtic art, Native American petroglyphs, African art, Japanese rock gardens, and Peruvian Nazca lines. Spirals all over the place.

---

1 Spirals have always fascinated people. Math fanatics love them. Architects draw them. Spiritual gurus revere them. Hundreds of thousands of people visit labyrinths every year. They're that cool.

While spirals have long been held sacred, not all spirals are constructive. They can be powerful in dangerous ways, too, as with tornadoes. These funnels fueled by air spirals can produce up to 500-mile-an-hour winds. *Not as cute as a little innocent snail, for sure.*

On the human behavior side of things, psychology's legendary spiral reference has always been the downward spiral. It's the infamous descent to rock bottom that we're taught to avoid at all costs—the one we're incessantly warned to believe will wipe us out, just because life is messy and hard.

Are you lost—or right where you're supposed to be?

As a result, we often struggle to trust the process. We numb out instead of realizing that we're designed to return to homeostasis, even after our worlds have been thrown off-kilter. For many of us, it's not a matter of poor memory recall. We just weren't taught correctly in the first place.

Historically, we've approached our understanding of loss of control as a personal or moral failing, not as a natural response to environmental chaos. Our narrow paradigms cause us to draw the conclusion that when things go wrong for us, we're automatically on the downward path. Right from the get-go, life plops us front and center within a chaotic universe, and our life journey becomes about how we ride out the storms and embrace our unique spirals.

The way we approach the storms of life depends on many factors. Along with primitive instincts, social conditioning, developmental stage, and generational perspective, our cumulative experience with turbulence directly influences our behavior.

The force of the spiral is inevitable. What will be your resulting direction?

All of us are subject to various forms of adversity as the seasons of our lives unfold. Whether cloudy days, rainy patches, torrential downpours, or full-out tornadoes, each of us develop behavioral patterns in response to life's intense conditions. Once we've endured endless storms, a variety of reactions can result. Sometimes nothing seems to phase us because we're so used to turmoil. At other times we clamor at the thought of one more gust bearing down upon us.

Storm Approach Types

The Storm Chaser. The minute the winds pick up, you're stoked. You love novelty and variety and get a rush from getting as close a view as possible. You live for experience and adventure, and are insatiably curious. You have a lot of colorful stories to tell. You don't sit and wait for things to happen—you are always on the hunt for stimulation. When taken to the extreme, you find yourself a bit impulsive and careless, sometimes putting yourself in harm's way. You find yourself regularly dissatisfied, sometimes even creating chaos to offset lulls. You can feel misunderstood but are admired for your experiences. You break tradition and convention.

The Storm Watcher. You are intrigued by storms but prefer to watch from a safe distance. You appreciate the beauty and power of them, enjoying the percolating energy brought about. Still, you are not inclined to get too close. You love being in the know, carefully gathering facts and sharing information you've accumulated, but many times it's more apt to be from indirect experience. You pride yourself on being a good protector, and you relish in the chance to warn others of pending danger. You are highly observant, dependable, and patient. You are an excellent resource for storm chasers who sometimes find themselves a little too close to danger.

The Storm Avoider. Storms petrify you. You've seen your fair share of them and try everything you can to stay away from anything risky. If there's a hint of storminess, you make your way to the basement, where you've stockpiled resources. You are well prepared and an anchor to chasers and watchers. You prefer control of your surroundings rather than exposing yourself to life's elements. Sometimes you feel alone, but your curiosity has given way to fear. Your storm aversion keeps you safe in some ways—but the hiding sometimes makes you feel isolated. The anxieties you experience are a natural response to the storms you've been through, but your chances of healing will be slow if you stay in the basement instead of making your way up the steps.

Tune In to Identify Storm Approaches

The constant twists and turns of life can help us build agility, but they can also shake us so badly that we do everything possible to avoid being exposed. Sometimes we're open to experiencing the forces at hand; other times we want to batten down the hatches. There are endless ways we can approach storms, and it helps to think about the main responses that we choose to either cultivate resilience or disrupt it.[2]

Don't be fooled into thinking you are safe because you are hiding out in the basement of life. Doing so might create its own stormy conditions that damage us more than the original or even attempted intrusion.

No matter where we find ourselves on the storm response spectrum, we all face dynamic instability—but it doesn't mean that we are one and done when we've weathered hard storms. In the face of chaos, unlearning and pivoting are vital to help us keep our spiral moving up. Just like the timing of a butterfly wing flap, the new insights we develop can dramatically change the course of our lives. A lifelong learning mind-set can provide the gumption we need to keep progressing. With all the pending storms on the horizon, we need to tune in to see how we can become more resilient.

Become a Forever Learner

The research question driving my entire study was, "What contributes to student identity and resilience?" Two of the predominant codes that ran consistently through my research were empathy and community. The majority of my students originally bought into the prevailing thoughts about one-and-done so-called failures. But then they tuned into the fact that the compromising moments in which their lives seemed to have spun out of control were the very ones that helped them develop empathy and find community. As Poonam put it,

> *My family has high expectations for me to come to study and end up a doctor. When I arrived to the U.S. I thought this was my dream—my*

---

2 The storm types shown in the box are not rigid categories. We might find ourselves as a combination of all three, varying across the different types of storms we face. Most of us have one predominant method of facing life's chaos, based on prior storm experiences.

destiny. I was miserable and was only sleeping like three hours a night. I fell into a pretty bad depression and stop communicating to people. I thought I was all done, and I didn't want to face life anymore. My family's expectation for me started to really bother me. I love them, and they love me, but I didn't want to have to keep looking, you know, for some kind of perfect path that doesn't exist. I just wasn't happy. I started volunteering at a nonprofit and fell in love with the

Resilience isn't linear. It's more than just falling, bouncing back, and being gritty. It's a process that takes time, massive redos, and backbreaking work— and not just by one person. It happens through the presence of community, one that never stands with fingers pointed or brows furrowed, but arms thrust open, no matter what.

work. It was healing, because in a lot of ways the stuff people were going through was the same as me. I had a big heart for them and realized that if I hadn't gone through my own low moments, I wouldn't have really understood them like I do.

Mikhail had a similar realization about arriving at a place of greater empathy and connection:

Sometimes I wish I didn't have to go through all this. But it really helps me put myself in someone else's shoes. I used to be so embarrassed about myself, thinking I had messed up royally, and that I was way behind everyone else. A lot of my friends had already graduated college and some even had kids. It seemed like everyone had their life together except me. But they all come to me for advice, I think because they know I won't judge them, and I also think that the things I've gone through have taught me a lot of lessons that make me who I am. I think the crappy moments ended up teaching me more than other things that are supposed to make you smart. Now I see it differently. And I'm not afraid to talk about it anymore. I think my openness has helped people open up, too. I think as soon as you get to know someone, you realize that most people are feeling like they could do better, but life is just life and we all end up getting to the place we're supposed to go.

When we face trials, we develop a newfound appreciation for human hope and healing. We understand life isn't black-and-white, and challenges aren't of simple origins but a mix of complicated factors. Going through difficulties is humbling, but chaos is a denominator we all share and has the potential to bind us together in our common humanity. Difficulties allow us to recognize that while certain points in our development can be completely out of control, we can still be okay. We learn by experience. Loss, letdowns, and change are our best teachers. We are not epic failures when things don't go as planned.

Learning is everything. Everything is learning.

The outcomes of our experiences are very seldom what we expected. We show up to our classrooms, jobs, or new places thinking we are here for one certain reason—to gain one particular thing. Then things don't go as planned. We beat our brows for a while. Sometimes we even feel sorry for ourselves. We ask why. We struggle to make sense. Eventually, we start to shift our attention to all the learning and growth that transpired. And we realize it didn't happen in spite of, but because of, the disruption.

It wouldn't surprise me if you've had similar moments where you've tuned in to how challenges have cultivated resilience, empathy, and community for you. This comes from seeing that *learning is everything and everything is learning*. See if you can relate to the mind-sets and behaviors of a *forever learner* that came out of my research findings:

- **You believe learning is everything, and everything is learning.** You don't just say it, you mean it.
- **You live to learn.** When you don't know something, it excites you, instead of frightening you.
- **You are a tireless discoverer.** Always bursting with the latest NPR story, deep soul excavation, construction of a new theory, and golden nuggets of wisdom from your last podcast binge, you're on a never-ending curiosity mission.
- **Growth is your lifeblood.** Stagnation is the disease you want to avoid. You hit plateaus, get itchy, and want to bring it to the next level.

- **Learning is your air.** Innovation is your middle name, and creativity your core. The librarians know you by name. You're that interesting person people love to get seated next to. You go into withdrawals without daily intellectual stimulation.
- **Your hunt for answers leads to more questions.** Uncertainty fires you up more. And even though it can get a little lonely, you don't give up on the people who've had their curiosity fires stomped out.
- **People with one set way of seeing life don't really get you.** And it's hard to get them, too. You want to go beyond superficial, but a lot is getting in the way. Other people's formula for living seems so limiting to you. You want so much more for them. It's tempting to hurl insults, but you know their tunnel vision makes them feel safe—and wasn't their idea in the first place.
- **You refuse to accept a myopic worldview.** Any optometrist who handed out the same exact prescription to every patient wouldn't stay in business for long. That we let teachers, parents, and religious leaders get away with their own versions of universal prescriptions troubles you to your marrow. You can't accept that we're handing out monocles in our global twenty-first-century world when we desperately need kaleidoscopes. You're convinced that the complexity in our world cannot be met with simplicity.

> **"Lessons always arrive when you are ready."**
> —*Paulo Coelho*

It takes time and intention to understand how to welcome these teachers in our lives and pull something useful from the lessons they offer. Our instinct is to resist. Not until we look back do we realize how much we've grown in the face of chaos. Reflecting in such a way helps deepen our appreciation for our so-called failures just as much as our so-called successes. Reflection helps us get to a place of new stability and resilience, one that helps us know we are never one and done, even when chaos is enveloping us.

> **"There is no birth of consciousness without pain."**
> —*Carl Jung*

Session Seven Worksheet:
Embracing Your Spiral

Objective:
Unlearn one-and-done indoctrination that breeds instability.

Pivot toward resilience.

Rethink It:
Move from One-and-Done to Resilience

With all the conversation swirling about resilience, there is little talk about the chaotic environment at hand. Instead, we fall for romanticized stories of individuals moving from setbacks to comebacks, without looking at the bigger picture. Stability comes when we harness empathy and community to get to resilience together.

Resilience Check

- Have I ever felt like I'm done after a setback?
- What makes me feel stable? What makes me feel unstable?
- What kind of storm responses (storm chasing, watching, avoiding) do I typically identify with?
- What aspects are helpful, and which do I want to change?
- Are there any areas of life in which I'm hiding in the basement?
- What or who can help me start climbing the stairs toward healing and new mind-sets?
- What key lessons have I learned from challenging experiences?

Action Steps:
Embrace Your Spiral

When reflecting on our lives, we sometimes overlook that everything we experience is part of a system of dynamic instability. Opportunities to learn and grow are always available, but a sense of adventure and perpetual curiosity are needed to harness the forces at hand. To adopt a forever learning approach, we need to embrace our unique spirals and tune into the ways they teach us.

1. **Breathe new air.** Think about the common ways you've thought about your challenges. How have they deepened your empathy and resilience? Write out three main areas you've struggled with and try to come up with a corresponding lesson you've derived and used to cope with later challenges.

2. **Factor in the forces.** Consider your age/stage. What moles are popping up for you right now? What developmental challenges (e.g., moving

away from home, retirement, or a new relationship) are requiring your attention? Are the emotions you're facing making you feel as though you are spinning? Find someone in your network whom you think might be going through something similar. Ask that person to meet for a walk or coffee to talk about the ways they cope.

3. **Keep your eye on the good life.** The good life isn't without strife. Be sure you are working to cultivate resilience in community. Staying burrowed in the basement won't promote growth. Ask a friend or someone at work to remind you of your quest to adapt and remain stable in the face of trying times.

4. **Embrace your spiral.** Select your favorite forever learning mind-set and work at using it as a mantra for one solid week. Pay attention to the kinds of shifts you experience. Try on a few of them and see which ones help you embrace resilience and reduce any one-and-done mind-sets that breed instability.

You may have experienced what seem to be **UNSPEAKABLE ATROCITIES.** But **HEALING** is always a possibility— one that **INCREASES** in probability according to its own **UNIQUE** rhyme and reason—and not because someone **SAID** so or **DID** so, but because you stayed on the **LOOKOUT** for countless variables that ended up nudging you **AWAY** from a process of resignation and relegation. Embracing **INSTABILITY** has its own way of **STABILIZING.**

Unfriending Chicken Little

Objective:
Unlearn sky-is-falling indoctrination that breeds fear.
Pivot toward critical thinking.

*A reliable way to make people believe
in falsehoods is frequent repetition, because
familiarity is not easily distinguished from truth.
Authoritarian institutions and marketers
have always known this fact.*

—Daniel Kahneman

C hicken Little gets hit by a nut, and the rest is history. He manages to convince the whole town that the sky is falling. Doomsday is here. For centuries, the tale has been told in various iterations, proving that mass paranoia and hysteria have always been in style.

Even before Sean Hannity and Rush Limbaugh, there have been plenty of town criers flagging us down, getting us shaking in our booties because the world is coming to an end. *Where's R.E.M. when you need them? I don't feel fine.*

The bad news baits us 24/7. Not only do our screens flood us with images of chaos and negativity, but they follow us everywhere we go, clucking at us and activating each last nerve of our limbic systems. We receive our information *faaast*. We skim off the top of our feeds, Google-and-go in .003 seconds, taking in the equivalent of 174 newspapers a day. That's a lot of breaking news about epidemics, pandemics, and the latest catastrophe. Crisis sells. Otherwise, maybe we'd have some *serenity*.

The news about "dead truth" is catchy, given our reality-show president. The March 2017 cover of *TIME* magazine jostles us with, "Is Truth Dead?" a fair question considering the "alternative facts" encircling us. Lies are dangerous and scary, especially when told by those in power. We'd be disillusioned to think there's ever been a point in history when authorities have held a steadfast commitment to truth telling.

The world has long suffered its own versions of misogyny, predatory behavior, and corruption. Politicians simply weren't exposed as quickly.

Cover-ups aren't new. There just used to be fewer unbridled options available to tantalize the likes of those who take to Twitter and Tinder to display their dirty laundry. Discretion also seems to be dead. While we're at it, let's hold a funeral for humility, decency, virtue, diplomacy, pluralism, and bipartisanship.

Lay Off the Chicken Little Stew

We can't hold a funeral for something that was never a thing, but we can't roll over either. Mark Crispin Miller, professor of media studies at New York University and author of *Boxed In: The Culture of TV*, warns about media manipulation, citing it as "more efficient than it was in Nazi Germany." With the volume of information that blasts us, we end up with the false pretense that we are getting the full story. Miller worries that this misconception prevents us from even *looking* for truth.

In 1983, fifty companies controlled 90 percent of the media. Today, six companies—GE, News-Corp, Disney, Viacom, Time Warner, and CBS—have it wrapped up. The information they sell isn't just half baked—the ingredients they use are toxic. And like McDonald's, although the unhealthy ingredients are widely known, they manage to keep people coming back for more. Here's their not-so-secret sauce:

Ingredients

Lead-and-bleed headlines *(choose the cut that evokes the most fear)*
Anecdotal stories *(the more dramatic and unscientific, the better)*
Fatalistic thinking *(this ingredient cannot be substituted)*
One ripe audience *(provoke with fear and anger, then pick 'em)*

DIRECTIONS

1) Start by whipping up the audience with a swift and sturdy hook. Next, throw in some anecdotal stories and spin it on high, repeatedly. There is no risk of overdoing it. Add in heaping amounts of fatalistic thinking and then allow it to crawl across the screen over and over until the heaviness sets in. Use a very broad brush to present your final product. Serve to an audience hungry for comfort food that's familiar to them. Repeat the steps as often as possible to keep them coming back. It never hurts for the chef to dress seductively or yell loudly to keep people's attention.

This recipe works. The *Washington Post* called the 2016 campaign a "gusher" for CNN, which approached a record-breaking $1 billion gross profit, the best-ever in its thirty-six-year history. Fox News also boasted its most lucrative year. MSNBC's percentage growth rate exceeded CNN's and Fox's. Our anxiety becomes their profit.

We have to learn to tune out before we can tune in.

Given the information overload at hand, we need to examine what's being served up. If we are what we eat, are we what we watch, too? We have information consumption choices that will either nourish and sustain us, or leave us depleted. Rotten ingredients, sketchy chefs, and empty calories hailing from WWE-type media can poison us if we're mindlessly consuming what's being served up writ large.

The indigestion from mainstream media has opened the door for alternative news sources and podcasts. There's a midnight cruise buffet being served—with a taste for everyone—ranging from conspiracy stew to scientific data à la mode. *I recommend generous helpings of science, culture, art, philosophy, and spirituality. Balanced diet. And lay off the Chicken Little stew. It's linked with acid reflux and brain fog.*

What if the media took a cue from positive psychology and adopted a strengths-based perspective in their reporting? The sensationalistic approach sells, but it also blocks us from seeing the progress and potential gains we are, and could continue to be, making.

Know the Science and Roots Behind Mass Hysteria

When we face uncertain times, we can't help but seek explanations. The trouble is, we can end up making judgments based on raw emotions, not facts.

We are prone to buying into fear-based marketing of the news and companies because of the brain's tendency to trigger physiological symptoms. Dr. Gary Small suggests that when we are excited and scared, we tend to hyperventilate, causing lower carbon dioxide levels and heightened sensitivity to physical symptoms.

Bruce Shneier, author of *Beyond Fear*, mentions that despite the irrationality of our thinking, we tend to make judgments on our feelings, not facts. He emphasizes that we often exaggerate risks, especially to children, to keep them safe—but we also foster a situation of overlooking facts in favor of emotional conclusions.

Here's a truth bomb you're unlikely to hear: we live in the most peaceful and prosperous time in history, with the greatest advances in democracy.

Instead, we're told it's The Worst Time Ever. The sky is falling, and that *No One Has Ever Had It Like This.*

We are certainly not the first generation to face brutality, terror, and trauma. The partition in India. China's Great Leap Forward. Biafra.

Vietnam. Khmer Rouge. South Sudan. Rwanda. The Holocaust. War after war after war.

The truth is, we've evolved quite a bit as a species. The world we live in is technically safer, with better outcomes than ever before. We live longer. Literacy rates are better. We have technologies and advances that were once the stuff of dreams.

Yes, there's far too much violence, but we don't bludgeon each other like we used to. Evolutionary psychologists say we're apt to cooperate more since it helps ensure survival.

We're still in a lot of hot water. Our health care systems, schools, and governments have come a long way, but have far to go. Public health experts from the Robert Wood Johnson Foundation report that zip codes predict health outcomes. Massive disparities based on socioeconomic status and race limit access and affordability of care. You don't have to look far to see injustice.

It's time to unfriend Chicken Little. We're not characters in his hysterical tale of woe. Even though today's challenges are extraordinary, so is the progress that we've made, and will continue to make, if we stop listening to hysteria and work together to confront our greatest challenges.

We've made significant gains in reducing communicable disease in many parts of the world, but we are obese, addicted, and medicated. By 2030, the World Health Organization says stress-related, noncontagious illness will be our prime concern. It's not ideal to get sick or die in either case, but the truth is we're living longer. We have the resources to keep improving our outcomes.

Saying that the world is as it should be would be like seeing with only one eye. Around the world, violence, terrorism, and political unrest are rampant, but they're not new kids in town, like the media want us to believe.

It's better than it used to be, but we still have much to overcome. When we deny the pervasive violence, inequities, institutionalized isms, war, poverty, lack of access to education and health care, and polarization in our current global sociopolitical climate, we might reify the root causes that perpetuate them in the first place. *We need Chicken Littles to keep us woke, but we don't need to eat Chicken Little stew every waking minute either.*

We all have Chicken Littles in our lives, and not just on the media and political fronts. Church ladies doused in Jean Nate perfume shake their fingers at us, warning that we're going straight to hell without passing Go; that doomsday is here. Some scientists deny any existence of the divine. They lump together as *pseudoscience* anything that doesn't have a double-blind peer-reviewed process and cannot be precisely measured.

Keeping fear from spreading takes our collective will. Subjectivity and partiality reign. If we look at life through too narrow a frame, we miss the chance for integration of knowledge from a wide range of sources. If there's one thing my work in grounded theory research has taught me, it's the fusion from all the worlds—science, spiritual, philosophy, arts, and beyond—that helps us inch our way just a little closer to understanding.

> **"We shouldn't be looking for heroes, we should be looking for good ideas."**
>
> —Noam Chomsky

In order to do so, we cannot blindly follow down the road led by one so-called expert whose agenda might be led by fear, not getting us all to the good life. The mass hysteria that our leaders promote diverts our attention away from their outlandish tactics to keep us from tuning into the problems that need our unwavering focus.

Get Off the Yellow Brick Road

In the Land of Oz, Dorothy Gale has one set mission: Find the Wizard. As she journeys through the dramatic twists and turns along the yellow brick road, she and her companions underestimate their gumption as they channel all their energies on getting in with the "expert" who will surely impart his wisdom and grant their wishes.

The moment of truth arrives in Emerald City. Luckily, Dorothy's dog, Toto, puts an end to the whole scam. When he pulls back the curtain, he exposes the sweaty phony dude sitting on his perch, pressing everyone's fear buttons. *Go, Toto! Leave it to a dog to sniff out the truth. Little smarty. Get him!*

So many aspects of this plot from one of the most popular movies of all time are familiar. Across the world, societies have touted the idea that one all-knowing leader will magically wave a wand and remedy all our problems. All institutions have been built on this very premise—that solutions come solely from experts and those in power, not from varied sources and perspectives.

We're introduced to these ideas before we can safely eat honey. From an early age, we're taught to sit at the feet of teachers and authorities, with bated breath, ready

> **"Too often we enjoy the comfort of opinion without the discomfort of thought."**
> —*John F. Kennedy*

to absorb the secrets that will set us straight. We're supposed to revere people in power—from teachers to clergy to celebrities, mimicking their alleged formulas for better living.

We're taught not to question authority, to show respect, all while some jackass behind the curtain is scamming us. Across societies, power is misused and abused, diminishing the worth and credibility of anyone outside the few dominant-group key holders to the city. Those in control push their agenda by defining whom they see as "good and worthy," while marginalizing and stifling the voices of the masses.

Across generations, culture, time, and space, dominator systems have left whole groups of people in the dust. Whether because of class, race, gender, sexual orientation, age, ability, religious affiliation, appearance, or other social identity categories, much suffering has resulted.

These time-honored traditions cause a lot of damage. People who use their power for their own glory and to the detriment of those they are supposed to be serving are *@RealCowardlyLions*. If they were more evolved, they would share their power. They would stop talking and start listening. They would care about the greater good. But with too many benefits for them, they keep us hustling along the yellow brick road. When we finally arrive and peel back the curtain on the expert we've been seeking, we're likely to find a shriveled dominator who's far from heroic.

> **You don't need to be rescued or saved. You just need spaces that allow you to expand and rebuild.**

Dominators are demagogues who hoard all but a few scraps of bread. The crumbs they scatter leave us stampeding, knocking each other down without a second thought. The promise that we, too, can live the dream by working hard and doing our very best sends us in a frenzy to beat the odds, and to beat each other out. They intentionally whip up crowds to shut down reasoning. They tend to use immediate and forceful means of addressing conflict, and when questioned, they respond defensively with accusations of lying and disloyalty.

Demagogue

Academic Definition

A leader who gains followers by exploiting fears, prejudices, and ignorance among the common people. Demagogues are known for their ability to agitate and rabble-rouse.

Street Definition

A demagogue is a trash talker who loves to stir up trouble and get everybody against each other. #trashtalk

---

With not enough to go around, we're pitted against each other. Common bonds are hard to find when primitive survival instincts are activated. It's a smoke screen that keeps us from seeing what's really going on. When we're facing off against each other, we'll never see who we should be fighting against. We'll just keep accepting the truths of those pretending to have the answers, but who really have an agenda to keep us from rethinking what we're dangerously being sold.

> Stop searching for wizards and wands. Don't buy into the belief that you don't have the brains, heart, and courage to make it. Link arms with your fellow travelers and never let go. Hold each other up so that you can see your own magic.

Hold onto Your Pop

The little Tootsie Pop boy's curiosity was no match for his impulses. He needed some help, but Mr. Cow, Turtle, and Fox were self-identified biters, too. Surely, Mr. Owl would impart his wisdom to solve the burning licks-to-the-center question. He postures himself and 1-2-3 . . . *chrrruuhck!* He bites. Neuroscience wins. The world will never know the answer. The lure of instant gratification was too much—even for Mr. Owl's stellar brain.

This vintage 1970s commercial shows that even the wisest among us fall prey to the impulse for the quick and tasty. Our brain is hardwired for the immediate fix. Even with strong wills and the best of intentions, we easily succumb. When students at Purdue University reenacted the commercial in a laboratory experiment, they found that getting to the pop's center took 252 licks. Now, that's restraint.

> Truth isn't dead, but it is subjective. We need to join forces and look carefully at varied sources to get closer to accuracy.

Like Tootsie Pops, fallacies are hard to resist. The word *fallacy* originates from the Latin *fallacia*, meaning "to deceive." We bite down quickly on information, preventing us from critically thinking and overcoming our mind's natural inclination to being tricked.

Critical thinking helps us tame our bite reflexes and move beyond impulses to believe what we want to believe. The discipline it gives us is worth it. We end up with lenses to evaluate information carefully, getting us closer to clarity and accuracy. It helps us cultivate the skills we need to raise questions about what we're being sold, gather and interpret information, arrive at well-reasoned conclusions and solutions, and think more open-mindedly.

Critical Thinking

Academic Definition

Disciplined thinking based on intellectual standards of clarity, accuracy, relevance, precision, breadth, depth, logic, significance, consistency, fairness, completeness, and reasonability.

Street Definition

Thinking about thinking while you are thinking to make it more on point. #think #questioneverything

Critical thinking is truly essential to get us to the good life—and not destroying the center. We're not taught or automatically inclined to think well. It's a practice to be adopted through our lifetimes. Like anything important in our lives, it is built upon a set of virtues. Understanding essential intellectual values helps us move away from egocentric thinking and tune in to becoming less self-serving, or being bamboozled by Chicken Littles, wizards, and demagogues.

Know the Essential Intellectual Virtues to Combat Egocentric Thinking

Dr. Linda Elder and the late Dr. Richard Paul assert that we do not naturally appreciate the views of others, nor the limits to our own points of view. We believe in our intuitive perceptions and use self-centered measures to decide what to believe or reject.

Elder and Paul suggest that we commonly accept things as true for the following reasons:

- Because I believe it
- Because we believe it
- Because I want to believe it
- Because I have always believed it
- It's in my selfish interest to believe it

Their Thinker's Guide Library highlights steps we can take to move from being unreflective thinkers to accomplished thinkers who demonstrate these core values:

- Intellectual humility versus arrogance
- Intellectual courage versus cowardice
- Intellectual empathy versus narrow-mindedness
- Intellectual autonomy versus conformity
- Intellectual integrity versus hypocrisy
- Intellectual perseverance versus laziness
- Confidence in reason versus distrust of reason and evidence
- Fair-mindedness versus unfairness

> When we commit to lifelong practice to cultivate intellectual skills and virtues in our lives, they can eventually become second nature—but not without tuning in and working to get beyond our natural tendencies to think narrowly.

When we stop listening to town criers and take the opportunity to listen to varied voices, it can help undo a fear-based, sky-is-falling indoctrination that prevents us from critical thinking. It's easy to get cynical given the contradictions at hand. Cynicism keeps us stuck. We can instead adopt a "skeptimistic" mind-set that blends the traits of a skeptic and optimist. Our skeptical side is always seeing through issues and asking important questions:

- Who says so? What wisdom, experience, and expertise do they have?
- Why? What is their underlying agenda or motivation?
- What lens is represented in their assertions? Is it comprehensive enough or built on myopic thinking?
- Are there alternative views to consider? What else needs to be discovered or taken into account?

> "In a world where critical thinking skills are almost wholly absent, repetition effectively leapfrogs the cognitive portions of the brain. It helps something get processed as truth. We used to call this unsubstantiated buy-in. Belief without evidence. It only works in a society where thinking for one's self is discouraged. That's how we lost our country."
>
> —Laura Bynum

Our optimistic side believes we can find answers and knows that since life is rich with mystery and ambiguity, we can't expect a single source to provide our definitive formula. Like Dorothy Gale and her Oz friends, we have the resources we need to get to better thinking and to avoid believing that the sky is falling and we can do nothing about it. We can become mindful skeptimists who honor the voices of scientists and morally conscious faith-based leaders just as much as we do the lovers, dreamers, poets, artists, and athletes. We can learn from all of them: Alanis, Marie Curie, Noam Chomsky, Adrienne Rich, Venus and Serena, Buddha, and Glennon Doyle.

We're so much better off when we appreciate each other's lenses, instead of bickering and raising constant fear. Combining varied perspectives helps us pool our resources and become better equipped to stand on guard against oppressive regimes, sensational media, and sneaky marketers, who want us to be so busy watching the sky fall that we can't see the rainbow on the horizon.

Session Eight Worksheet:
Unfriending Chicken Little

Objective:
Unlearn sky-is-falling indoctrination that breeds fear.
Pivot toward critical thinking.

Rethink It:
Move from Fear to Critical Thinking

When Chicken Little is constantly in our ear, telling us how scared we should be, it blocks our ability to think critically. We let fear, not quality reasoning, rule. Between the media, people in power, and our own tendencies to make errors, we need to find and use our mindful lens to ensure we are living out intellectual virtues that help keep us from thinking the sky is falling, and instead look for rainbows on the horizon.

Critical Thinking Check

- Are there any Chicken Littles in my life? Do their messages get to me? Are there any forms of sky-is-falling indoctrination stew baiting me in my life that need to be purged and eliminated from my diet?
- What resources do I have that help me stay off the yellow brick road, and instead steer clear of the dominator's ideologies? Is there anyone with whom I can join forces?
- Of the reasons that Drs. Elder and Paul say we tend to believe things, which ones do I typically fall into (e.g., It's true because I believe it, we believe it, I want to believe it)?
- What steps can I take to go beyond my first instincts to believe something?
- Which intellectual value(s) do I already demonstrate? Which one(s) do I need to work on the most?

Action Steps:
Lick Your Way to the Center

Critical thinking requires us to take time to rethink our impulses to believe what we are being baited with, or to go to one source alone. It helps us ensure that we are engaging in a process that fosters intellectual virtues and upholds standards in which we can have more confidence. To accomplish this, try the following:

1. **Lay off the Chicken Little stew.** There's plenty of good to be found when we look for it. It doesn't mean there aren't plenty of problems, but we can look for positive data sources and news to help balance the

predominant negativity. Take time to review news stories from positive news sites or credible sources such as the BBC. Don't limit yourself to local lead-and-bleed sources.

2. **Get off the yellow brick road.** Revisit your VIA and SWOT analysis to reflect on your character strengths and values. Remember that you don't need to be ruled by an expert or leader. You can wield your mindful lens to tune in and see beyond their tactics and take control of your own thinking and behavior. When you link arms with fellow travelers in this way, it helps push back against systemic forces that get in the way of moving us closer to the good life.

3. **Hold onto your pop.** Don't fall for the impulses of your mind. Mindfulness takes us further than mindlessness. We are inundated with constant fear-factor information, filling up our feeds and flooding our minds. Take time to look at varied sources and put information up to the test of intellectual standards. Don't make quick assumptions or judgments or take information from one person, group, or place. Pick an intellectual value to work on for at least a week. Take notice of information you are presented, and take the time to think through it before making assumptions. Adopt a skeptimistic lens that asks questions, stays optimistic, and works together with varied sources to help you see and do better.

Waiting for Marshmallows

Objective:
Unlearn consumeristic indoctrination that breeds waste.
Pivot toward gratitude.

*Advertising sells you things you don't need
and can't afford, that are overpriced and don't work.
And they do it by exploiting your fears and insecurities.
And if you don't have any, they'll be
glad to give you a few.*

—George Carlin

It's Christmas day. By the explanation given, you'd think it was my mother's best friend, not QVC, who supplied her with the thirty-seven Lock and Lock containers for each of our extended family members.

The house is brimming with flameless candles and Today's Special Value appliances. Mama unveils the handy pocket LED light/pen she's gotten each of us. No more fumbling to open our car doors, and if we ever need to sign an autograph on the fly, we'll be in luck.

Most of my nephews and nieces are too busy on their screens to bother to look up and remind her there's already a flashlight built into their smartphones-turned-appendages. No one has the heart to bring up key-less car entry. *Or how picky and nerdy I've become about my pens.*

Mama has always been the ultimate gift giver. She can sound off our favorite colors and taste in jewelry like she's a Scripps National Spelling Bee champ. *Kristen likes g-r-e-e-n, Kellie purple, no hoops for Melissa.*

And, like all of us, QVC loves Mama and her *generous spirit*. QVC and Mama have been chatting things over, living room to living room, for a long time now. QVC's learned a lot about Mama over the years:

- Boomer
- Definition of love
- Would die for fam
- Loves a good sale
- It's generally hard to get anything past her

In turn, Mama knows all about the QVC hosts and their guests—the vineyards they own, the countries they travel, and even the secrets behind their glowing skin. Their gorgeous lined $29.99 *plus tax* mouths tell her that shopping is "best enjoyed with friends." It's a fitting slogan, since they rake in billions of dollars from jolly new playmates every year. In 2016, QVC made $6.1 billion and HSN (Home Shopping Network) $2.5 billion.

The network hosts are so smooth and shiny, they make us think we can surpass Dale Carnegie's how-to-win-and-influence advice, with just the right pair of ankle booties and pearls. They never bring up that life is transient, always changing. That all of life's treasures are short-lived, and that the best aspects of life aren't delivered off big brown trucks. Instead, they are masters of the art of "parasocial marketing," stoking illusions of connectivity. They bring us into their must-have in-group, promising ease and status so that they can unload onto us the fifteen football fields' worth of goods behind the scenes.

With over 50 million customers worldwide, QVC's quest to convince us how they can make our lives easier has become big business. We are friends worth keeping. They're picking our pockets, but we're too busy enjoying the glamour grommets on our organic cotton Capri pants that go with everything—and will make us *the star* of the cookout—to even notice.

The picture-perfect hosts receive more training than most people receive across their entire career span. Their performance is measured in real time; if people are calling, they are egged on to keep repeating their lines. They know exactly how to climb into our brains, pressing just the right buttons to light us up.

In 1960, Walter Mischel initiated one of the best-known early examples of measuring those instant gratification lights in us. His now famous Stanford marshmallow test gave preschool children the option to earn two marshmallows if they waited for the researcher to signal them. If it was too hard to wait, they were instructed to ring a bell, knowing that they would only get one, but it would be right away.

In 2011, Mischel and colleagues tracked down fifty-nine of the original subjects, now in their forties. The same levels of impulse control were in effect: those who waited for marshmallow #2 in the 1960s still demonstrated better restraint than their peers who couldn't resist the bait of #1. One of the participants admitted she hadn't saved any money for retirement because "when I see a hot motorcycle, I buy it!"

The experiment went on to become a springboard for the study of self-control. Many scientists and economists draw a similar conclusion to Northeastern University economist William Dickens's take: "Pleasure now is worth more to us than pleasure later."

There are a lot of marshmallows in front of us. The clock ticks, and we worry we'll miss the once-in-a-lifetime offer if we don't hit the bell. It's hard to get excited about the marshmallows we can't see. We don't realize that having the cool ice cream maker now might leave us short on a down payment later. It's doesn't matter that gadgets break or we'll become too lazy to yank them out of the back of the cabinet. We have a hard time staying focused on building a nest egg for rainy days when there are so many bells to ring.

Know the Science Behind Buying

Neuroscientists are working to uncover why humans—especially Americans—have such an itch to spend. Delaying gratification has become increasingly challenging in our bell-ringing culture.

The measurable differences being noted between brains of spenders and savers are of great interest to scientists and marketers alike.

Magnetic resonance imaging (MRI) machines have helped identify the regions that influence whether we tend to spend or save. The prefrontal cortex is an area of our brain that helps regulate decision making, and neuroscientists are demonstrating that the dorsolateral or back side seems to be helpful in slowing down our impulses to splurge.

Companies like QVC, HSN, and Amazon know that putting enticing marshmallows under our noses works wonders for their bottom lines. Not only are they offering less of a ripoff than other retailers, but they are master tantalizers. They give us overnight deliveries, easy-pay options, and loyalty rewards. They know just how to keep the pleasure of the purchase in the forefront of our minds—and the pain to our wallets in the back—so we keep spending to the point of no return.

Get Off the Treadmill

James Gustave Speth, author of *America the Possible: Manifesto for a New Economy*, says that in the face of our consumer society, our tendency to compare ourselves becomes "grotesquely exploited." Keeping up with the Kardashians is hitting us hard. We're saving 5 percent of our money every year if we're lucky. Uncle Sam and his minions count on us to support 70 percent of the gross domestic product.

That's a lot of stuff to cram into our houses and psyches. Consumerism and materialism lead to waste. Ninety percent of what we buy goes to the trash within six months. But somehow, companies convince us we need inflatable Santas for our roofs and heated seats to keep our super-size-me asses comfy. They want us to sport $25 Tervis cups to keep our caffeinated beverages tempered so that we won't lose ours—except for when they break or we lose them and *must buy* new ones.

For those resilient enough to brave the stores in person to find that the Halloween candy is out by spring and Mother's Day stuff by Groundhog Day, you have some serious warrior in you. Since there's always another holiday or occasion that necessitates more stuff, the stores are always at your service, except for when it's June 1 and you cannot find a bathing suit to save your life unless you're a size 00 or 14, or happen to rock a purple leopard-print look.

The endurance for the never-ending Macy's One-Day sale is a feat. It used to be that "one-day" meant just that. Now it means Wednesday to Sunday, four times a month.

This is the fun of living in a consumerist culture. In his book *Consuming Life,* Polish sociologist Zygmunt Bauman says our departure from a time when we used to make things to one in which the prime objective is to consume them leads us to trouble. We're in a permanent state of busyness and the constant feeling of being in a state of emergency.

We're caught in a cycle of overworking and overspending, frantically trying to soothe ourselves from the resulting overwhelm.

We're professional hunters for the newest style, latest upgrade and 4-D experiences. We pride ourselves on being smart consumers, which seems to be oxymoronic.

We flip for Groupons and 50 percent–off outlet purchases from stuff marked up by 62 percent to begin with. *Look at this dress* (to be worn only once because of social media) that was supposed to cost $375 only costing $150. *OMG.*

We've been baited into buying beyond our needs and means. We are ripe for the picking because we think stuff will help us secure identity and meaning. Speth says that "the stamina of shoppers is crucial for global growth." We seem to be keeping pace, proving we are more than willing to shop until we drop. The trouble is, our stuff seems to be doing nothing more than pacifying us until the next want surfaces.

We're running on a treadmill that's hard to dismount. And the more stuff we have, the less it seems to matter to us. We fall prey to getting stuck

Buying may well be our rebuttal to the rather unsettling matter of transience—that nothing lasts or stays the same. We're cramming everything we can into our brains, our guts, our dwelling places. It may not be our gluttony that defines the problem in totality. Maybe stuff represents some measure of consistency, an unspoken but sought-after comfort. Maybe it gives us a sense of control. We think it will soothe our unquiet souls. And then the question becomes, is it working?

on a *hedonic treadmill*, a metaphor that psychologists use to debunk the myth that more is more.

Our "Will Work for Stuff" signs aren't making us happy. The more we have, the higher our expectations climb, with no permanent gain in our well-being. University of California–Riverside psychologist Sonja Lyubomirksy explains that happiness has a set point, remaining relatively steady—whether we find ourselves in the face of crappy or cheery circumstances.

During good or bad times, we are wired to get used to things. When the going gets tough, the agility comes in handy. But it can turn into a negative when we're on the up and up. No matter how high we climb, it's never enough. Stuff doesn't magically wipe out our underlying insecurities and natural unsettled responses to transience.

Lyubomirsky's research also revealed that our happiness is dramatically impacted by social comparison. In her book *The Myths of Happiness*, she unpacks some counterintuitive findings. She found that people in her studies were more willing to accept a worse end-result than to be outdone. Her participants were more willing to accept doing poorly, as long as someone else was worse off. In situations when they had a positive outcome, they weren't any happier if people were doing better than them.

Watch Out for Social Comparison

Besides there being little time to share or appreciate what we have, our merry and bright grow dim in the face of social comparison. Even good-natured people who are happy to celebrate the successes of others are exposed to the germs of our day. The national affluenza contagion, complete with clutter, frenzy, and disconnect, seems inescapable, and to be spreading fast. *Isn't there some sort of fruity antibacterial gel for this?*

Now we've got to show up ready to charm our friends with just the right hostess gift, even though everyone's squawking about their messy, cluttered houses.

> "The unhappiest people in the world are those who care the most about what other people think."
> —C. JoyBell C.

Gone are the days when we could show up with a six-pack and loaf of homemade banana bread. Handwritten cards have been replaced with airbrushed, professionally photographed family pictures with clever salutations.

We don't feel worthy unless we arrive with an organic bottle of wine in tow wrapped in a perfect glittery gift bag that says something magical like "Live. Laugh. Love" on it; even though everyone in the room knows there will be *no damn time* to do such novel things, since this is only stop number two of seven of the holiday madness.

We've gone from giving our kids coloring books and A Barrel of Monkeys to handheld electronics that give them the entire world in their hands but only last for the next thirty-six days until the next must-have upgrade becomes available.

What happened to being able to sustain a full fifteen minutes of attention with Silly Putty and newspapers—when the highlight of the birthday party was the Carvel Ice Cream cake with the cone-shaped nose, not matching tablecloths, napkins, balloons, and $20 themed goodie bags from Party City.

The stuff that's supposed to be making our lives easier seems to be having an opposite effect. We obsessively overwork, overspend, and overjustify. We *deserve* to pamper ourselves and take overpriced vacations, given how hard we friggin' *work*. But our overstimulated brains,

> "Consumer markets breed dissatisfaction with the products used by consumers to satisfy their needs—and they also cultivate constant disaffection with the acquired identity and the set of needs by which such an identity is defined. Changing identity, discarding the past and seeking new beginnings, struggling to be born again—they are promised by that culture as a duty disguised as privilege."
> —Zygmunt Bauman

fragmented souls, and exhausted bodies don't seem to be responding well to retail therapy.

Know the Difference Between Wants and Needs

Wants are things that we hope to get but are not necessarily for survival and won't live up to their promises—they are more *the goods life* than the good life.

Needs are things that we required to stay healthy, like water, nutritious food, shelter, and so on. Everything else is a bonus, and remembering that actually boosts our health and helps us live with simplicity and allows us more generosity—markers of the good life.

Dr. April Benson, an expert on slowing down want impulses to better determine needs, says when you're about to make a purchase, ask yourself: *Why am I here? How do I feel? Do I need this? What if I wait? How will I pay for it? Do I have something like this already?* Benson says that putting time between the impulse and action helps prevent unnecessary indulgences.

We even spend money on stuff that helps us with stuff, like plastic totes, storage space rentals, and personal organizers. Marie Kondos's 2014 book, *The Life-Changing Magic of Tidying Up: The Japanese Art of Decluttering and Organizing*, became an international sensation, with over 2 million copies sold. (I lost my copy under a pile somewhere.)

It's hard to get unhooked from Lock and Lock when it starts so early.

What you consume can end up consuming you.

There are now Baby Keurig machines and toddler bidets. Kids are getting iPads and smartphones before they lose their first tooth, at which point they're greeted by a twenty-first-century tooth fairy who has upped the ante of its two-quarter-giving predecessors.

As adults, we can become like kids in the marshmallow test experiment, impulsively downing all the first marshmallows with little thought about the long run. We forget that stuff breaks—that even though it can make life easier, stuff makes it harder, too. You'll be too tired to dig out the password for your lifetime guarantee. You'll trip over your stuff and become a slave to it. Then when you go to resell stuff, you'll only get four cents on the dollar on eBay. What you consume can end up consuming you.

Even with designer nursing pillows and ergonomic carriers, parenting will still break your back. Special reading glasses and antiwrinkle creams might assist with the sting of aging, but can't stop time. Having smoky eyes, rock-solid abs, Rihanna X Puma sneakers, and Givenchy shades won't be the magic bullet. Even really cool stuff won't meet our deepest desires for connection and meaning. Rising numbing behaviors like over- or undereating, cutting, drinking, drugging, hookups, and benders might be our rebuttal to the pressure to have it all.

Stop trying to cram your brain and guts with stuff to fill the void in your soul.

It's not that Veggetti, the right eye-shadow palette, or new smartphones don't have their redeeming value. Returning to the days of washboards and flip phones would have its own perils. But the nonstop trips to Stuff-Mart we hope will build us up seem to be tearing us down.

No matter how full our guts are, we are like Jack Sparrow from *Pirates of the Caribbean*, gorging ourselves on a consumeristic, materialistic diet that is leaking out as fast as it goes in. Buddhist tradition names people with intense emotional needs that act in animalistic ways as "hungry ghosts." When we live our lives this way, the deeper pain we're trying to mask goes untended. We barely pay attention to the things that could bring healing to our minds and souls.

Focus on Gratitude and Giving

Practicing gratitude is a start toward shifting our attention to mind and soul care. Gratitude is rarely controversial. You never meet anyone who explicitly balks at it. It's one of those rare instances where science and religion agree. Spiritual people call it *counting your blessings*, a way of expressing thankfulness and appreciation. New science is showing that practicing gratitude is more than just minding your manners or being a polite-bot.

Robert Emmons, the world's leading scientific expert on gratitude describes gratitude as the "queen of the virtues," and ingratitude the "king of the vices." He warns that our accumulation of "things" and hyperfocus on materialism are bought at a cost. He believes that our transactional ways of making purchases spill over into relationship domains, making us even see each other as disposable.

What would happen if we started taking care of the treasures we already have, instead of wanting more?

In his Expanding Gratitude Project at Stanford University, Emmons and his colleagues have reported new findings that affirm priceless returns for people who practice gratitude regularly. Their research discovered stronger immune systems, higher levels of positive emotions, and less inclination toward loneliness and isolation among those who gave intentional thanks. These are all things that money cannot buy.

Know the Science Behind Gratitude and Giving

In the first set of studies designed to solicit expressions of gratitude, Emmons and colleagues asked one group of participants to write down five things they were thankful for once a week for ten consecutive weeks.

The control groups were instead asked to take note of their hassles or to track random everyday events. The studies revealed that those asked to express gratitude reported higher levels of optimism and satisfaction with their lives than those in the control groups. They also reported fewer physical symptoms and better lifestyle behaviors such as exercise.

Sonja Lyubomirsky found similar results in her lab, with the caveat that her participants reported more positive results through a once-a-week practice versus three times a week. The practice was at its highest impact through weekly practice, not several times a week, when it seemed to take on the nature of a chore. Her findings are not suggesting that merely scheduling a rigid weekly ritual will be the magic bullet, but that keeping our strategies fresh without overpractice can help. The key is to avoid becoming rote in gratitude practice. Lyubomirsky emphasizes that "variety—the spice of life"—is extremely important to helping us accomplish this.

Social psychologist Liz Dunn reported that, in her control groups, those who held onto the money they were given had higher cortisol levels than those who donated it. Stephen Post, professor of preventative medicine and bioethics at Stony Brook University reported that brain scans of people who were merely planning to make a donation already became happier.

Besides the many returns on practicing gratitude, giving is another pathway to the good life that reaps benefits. Lynne Twist, philanthropist and author of *The Soul of Money: Transforming Your Relationship with Money and Life,* warns that we have assigned too much authority to money, even when science proves it brings more happiness when we use it to help others. Some scientists are calling this the "givers' glow" and "helpers' high." Stephen Post, author of *The Hidden Gifts of Helping and Why Good Things Happen to Good People,* says that "when the happiness, security, and well-being of others become real to us, we come into our own."

In addition to money, we can be generous with our time. Volunteering is another way to boost individual and collective resilience. When we pay it forward, the rewards are priceless. Even when we're cash- or time-strapped, there's often a way to give up something we don't need to make room for something that would bring higher social impact.

Practicing gratitude and giving turns out to be an amazing seal for us to use as our own version of Lock and Lock, helping to preserve and store optimism. Each day, we're given the opportunity to indulge in the true jewels of nature, whether we have a cent to our names or not. Barely noticing is perhaps the biggest waste of all. When we offer thanks to earth and sky, seaside and laughter, we are more inclined to recognize that the most beautiful aspects of life seldom involve consumption. When we

What would happen if you stopped cramming your brain and gut with stuff to fill the void in your soul, and started to feed it what it really needs?

share, we move closer to the good life. We enjoy presence with one another, being lost in timeless moments when we are creating, relishing in their value. These are what help keep us full—not stuffing down every last marshmallow coming our way.

Session Nine Worksheet:
Waiting for Marshmallows

Objective:
Unlearn consumeristic indoctrination that breeds waste.
Pivot toward gratitude.

Rethink It:
Move from Consumption to Gratitude

We are inundated with messages of consumption, even when in utero. Our parents leave their baby showers with a truckload of stuff to welcome us, and from cradle to grave we're false-promised that a better, happier life will come with a lot of plastic that lasts seconds in the grand scheme of life. Our brains light up in the face of all this stimulation, and our deeper soul needs make us vulnerable to falling for retail therapy to fill our voids. It takes deliberate attention to hold onto our wallets and to tune into the true joys of life, those that are priceless and won't ever waste our time and money.

Spending and Gratitude Check

- Where do I invest most of my time and money?
- Am I paying the price for overactive indulgences in any areas?
- How driven am I to make a good appearance?
- Do I regularly stop to appreciate life?
- What are three blessings for which I am grateful?
- What changes can I make in spending to become more generous?

Action Steps: Pinpoint Opportunities
for Gratitude and Generosity

It's easy to get swept away when you live in a marketer's heaven and a consumer's hell. Consumerism leads to wasted time and money, distracting us from the true joys of life. Stuff can be like a collar around your neck, with companies pulling you by their mega-leashes. Consider unhooking yourself by engaging in the following activities:

1. **Take a stuff walk.** Spend five minutes in each room and closet in your house. Take note of your clothes and shoes. Are there any tags on clothes that you bought and have never worn? What percentage of your wardrobe do you wear? Do you have items that have lasted the test of time? Anything you've worn only once? Check out your personal products. Have they delivered their promises? Are the name brands you pay for worth the hype? Sometimes we don't even realize

how much stuff we have. Very often, taking inventory of what we have can serve as an appetite suppressant for shopping.

2. **Do a mental fire drill.** Pretend that where you live is on fire and you have ten minutes to evacuate your house. What essentials would you take with you? How much of what you would have to leave behind would be truly missed? What does what you would keep or abandon say about what you value most?

3. **Review your budget.** Look at your last few bank statements. What areas are you spending most on? Housing, transportation, and food tend to be biggies for everyone. Review your personal expenses, such as entertainment, going out to eat, and so on. How much are your weekly coffee, takeout, or entertainment bills? Are there ways to reduce spending in any of the areas? Are there any "unbeatable" discounts that are backfiring on you (buying three to get the fourth one free on a product you wouldn't generally consume that much of)?

4. **Reflect through music.** Listen to the "Christmas-Can Can" song by Straight No Chaser. Does any of it seem familiar? Do holidays, birthdays, weddings, or other occasions that are supposed to bring joy have an opposite effect on your wallet and psyche? Is the stuff getting regifted anyway?

5. **Move from *ahhhh!* to *aha!*** The constant *ahhhh!* hustle of life that entices us to acquire stuff draws us away from the true treasures of life: relationships, health, opportunities for growth and impact. Take time to get away from the hustle to practice gratitude and connect, to find your aha moments of full appreciation and contentment.

6. **Dial up your gratitude and giving.** Instead of mindless screen sucking or purchasing, use your phone and social media as creative outlets to track gratitude and generosity. Take pictures of things you appreciate and post them with your reasons why. Most nonprofits and charities have easy text options to contribute, and automatic withdrawal systems. You can also use your phone to track the amount of time you spend volunteering, instead of screen sucking. Giving our time away is another amazing way to bring about the good life and to boost along our collective progress.

Our phones and wallets have become our **TEDDY BEARS**. We **SNUGGLE UP** to them, **NEVER** leave home without them, and **RELY** on them as **SOLE COMFORT**, when what we **NEED** is **SOUL COMFORT**.

They hold their place, all while our nearby hearts are pining for a **NEW KIND** of absorption to take over—one that **RELISHES** in the eyes of a lover, squeals of children, glamorous sunsets, the smell of ocean.

The heart **WAITS** to be **UNTETHERED**, but the **VICES** of consumeristic culture **CONFUSE US** with a neurochemical rush that seems at first to resemble **EXCITEMENT** and **JOY**, but pales in comparison to a heart that is **FLOODED** with **GRATITUDE** and **PRESENCE**.

Embracing Impermanence

Objective:
Unlearn happy-talk indoctrination that breeds mindlessness.
Pivot toward mindfulness.

Nothing in the world is permanent,
and we're foolish when we ask anything to last,
but surely we're still more foolish not to take
delight in it while we have it."

—W. Somerset Maugham

Jackie drops her kindergartener Lexi at school, where the five-year-old starts her day on her mat, listening to her teacher read *Sitting Still Like a Frog: Mindfulness Exercises for Kids*. Jackie heads to work, where the lunch-and-learn session of the day is *Mindfulness: How to Cultivate Presence Amidst Your Busy Workday*. Later that day, her wife, Peggy, comes home gushing over NPR's story on Buddhist monk Haemin Sunin's promotion of peace and mindfulness via Twitter, of all places. As she curls up into bed, she flips through the special "Mindfulness" edition of *TIME* magazine she bought a few months back but had been too busy to read. Maybe there was something to all this.

Mindfulness seems to have become an overnight sensation, even though it has been around for more than 2,600 years, originating within Buddhist teachings. Ever since molecular biologist Jon Kabat-Zinn introduced it in the late 1970s as an antidote to stress, it's been gaining traction. At first, it seemed to draw a radical type of New Age crowd, but soon became accessible even to those who wouldn't necessarily be inclined to walk across burning coals or drink Kombucha, but would still welcome a little Zen in their crazy, busy lives.

Mindfulness has become as mainstream as sushi and acupuncture. *Thank you, East, for all these wonders of life.* Zinn defines mindfulness as "paying attention in a particular way: on purpose, in the present moment, and nonjudgmentally."

Mindfulness

Academic Definition

Mindfulness, a state of active consciousness and conscientiousness, is defined in a wide variety of ways across the scholarly literature and therapeutic realms. Mindfulness helps us observe, acknowledge, and accept feelings, thoughts, and bodily sensations without judgment.

Street Definition

Mindfulness is like a first cousin to consciousness. It helps us step out of the ring from our thoughts and feelings, and watch them from afar, without having to declare them as winners or losers, but just calling the shots in real time. It steers us away from overreacting to difficulty, but not in a way that forces us into pretending to be shiny, happy people. Mindfulness helps us better appreciate positive circumstances and tolerate unpleasant ones. #observe #acceptance #nonjudgmental

Ironically, mindfulness—the very thing that's supposed to help us empty out and breathe a little deeper—seems to be for sale. You wonder what the Buddha would think about it becoming a white-hot commodity, generating over $4 billion in sales in 2016. There is palpable enthusiasm for everything from the 12 million adult coloring books sold in 2015 to the 100,000 mindfulness books sold, to the 700-plus apps emerging to help us eat, walk, commute, and work a little more mindfully. The "new" antidote for modern living is everywhere we turn.

Entrepreneurs are experimenting with mindfulness as a success hack, using it to improve instincts. Companies eager to boost employee productivity are paying a fortune to set up quiet spaces and teach employees to "focus on regulating breath" and "notice sensations without judgment." Schools are bringing in peace teachers and building mindful moments into classroom routines, eager to improve student performance and behavior.

Mindfulness isn't a drive-thru option for quick relief. We need to be careful not to jump on a bandwagon, grab our fix, and then head right back down the same path of constant stimulation and reactivity that begged us to be more mindful in the first place.

Embrace Your Periphery

Mindfulness doesn't come as fast as marketers trying to sell it would like us to believe, but it can be put into place without a lot of fanfare. The term itself often gets used interchangeably with the activities that help us corral ourselves toward a more neutral, observant state. The most well-known pathway is meditation, which helps bring mental processes into greater focus. Like metacognition and critical thinking, mindfulness practices help us check in on our thinking, bringing us to awareness that allows us to make needed tweaks and build agility. We enhance our calmness, clarity, and concentration.

While mindfulness has certainly had a lot of help from entities eager to sell it or improve their bottom lines, it's not just another gimmicky self-help intervention or way to line someone's pockets. Science backs it.

Not only has the concept originating from Buddhism become a great source of fascination in the popular press, but mindfulness is rocking it across the academic and scientific literature. Researchers have put in overtime mining for the reasons behind its benefits to our well-being. They seem to have struck oil—demonstrating that mindfulness practices can rewire the brain's responses, helping with learning, memory, rational thinking, empathy, and compassion. No wonder it's selling like hotcakes.

Know the Science Behind Mindfulness

Mindfulness isn't just the latest fad. It has empirically supported benefits. Research affirms its power in helping reduce rumination through meta-awareness. It helps us shift from unproductive thinking to new states of attention and awareness that aid in keeping our emotions in check—aka *emotional regulation*.

In 2008, for example, researchers Richard Chambers, Barbara Chuen Yee Lo, and Nicolas Allen took twenty new meditators to a ten-day intensive mindfulness meditation retreat. After all was said and done, the retreat participants reported fewer depressive symptoms, the ability to stick with tasks longer, and improved affect.

In addition, Hoffman and colleagues meta-analysis (for them, this meant analyzing the findings of twenty-nine studies) exploring the use of mindfulness-based stress reduction and mindfulness-based cognitive therapy affirmed its benefits in improving affective and cognitive processes that commonly accompany anxiety and depression symptoms.

Another line of research suggests that in addition to helping people become less reactive, mindfulness meditation may also give them greater cognitive flexibility and agility. One study found that people who practice mindfulness meditation appear to develop the skill of self-observation, which neurologically disengages the automatic pathways that were created by prior learning and enables present-moment input to be integrated in a new way. It also helps spur on adaptive responses to stressful situations.

Mindfulness is like medicine for the brain—and our weary souls. It helps us take pause from our shopping, running around, and overworking. It helps us to simply notice what's happening, almost like we are a fly on the wall of our brains. When something stimulates us, we don't immediately rush to conclusions. Instead we take stock of what thoughts are percolating and what sensations are bubbling up, and we simply observe, rather than try to immediately appraise or solve it.

Mindfulness helps us avoid disproportionate extremes in positivity and negativity. In other words, we don't have to be all hunky-dory when things are off-kilter, sugarcoating the hard stuff. We don't have to take the bait of our racing hearts and raging emotions when we're raw and uncut either. We can ride out the disruptions happening in the periphery, outside the realms of our control—the ones that are harder to manage because we rarely bring them up in our happy talk.

As we improve in our abilities to experience this on-the-spot full-picture neutrality, we can transfer it into a variety of areas of our lives. We can hang out in the periphery without totally freaking out. It helps us remain present even in precarious situations, seeing through a more holistic and realistic lens. It doesn't happen magically, but it doesn't take a rocket scientist either. It starts with revamping the way we talk about life.

Make Room for Grief and Praise

Happy-talk indoctrination floods our consciousness from an early age. There's an endless plethora of self-help accolades: "You can do it. You can do anything. Just put your mind to it." We're always taught there's a light at the end of the tunnel, but skip over the dark forces of the tunnel. We're told "keep typing yellow smiley faces and things will get better. Everything is going to be fine." We long for these messages to be true, to be able to soften life's blows with expedient relief and simple strategies.

It's not just the strains of modern living that we're dealing with. A tremendous amount of conscious and subconscious work is required to come to terms with deeper life cycles, ones that are hard to reconcile, ones that do not resolve even when Tony Robbins

Mindlessness is when we try to "Carpe diem" our way through life in reckless and haphazard ways— or when we completely check out, living in our superficial sphere, satisfied by happy talk, tuning out all other dimensions . . . the ones that could help us integrate. Mindfulness opens the space for the dark emotions to be held, the ones that swallow us whole and sink us at first, but then provide needed contrast for our lighter moments to have the chance to stand out and be relished.

shows up at your house for a private motivational session, or that Leslie Knope and all her binders couldn't fix. The kind of cycles can keep you from laughing even after binge watching Ellen DeGeneres for days.

Humor and motivation help us through dark moments, for sure. Sometimes we take life way too seriously and make things more complicated than we need to. A strong dose of fun and positivity can work wonders, contributing powerfully to coping and resilience.

At the same time, overreliance on trite sayings can become dysfunctional, too. We explain complexity with simple slogans. We try to avoid confronting realities of the human condition that even the Great Houdini couldn't escape, the kind that make even the most agile of us want to numb out: unwanted change, oppression, discrimination, war, poverty, losing people we love, aging, our own imminent death. Deep cycles of generational suffering permeate our lives.

> **"Grief is love's souvenir. It's our proof that we once loved. Grief is the receipt we wave in the air that says to the world: Look! Love was once mine. I love well. Here is my proof that I paid the price."**
>
> —Glennon Doyle

Glennon Doyle, author of *Carry On, Warrior: The Power of Embracing Your Beautiful, Messy Life*, calls life "brutiful," saying that both the beauty and brutality of life need to be embraced to live and love fully. She says, "Grief and pain are like joy and peace; they are not things we should try to snatch from each other. They're sacred. They are part of each person's journey. All we can do is offer relief from this fear: I am all alone. That's the one fear you can alleviate."

When we rely on too much happy talk we turn our backs on the chance to embrace life's "brutiful" nature, to offer the simultaneous grief and praise that Martín Prechtel writes about in his book *The Smell of Rain on Dust: Grief and Praise*. He calls grief the "art behind all real art," explaining the connections between both processes—praise being an expression of grieving what we love but know will eventually lose; the grief a form of praise for love that is lost. He emphasizes the interconnected presence of both in our lives:

Grief permeates life and can take many forms, but grief can never be outrun or simply thought away, transcended or meditated into non-existence. Necessary grief when shunned or unattended can easily hide for years, even generations in the skeletal structure of the family collective psyche. Like light, matter, sound, and energy, grief will eventually manifest even among those who did not consciously experience the loss.

I first learned about Prechtel's work at an intimate coffeehouse show featuring American musician Glen Phillips, who was mourning the loss of his twenty-plus-year marriage. I've followed Glen closely his entire career, a committed if not obsessed fan of his melancholic music since my friend Karen Porter handed me half her Walkman muff pumping out a "Fear" cassette at our high school lunch table.

That table was the sacred place where we joked, sang, grumbled about our teachers, and planned our futures. Margo wanted to be a flight attendant so that she could see the world. Karen wanted to be a vet because every time she saw a dog she freaked out, in a good way. Gina wanted to be a fashion model. It didn't matter that she was five-foot-two; she was gonna rock the runway. Ashley wanted to do it with every guy in our grade, and she was making good progress. We were committed. A lot of guys in our class sported mullets, so I let Ashley do her thing, and instead I wanted to be the first female president, or own a Harley.[1] It was the time of life to entertain our tangential fantasies with the full bravado of seventeen-year-olds ready to take the world on by storm.

We sang along with Glen Phillips and his band Toad the Wet Sprocket's (love those '90s band names) "All I Want," like the unstoppables we thought we were.

We didn't know that just a few weeks later things would never be the same. Margo, along with our guy friend Jamie, were our most hyped classmates. Pretty much every kid in the school had a crush on them. They were our little high school's version of Brad and Angelina, the pair voted Best Looking in our yearbook superlatives, and that made us all swoon.

---

1 Note to seventeen-year old self: You could've done both. If you're going to blaze trails, do it right. Go big or stay home.

Three days before graduation they were killed. It was so classic high school tragedy it was almost cliché: graduation party–meets 100-mile-an-hour car into tree–meets hospital–meets cemetery. "All I want is to feel this way" was over.

We'd all come of age together, and this was supposed to be the happiest time of our lives. The joy we'd had was directly proportionate to our grief. Best moments turned to worst. The grief and praise were inseparable, just like we had all been. We didn't know when we first started listening to that "Fear" tape at the lunch table how much we would come to rely on it to help us process and grieve in the spaces ahead.

At the coffeehouse, Glen belted out his song "Grief and Praise," and I was touched by how his words resembled the very same themes of not only my research but my own personal soul excavation. At the time, I was experiencing several losses and transitions, and finding it excruciating to integrate my own grief and praise. The lyrics reminded us that even though all we love is eventually taken, the reason we hurt is because we had something good to be thankful for in the first place.

Glen must have known that I was having trouble because he followed with Toad's best-known hit, "All I Want," the same one that kept our 1992 lunch table rocking out.

We're trying to pave over ambiguity, but the bumps are still there underneath, bursting out from the concrete, proof that pain is always present, an inescapable contrast to what is beautiful and smooth.

There I stood, grieving and praising with full gusto, acknowledging the pain but still singing. I started accepting the contradictions that were burdening me at this stage in life. It's not easy being immersed in such an intense research process over so many years. I was living and breathing human analysis. Working to understand my students' psyches was forcing me to rethink every emotional crevice of my own life, at a time when I already felt entirely overloaded and unhinged.

After my own breakdown—err, *mindful moment*—in the middle of the concert, I didn't necessarily leave elated, but did find a new sense of resolve and peace I hadn't experienced for a while. I paid homage to my pain, knowing it was deeply connected to the many blessings I'd also experienced. It was a lesson I had begun learning after traumatically losing Margo and Jamie, and one that continues to teach me as I make my way through life's inevitable losses and changes.

Like my students, my ability to integrate and remain agile was under serious test. Thanks to Glen, and as only music can do, I had a new way to process some of the messiness. "Grief and Praise" became part of my new playlist, and I ordered a copy of Prechtel's book, too, since, besides music, *reading is my air.*

We tend to believe what we want to believe. In all our pining for expedient relief, we try to decipher complexity through a lens of simple, happy talk that conflates reality to something it is not, leaving us more apt to become disappointed and confused when trite slogans and three-step solutions don't hold up. Acknowledging grief can help us make way for praise.

Put an End to Happy Talk

Happy talk to avoid pain ended up being an entire code in my research. My students repeatedly revealed their abandonment of it in favor of confronting life's hard realities. At first unsettling for them, it eventually helped them come to accept and embrace impermanence. Many of them named it as the turning point in their healing process. My students were recovering happy talkers. As Seema put it,

I've probably read every self-help book out there. My colleagues even call me the Queen of Positivity. I watch motivational speakers like Tony Robbins like it's church. I even was addicted to watching Joel Osteen for a while. But then I dug in and learned about "prosperity teaching" and really started to analyze the messages. It felt like they were trying to sell happiness—if you believe, then good things will be a given. It was almost superstitious. This went directly against my experiences. I've always been the kind of person who gives a lot and does everything by the book. But I've never really seen that kind of luck come in. I've actually had terrible luck when I really think about it. I wish I could have all that time back where I was frustrated with myself because I couldn't just magically will big things into existence. It totally stalled me out. I sat around. I even gained weight—food became my crutch. Then I went from a glass of wine a night to three or four. No one would've guessed how numb I was becoming to life—and it wasn't like I was going through some big catastrophe. I think I kinda gave up just because I hadn't been delivered some mystical prize the sky was supposed to open up and deliver. Reality wasn't even that bad, but I think that all that happy, you-can-have-any-thing-you-want talk was making me think it was. When I started to see through it all, I turned things around. I was able to accept that things weren't going to rain from the sky, but my outlook was still decent.

Stephen also had his misgivings about happy talk:

I'm not a negative person, per se, but I think that a lot of the self-help movement tells us what we want to hear, and isn't really that helpful. I don't think you have to be all happy-go-lucky 24/7 to be okay. . . . I've been through a lot in life, and at first I was so ashamed of my story. I didn't want people to think bad of me. But I honestly think that most of my best relationships have come by being honest with people—and myself. Life is a shit show. Everyone has their cross to bear. I just know myself better now and think I'm stronger because I've been able to face stuff more head on. And when things go well, I feel like I appreciate it more. I try to remember that things will get better, and things also get worse. It helps me get through the bad times and try to enjoy the good ones, instead of thinking it's gonna last forever.

Everything is temporary. The highs. The lows. Nothing stays the same. We all take turns soaring and suffering. Mortality is inevitable. These are heavy, hard, and disruptive truths, ones that can potentially sink our spirits into despair—but that also have the power to help us live fuller, truer, and mindfully.

Seema and Stephen were just two of my students who had worked at rethinking happy-talk indoctrination. It meant different things to everyone, but one theme that consistently presented was working to disengage from the opposite of happy talk: crippling negative self-talk. At first, many of my students were drawn to happy talk because what was going on in their lives was so dark and difficult. In a world where shaming is blood sport, my students were eager to get into a new arena, ready for respite from the heinous cut-throat competition. But they also found that the hatch-door happy talk provided only led them to places of numbing and more despair. They realized that either extreme would interfere with progress.

> "Nature's first green is gold, her hardest hue to hold. Her early leaf's a flower; But only so an hour. Then leaf subsides to leaf. So Eden sank to grief, so dawn goes down to day. Nothing gold can stay."
>
> —Robert Frost

After the Glen Phillips concert, I went back to the data to reexamine my students' shifts from self-crucifying to happy talk to more mindful practices. There was a lot to weed through—hundreds of students from across the world over years of teaching. This was the biggest research project I'd worked on, and I had to get it right. I found several summarizing passages toward the end of my research journal that captured their progression:

- **Initial aversion to change.** Not wanting good things to change and not wanting bad things to last. Keywords: resistance, frustration, struggle, holding on, hating change, fighting myself, wishing, anxious, sad, loss, lost, "thought it was over."
- **Wake-up calls.** It took negative experiences, framed as wake-up calls and hellish moments that brought newfound appreciation of the fragility and beauty of life. Keywords: devastated, shocked, worried, all alone, scared, "not thinking I could make it."
- **Someone holding space.** The grief couldn't be "hurried up." It took time and the safety of relationships for healing to begin. Keywords: time, caring, friends, pain, unleash, waiting, "knowing that I didn't have to rush through it."
- **Acceptance.** Even through major losses, trials, and heartaches, healing took place. It didn't mean there weren't tender scars and ongoing burdens to deal with. It meant "taking the good with the bad." Keywords: survive, gonna make it, coming out of the dark, appreciating life, mindful, acceptance, becoming more tuned in.

Their process was strikingly similar to the work I had helped my own patients move through over the years. It also closely resembled my process with Lyla, my own therapist, who has earned more than a few stripes working with me. Therapists are not the easiest breed to work with. *We think we know everything, but we can only apply our skills to our own lives so much.* The idea of "holding space"—not feeling like we have to fork over the Kleenex or break out the magic wand for someone who is grieving—is a big antidote to happy talk. That kind of presence is the exact embodiment of mindfulness that can help us undo the indoctrination and human tendency to keep "All I Want" on repeat, instead of integrating "Grief and Praise" on our playlists, too.

"Once we know that LIFE is difficult— once we truly UNDERSTAND and ACCEPT it—then life is NO LONGER difficult."

—M. Scott Peck

Session Ten Worksheet:
Embracing Impermanence

Objective:
Unlearn happy-talk indoctrination that breeds mindlessness.
Pivot toward mindfulness.

Rethink It:
Move from Happy Talk to Mindfulness

Happy talk can serve a purpose. It gives us the muster we need to keep calm and carry on, to seize the day in front of us. But if we make it out to be all rainbows and butterflies, happy talk can have the opposite effect. We can end up numbing in excess to try to escape sitting with grief. Our attachments to the idea that everything is supposed to be fine can cause pain. Happy talk can mislead us and bring about more harm.

Mindfulness Check

- What types of mindful practices am I most drawn to?
- What parts of my life are the most beautiful? Brutal? What helps me sit with discomfort?
- For what do I have cause to praise?
- What am I grieving?
- Do I engage in excess happy talk?
- What needs to change?

Action Steps:
Make Room for Grief and Praise

Often, when the realities of life shake us at our core, we entertain ourselves, numb out, and go on avoidance binges only to find ourselves still unsteady. In the meantime, we've missed opportunities to see the beauty of the edges and contrasts that bring us to better appreciate and absorb the gift of life.

1. **Get more mindful.** Instead of numbing pain, listen to its messages. Look for contrasts. Work on mindfulness activities such as deep breathing, meditation, coloring, being in nature. Work to become an observer of your thoughts rather than judging them. Let your brain clear its overfill, and don't be on hypervigilant alert over everything.

2. **Acknowledge the "brutiful."** Take a cue from Glennon Doyle. Pain has its sacred components, as it shapes our perspectives and helps us appreciate joy. Make a list of things that are beautiful and those that are brutal. Look for how the grief and praise are connected. Embrace

impermanence—nothing lasts forever—in some cases this works well for us, and other times it is heart-wrenching.

3. **Take the tombstone test.** What would you want your tombstone to say about you? Consider the following quote from Thom Hartmann: "Ask yourself how you'd live differently if you knew you were going to die soon, then ask yourself who those people you admire are, and why you admire them, and then ask yourself what was the most fun time in your life. The answers to these questions, when seen, heard, and felt, provide us with an open doorway into our mission, our destiny, our purpose." When people are told they don't have much time to live, they're told to "get their affairs in order." Pick three areas that you want to focus in on this month.

PART III

The Breaking-Out Sessions

Find Your Global Lens

Rethink the 4 forms of indoctrination that lead to insularity:

→ From Groupthink to Universal Thinking

→ From Binary to Real Thinking

→ From Bias to Solidarity

→ From Polarized to Common-Ground Thinking

The Breaking-Out Sessions help you unlearn four forms of indoctrination that lead to insularity. You will pivot to reclaim your birthright, become more multidimensional in your thinking, stop shoving yourself in restrictive boxes, lay off the Kool-Aid, and start mixing a new brew to develop your global lens. This approach will help you break the shackles of insularity, conformity, shame, and disconnection. Welcome to our new psychology of thinking: becoming unbound, global, twenty-first-century citizens. Are you ready to break out and be a free bird—and a fabulous one?

global

adjective | [glōbəl]

1. relating to the whole world; worldwide.

2. relating to or embracing the whole of something, or of a group of things.

Having a global view of life helps us see beyond boundaries and adopt a more universal perspective.

Purging Kool-Aid

Objective:
Unlearn groupthink indoctrination that breeds insularity.
Pivot toward universality.

*Either you repeat the same conventional doctrines
everybody is saying, or else you say something true,
and it will sound like it's from Neptune.*

—Noam Chomsky

Getting over 900 people to abandon country and family to move to a remote compound, labor from dawn to dusk, and drink deadly Kool-Aid takes some mad persuasion. In the fall of 1978, cult leader Jim Jones did just that. His promise of paradise in the South American nation of Guyana turned out to be a concentration camp for those he'd baited into his grips. Twenty-three years after founding the Peoples Temple, a religious movement that drew over 20,000 members at its peak, the troubled leader finally snapped.

The resulting mass murder was the largest modern loss of civilian American life at one time before September 11, 2001. Over one-third of his victims were children. Jones's perpetration of abuse and mental control

153

over his followers remains one of the most disturbing and harrowing examples of indoctrination gone wrong.

The Jonestown brainwashing unfolded over two decades. Peoples Temple members were robbed of their money, freedom, health, identity, families, children, and lives. The resulting carnage has been mourned, studied, and debated ever since. The horrific images and accounts elicit predictable responses: "How could he?" "How could they?" "Why, *I would never.*"

The perfect storm was brewing at the time Jones came to power. The polarized sociopolitical landscape was rife with turmoil. He appealed to citizens who were fed up with economic, racial, and social inequities. They were sick of being disempowered and bullied. Jones capitalized, becoming a dangerous predator who went from *praying for* to *preying on* people.

Jones's followers yearned for exile from oppressive conditions. Initially, their community served as a sanctuary. They were tucked away in a lush jungle, feeling safe from the devices of the outside world. The illusion of safety proved deadly for the victims of Jonestown. Understanding the psychology behind it—even when we think we'd never face such tragic and extreme outcomes—is critical to avoiding groupthink in our lives.

Peel Off Your Insulation

Jones's path to power relied on getting people scared and hopeful all at once. He promised a better life. He frightened them into thinking they had to isolate themselves to find it. He conditioned them for dependence.

The communities and social structures we participate in mold us into a common way of thinking and engaging—or disengaging—with the world. Every collective—whether a religious, governmental, occupational, or social group—has its own unique way of insulating us to one extent or another. The resulting barriers make it difficult to recognize that the very ideology that seems to protect can strip us of our senses. Recognizing our isolation is the start of being able to break out from it.

The word *insularity* originates from the Latin for "island." It involves staying in the bounds of your own affinity groups and associations and being detached from alternative viewpoints or ways of engaging with the world. We stay within a narrow frame of thinking. Jones wrapped his members tight in insulation. While few of us can imagine falling into such extreme ideology, we might be bound tighter than we realize.

By design, society sets us up this way. We stay with our own kind. It happens everywhere. Insulation is stuffed inside the walls of our lives. At work. School. Church. Within our social identity groups. The precise behavioral norms we're taught to follow are often instilled at an age before we have much to say about it.

Despite gains in civil rights, most neighborhoods, schools, communities, and churches are still homogeneous. We have secular and religious schools, black and white neighborhoods, gay and straight bars, cool kids versus nerds.[1] Why are we still such a weird combo of *Freedom Writers* meets *Breakfast Club* meets *Mean Girls*?

The persuasions we follow according to our own islands may seem inconsequential, but over time, sip by sip, they can cause us to lay down our discernment and succumb to groupthink. Not only can this compromise us psychologically, but it can prevent more integrated ways of understanding the world. Insulation needs to be peeled off. It rarely protects us the ways we're taught it will.

Groupthink

Academic Definition

The practice of thinking or making decisions in a group. Because of responsibility to and affiliation with the group, individuals relinquish their own interests in favor of keeping peace.

Street Definition

Group think is when you go along to get along. Because you don't want to ruffle feathers, you keep quiet and avoid bringing up controversy. #monkeyseemonkeydo

---

1 We have work to get to true integration. This is quite the mix of social identities here. Marginalized groups do not have access to dominant group benefits, and it's often unsafe to mix into unwelcomed spaces. We have a long way to go to overcome these divides that block us from the good life.

Social psychologist Irving Janis defines three characteristics of group-think that influence behavior. First, groups tend to overestimate themselves, falling prey to "illusions of invulnerability and inherent morality." Groupthink also produces close-mindedness and collective rationalizations of stereotypes about outsiders. Groups find ways to justify their judgments of people with whom they don't associate. There is also pressure toward uniformity, and consequences for those who dissent.

Groupthink favors coherence, even if it means sacrificing sound reasoning for less questioning and more following. The dictate of the leader and the resulting consensus go unchallenged. You stay in line with what all of your associates do.

From a brain science perspective, fear activates our amygdalae, triggering decisions based out of raw emotion and groupthink tides. When you first study Jim Jones, you might think you could never get sucked in. While he took it to the furthest extreme, many of his approaches derived from the very same structures our own indoctrination is built on:

The Promise of Fatherly Love and Protection

Jones's followers came to call him "Father" and "Dad," which seems contradictory when you think of the monster he was. Calling faith-based leaders "Father" or similar variations is common practice in religious communities around the world. The glorification of heavenly and earthly fathers is as old as dirt. Hello, patriarchy.

We're taught that we need protection, that fatherly wisdom is best. Women are told that if they didn't have the influence of a strong father figure growing up, they're screwed. You don't hear much about maternal influence and protection, or the dearth of research that contradicts these long-held incorrect beliefs. Just a lotta talk about Daddy issues.

Jones isn't the only father who has committed serious crimes against people. Countless church leaders have violated people's trust by perpetuating abuses of all kinds. Exploitation. Sexual abuse. Outside religious realms, the patriarchy continues to be a force. The old boys' network has been around a long time.

The Promise of Identity

Whether you are a Christian, Jew, Buddhist, Hindu, Muslim, or other humans are wired for a sense of safety and belonging with people of the same ethos. Even though we might be proud of our unconventional ways and not necessarily wanting to fit in, being alone isn't any picnic.

If you stay with the program, you will receive instant status and identity, protecting you from scrutiny. Your own authentic self will be relinquished, but you won't have to stand up on trial to defend your essence. Following keeps you low under the scrutiny radar. No need to explain yourself constantly.

The alternative is to take your place as the black sheep in a family, at work, or in a community. When you're not like the other sheep, you can also end up becoming a scapegoat, which is no picnic. The word *scapegoat* is based on biblical lore, telling the story of Aaron, who selected a strong (and perhaps opinionated) goat to cast the sins of the tribe upon, and then be banished. The displacement of anguish among the tribe provides comfort but leaves the scapegoat isolated, in danger, and faced with being a herd animal without a herd.

The emotional consequences of bearing the psychological discomfort of families and communities of origin are what I call paying *generational ransom*. You are atoning for everyone's pasts, pain, misdeeds, and anxieties. Instead of those issues being addressed, you become a needed diversion from their own issues and a target of their rage. Your contrarian behavior is seen as disloyalty. You are expected to take on all the pain without any of the comforts. Few of us can bear this load, so we hold onto identity that doesn't fit, but doesn't expose us, either. Generational ransom is costly.

Don't Be a Sheep or a Scapegoat

My first introduction to indoctrination came within the Baptist church I was raised in. It wasn't Westboro breed, or Jonestown, but there were similarities. There was a lot of us-versus-them talk. The world was a dangerous place, where "those people"—the wretched sinners, the lost, the ones not like us—lived in total abomination. We were the in-group, "they" were the out, but we were told "they"—the "worldly people" were the ones after us.

I always thought it strange that our pastor frequently warned about becoming educated—that it leads to too much self-reliance and indulgence. When any organization encourages us to give up thinking, it should be a *major red flag*. Encouraging people not to think for themselves is a way to maintain status and power.

The logic of education-as-evil never really added up for me, but at nine, the time when my former hippie parents "converted" and church became a weekly ritual, I was too chicken to fully revolt. At school, being smart was seen as a good thing, so I went for it there. But on Sundays, we bellowed, "God said it, I believe it, and that settles it for me"; memorized passages telling us to "Have faith like a child"; and sang songs like "I just want to be a sheep," animal noise effects and all:

> *I just wanna be a sheep*
> *Baa, baa, baa, baa*
> *I just wanna be a sheep*
> *Baa, baa, baa, baa*
> *I pray the Lord my soul to keep*
> *I just wanna be a sheep*
> *Baa, baa, baa, baa. . . .*

I was told to block my ears during evolution lessons and wear T-shirts that said, "No Scientist Is Going to Make a Monkey Out of Me." I was sent to Bible camp every summer and brought to abortion rallies. The church was our community, our culture, our whole world. We were told that the rainbow was God's exclusive promise to the Christians. Relationships with outsiders only existed with the intention of trying to get them to repent and become born again.

There were constant reinforcements to keep us *baa-baa*-ing. Our pastor showed a movie called *A Thief in the Night* that went right for my nine-year-old jugular. Back in the 1980s, it was an era when we let kids watch movies they weren't emotionally ready for. *Friday the 13th* movies were third-grade rites of passage.[2]

---

2 It was nothing like today. When my son Ryan was in third grade, he developed E.T. anxiety. He hadn't even seen the movie. It was the Universal Studios ride that spooked him. After that, we banned Reese's Pieces; any kind of E.T. talk in our house became taboo. I even alerted his teacher about the potential for E.T. triggering in the classroom. There was no worry about such things in the 1980s. It was a free-for-all, even in the Christian movie genre.

So, a few weeks into our induction to church, we sat and watched a low-budget depiction of the end times we were always being warned about. It featured a doomed secular family left behind after all their God-fearing family and friends were raptured to heaven.

This was my first introduction to *transference*—the clinical term meaning that we can overidentify with someone's feelings or situation because of their close proximity to our own. The little girl in the movie was right around nine—my own age, causing the kind of transference that made me shake in my chair and make a beeline for the bathroom.

She and her family tried to take on the smoking apocalypse landscape, but by the end of the movie, things looked grim. But alas, there was a way to be "saved" and ensure their ticket to heaven. All they had to do was publicly profess their love for Jesus. The trade-off? A trip to the guillotine.

The little girl clutched her red balloon in one hand and her mama's in the other. After the dreadful chopping sound that made the whole church pee their pants, the camera cuts to gray sky. Her red balloon floats away. That was enough to keep me sheepish for a while. I didn't sleep for weeks and raised my hand at every subsequent altar call (where you publicly profess your allegiance to God).

Even long after the movie was over, I was terrified. Fear was a mainstay. *When lightning strikes, you must've made God mad. If you sin, you're going to hell unless you pray a three-step prayer and make your penance. Don't drink, dance, or dress immodestly. If you touch yourself, your hand might fall off. There is no normal behavior; it's all a sin.* Secular music was viewed as of the devil. We even had sessions at church playing records backward so that we could hear Satanic subliminal messages. *No KISS for us.*

The fear was powerful enough to make me put a lid on my skepticism. I became a pro at covering up, making Bernie Madoff look like an amateur. Plus, church wasn't all bad: the promise of immortality was pretty enticing. The thought of being good and saved and experiencing the deep sense of belonging—the kind we're wired for—kept me hooked.

I was too scared to give all this up, so I went along even into my early adult years: teaching Sunday school, sending my kids to Christian school, and running Vacation Bible School every summer. Inside I was miserable, but too afraid of lightning, guillotines, and being alone to make my move, even though R.E.M.'s "Losing My Religion" was becoming my underground anthem.

As my pastor had warned, education gave me the thinking skills to critically examine my religious indoctrination. The stuff I'd grown up with seemed even more strange. Like how "love your neighbor" seemed to only mean the ones who think or look or love like you—not that *everyone is a neighbor and that the rainbow belongs to all of us.* Characters like Adam and Eve and Noah with his ark started to resemble Santa Claus and the Easter Bunny and her chocolate Reese's eggs. There were a lot of contradictions to overcome.

Get Off the Guillotine

When I first met Nadia, I was struck by her deep brown eyes and inquisitive spirit. We were sitting next to each other at an International Conference on Critical Thinking in Washington, DC. I was deep into my research at that point; the trip was part of my attempt to untangle things.

After being paired for various discussions, we realized how much we had in common, even though a casual onlooker might not have suspected such. Nadia was raised in a conservative Muslim family in Saudi Arabia. She was in the United States pursuing her PhD and had come to the conference with just as many conflicted thoughts as I had. She was also a first-generation college student; no one from her family had ventured outside her homeland. She was deep into her own process, a little frayed from her own excavation. She was getting a lot of heat from her family for all the changing she'd done. We were both textbook scapegoats, trying to pay the ransom we thought we owed.

Her eyes filled with tears as she quoted her older sister, who was not shy about making the family's disdain known: "She said to me, 'What's next? You're going to take off your hijab and start drinking beer, or start dancing? *Do you even believe the Qur'an anymore?*'" Nadia told me her family saw her venturing out from their framework as betrayal. Confrontation and tension were constant. She was trying not to let the fear grip her, but the grief was written on her face. Her pain was easy to recognize; it was the same pressure I felt. *Baptist guilt, like Jewish and Catholic guilt, are forces. Add Muslim guilt to the list.*

When your family or community of origin pulls out the betrayal card—"We've done all this for you, so where's your freakin' loyalty?"—it's almost a showstopper. Your anxiety tells you to retreat, to go along to get along. The last thing you want is to be disloyal to people you love—the ones who have raised you and sent you on your way. The guilt is almost unbearable when you're accused of "not being the same person" or thinking "you're better than us." Nadia and I hugged in solidarity, knowing we weren't without a herd after all.

When I got back home, I started to look over my data with a new lens. My students showed me that the church wasn't the only culprit. They had been asked to kneel down for all types of guillotines. At home, there was enormous pressure to follow family norms. At school, they faced the grades guillotine. At every turn, there were choices to make—go along to get along, or face rejection, isolation, and even persecution when you don't meet a defined standard. They seemed to know all about the agony of being scapegoated for going against the tide or breaking out of the mold. As Jamal put it:

> *Of all the emotions I remember the most growing up, the strongest is fear. It's what I ate for breakfast, lunch, and dinner. Anything that came out of my mouth was met with a look of disgust and concern, like there was no room to be my own person without getting hell for it. I felt like I was in constant hot water, just for being my own person, for having an opinion that wasn't the same. I felt like my teachers and my family took it personal, like it was some big rejection or rebellion. Like I was disgracing the family name. But really, I was just trying to figure myself out, to figure life out, and I didn't think their simple explanations were doing any justice. The biggie was coming out as gay. By the time I did, I wasn't going to take their negative reactions—I told them if they wouldn't accept me, then I wouldn't come around. I wasn't going to be a scapegoat for one more minute. Now people in my family come to me because they know I won't judge them, but it took a lot of fighting to*

get there. I think they passed so much fear onto me because they were scared, too.

Like Jamal, Allison took a lot of heat for her nonconformity:

I come from a family who emphasized making money—that was our religion. It's all they care about. All through school, I lived with constant anxiety—if I ever came home with anything besides an A, I was chastised, because it was going to mean I would end up a big failure or something. Everything in my family revolved around hard work and money; it was constantly talked about. No one was happy, but that didn't matter. It was our image that mattered . . . what people thought. It was nonstop brainwashing, just to impress people—but for what, or with what? Something not even honest? I saw through it, and finally went beyond the things that were forced down my throat since I can even remember. I work at a nonprofit, where the money isn't great, but the rewards of knowing I am doing something to change lives means a lot more to me than what car I drive.

Jamal and Allison chose to go beyond the indoctrination of their childhoods. They pivoted to a much broader definition of community, one that is universal. Like so many of my students, they recognized they didn't want to give up who they were to make everyone else happy. They couldn't hold on to everyone else's ideals and still be healthy. They realized that being led by someone else's superstitions and anxieties only created more for them. They wanted to have a mind of their own but also maintain connections to the world—and not just small pockets—in a dynamic way that allowed them to see common bonds even with people who at first seem different.

They pulled themselves off their guillotines—whether placed there by political, family, cultural, school, community, or social identity groups, or even professional disciplines. They broke out of fear-based messaging. It wasn't easy, but necessary to allow them to connect with the world in ways they never could have if they stayed in their insulated bubble.

Getting away from the guillotine is a risk that takes some careful maneuvering. The security blanket that comes from religion and other organizing frameworks brings comfort but can also insulate us in unhelpful ways. Breaking out can also cause backlash. Still, the cost of laying ourselves down, resigning ourselves to toxic Kool-Aid, isn't safe either.

When we unlearn groupthink and pivot toward universality, we begin our process of breaking out. Like my encounter with Nadia revealed, when we're sent away from our herds, we won't wander alone for long. We need to know that we belong to a universal herd, where we can also find protection and identity. We begin to form a universal bond that allows us to go beyond groupthink and fear. When we realize this, we open ourselves to interdependence that doesn't rely on insulation or paying ransoms that were never ours in the first place.

Session Eleven Worksheet:
Purging Kool-Aid

Objective:
Unlearn groupthink indoctrination that breeds insularity.
Pivot toward universality.

Rethink It:
Move from Groupthink to Universality

Insulation is sold as protection but often breeds groupthink that turns out to be harmful. When we recognize that questioning is a healthy part of life, we open ourselves up to seeing that the things we are projecting onto people who are different from us are misguided. When we let open-mindedness rule us, we are able to avoid paying the price for someone else's set of superstitions and instead integrate a wider perspective that sets the foundation for a global mind-set.

Insularity Check

- What types of groupthink have I been subject to?
- What are three groups that I currently belong to?
- What types of insulation do they provide?
- Do the groups welcome exchanges with people who think and live differently?
- In what ways are my associations protecting me? Hurting me?

Action Steps: Purge the Kool-Aid

Many of us have been taught lessons that slowly poison us into giving up our thinking. We don't always have to throw the baby out with the bathwater, but we do need to recognize whether our behaviors of going along to get along might be causing more trouble than good. It can help to have knowledge of your groupthink tendencies to make sure you are not sacrificing important parts of yourself for a cause that closes off potential for greater human solidarity and progress. Here are a few ways to peel off your insulation:

1. **Form dynamic circles.** Work to build diverse relationships with as many groups as possible. Be friends with everyone—no cliques or silos. Find spaces where you identify various parts of yourself, and engage in a process of co-nurturing with your fellow travelers. Go as global as you can in your reach with various people, places, and experiences. Don't limit yourself to proximity—widen your networks to avoid being stuck in stale groupthink.

2. **Don't be a sheep or scapegoat.** Read the poem "Please Understand Me" by Zoe Abel based on David Keirsey's book of the same name. Reflect on ways you might use this as a springboard for conversations with loved ones and groups you are part of, especially when there is pressure to conform.

3. **Listen.** Play Katy Perry's "Chained to the Rhythm." Do you think we are chained in the ways she describes? What can help set us free?

Getting Un-Thrust

Objective:
Unlearn binary indoctrination that breeds conformity.
Pivot toward Real.

*It's exhilarating to be alive in a time
of awakening consciousness; it can also be
confusing, disorienting, and painful.*

—Adrienne Rich

I t's 1971. Jim Morrison, lead singer for the Doors, climbs onstage and bellows out our collective plight, as riders on the storm.

Morrison nailed it. We are *riders on the storm*, trying to make sense of the simultaneous chaos and order of the universe. His "into this world we're thrown" lyric was based on the German concept *geworfen*, meaning "thrownness." European existentialist philosophers of the nineteenth and twentieth centuries were trying to expose certain trappings of convention and kinship, or "the matrixes of the past," the traditions of yesterday that influence our present and future.

As much as things change from century to century, these matrixes keep their hold across time and space. No one flags us down in utero and asks, "Hey, in there, just a head's up that we've been dealing with three generations of interpersonal violence over here, you still want the evite?" or "Oh, you've got a vagina—we're already painting your room pink, okay?" It's just the way it is, without our consent or collusion.

Before you're born, no one bothers to find out if you still want to drop in to the party even though "We plan to serve meat and potatoes night after night with no variation in sight?" or that "Your dad is a raging alcoholic but somehow your mom will find a way to blame you for everything that goes wrong for the next thirty-five years before your therapist advises you to put your foot down." There's no choice but, "C'mon down when you're ready for your induction into the Dysfunctional Family Hall of Fame; at least there's the obligatory holiday gatherings to look forward to."

You just show up to the party, let out a good scream, and get what you get. Your initiation is like a Mad Lib game meets the board game Life plus some cliché SAT-style circles that need to be filled in:

Welcome to the family. It's a _____ [gender]!

Here is your almost entirely _____ [Insert color here. If DOB is before 1927, insert pink for boys, blue for girls. If after, reverse.] blankie and wardrobe.

Next, please pick your game piece and partner. Be sure to take the ones we've assigned you. Do not deviate.

If you are a girl and you aren't *all sugar and spice*, we will start calling you

a. Bossypants   d. Hysterical
b. Bitch   e. Butchy
c. High maintenance

If you're a boy who's not all *snakes and snails*, you'll be pegged as a

a. Chicken   c. Pussy
b. Tool   c. Sissy
c. Crybaby

The ABCs of Identity

*Circle the choices that best describe you:**

Aggressive	Full of yourself	Neighbor
Airhead	Gifted	Ornery
Articulate	Girly	Outlier
Assertive	Hot	Pig
Bossy	Husky	Pretty
Brave	Impulsive	Queer
Charismatic	Independent	Quirky
Conservative	Intense	Rebel
Crazy	Intriguing	Republican
Creative	Jerk	Right
Creep	Jesus freak	Smart
Democrat	Kind	Stupid
Disabled	Know-it-all	Successful
Down-to-earth	Leader	Thug
Drama queen	Liberal	Trustworthy
Ethnic-looking	Loudmouth	Unlovable
Exotic	Manchild	Unreachable
Feisty	Maniac	Whiny
Foreigner	Moody	Whore
Friend	Nasty	Wise**

* Depending on the gender, race, and socioeconomic status we assign you, plus those you eventually agree to take on, some of these options will not be available to you. In some cases, they will automatically come with your package. Sorry, no substitutions allowed.

** Sorry, there just aren't enough endearing or disparaging terms available in the Vs and the X–Z range. You might have some luck on Urban Dictionary. And if this doesn't seem like a lot of options, don't worry. We will cover you up with an abundance of other choices to make—like twenty-six types of bagels and 101 shades of lip gloss to give you the sense you have some control.

Our social environment and prescribed norms are set in motion long before our arrival: the players at the table, pink or blue streamers, the game board, the menu—even before we could form a "Hell no!" on our little tongues and run like Forrest. Even Baby Mozart can't help us outsmart the matrix in our early years.

Like it or not, none of us have a choice about the circumstances that greet us at our grand entrance. At first we're too young to tell the difference. But not long into the event, the indigestion begins. Your aversion gets you looking around. You finally discover there are available substitutions, but not without cost, so you face the decision of whether to politely take your seat, choose from the limited menu, or even take extra helpings, or not. Either way there's a price. We will be called names either way.

The inherited frustrations, sufferings, and demands based on the way it's always been done by our family, culture, and society are tough to swallow, but we do it every day: it's the way we do gender, love, secrets, school, work, and play—all derived from past eras with different variables.

There are one-way signs all over the map we're handed. Everyone you know has been around the block a few times, so their path seems logical. The map serenades you like the "I'm the Map" song from *Dora the Explorer*.

Then the repetition starts getting on your nerves. The basic and prescriptive lyrics become annoying, but it's hard to get them out of your head. It's a little shocking that simple repetition works for so many people, but it does.

You need to tune into a different station. You're tired of crashing when you go down the one-way street the wrong way. You want to find your own path and not be dictated by what everyone else thinks is right. But the map has its appeal, too. There is some comfort in feeling like you know which direction you are going, yet it doesn't allow for anything but a linear existence and you know there's more to explore.

Are You for Real?

The irony is that people in adult life use the term "Real" to describe when you fit exactly within the prescriptive norms of the map. It seems the opposite of real, but most everybody else is doing it. You work tirelessly to "become," to morph into a more acceptable form. You are told to steer clear of the things that allegedly make you less of a man, woman, or person.

To become a lifetime member of the Real Men club, you've got to pay your dues. Don't cry. Real men have no fear and don't eat quiche. They don't let anyone correct them publicly or challenge their authority. They don't let women pay for dinner. Real men display their collection of sports and female trophies—the hotter their partner, the realer they become.

Real men like rough sports and rough sex—with women only. Real men are straight. There are no chick flicks or Zumba classes (unless it's to pursue a woman, then it's okay). Real men don't overdo the manscaping. They smell good, but not too good. Size matters. If you're tall, beefy, or well-endowed, you are the real deal. Real men can only show their feelings through anger, not sadness, even though there's plenty of reasons for the latter.

The key to being real is to never show how much you really care. Work yourself over the edge at work, but act cavalierly about it, like it was no big deal. Your girlfriend can break your heart, but suck it up and go out and hook up with someone else the next night. Not caring has become a cultural badge—for everyone. We're asked to work so hard to become real and not blink an eye when things don't work out. Our ways of defining real are unreal.

Stop trying to bend your mind around someone else's organizing framework.

Real women aren't too bossy, aggressive, or domineering. They are never nasty. They are submissive, gentle, and nurturing. They're not too skinny, not too chubby. Big breasts are always a plus. Real women are born with vaginas—if they are transgender and transitioned, they don't count as real. Real women smell like jasmine, taste like cherries, and don't pass gas, even though they are expected to eat a lot of salad. Real women dress to look attractive but avoid wearing something that might signal real men into thinking she's looking for it. They are expected to be freaks in bed, but not because they have gained experience by having a wide variety of sex partners. Real women are sex toys, but never promiscuous—sensual but not teases.

Real women are sous chefs in the kitchen, can fold a shirt like they work at the Gap, and are therapists to anyone who needs them. They send thank-you notes on time and make sure everyone is using their Sonicare toothbrushes. According to social media, they know how to take care of their man, and make their life easy. Real women know it's unbecoming to show anger, even though there's plenty to be angry about.

Supposedly, the highest honor bestowed on real women is getting called the "full package"—the ones who know their way around the bedroom, kitchen, boardroom, and even the gym. She's attractive and smart. Intelligent, but not pretentious,[1] a rare gem who can pull a lot off without being high maintenance. She's not needy, but not so strong she becomes a threat. Athletic, but not bulky. Successful, but down-to-earth. Knows it all without being a know-it-all. And she cares enough, but not so much that she becomes too intense—because everyone knows that's a real turnoff.

Even though it's meant to be a compliment, being a full package seems to be another way to reinforce the commodity mind-set of today—that you are nothing more than a possession or prize to be won over. That you are never enough unless you are everything. You are a full package and real deal only when you "have it all": the looks, brains, 2.5 kids, picket fence, Curves body, Fey humor, and the moves of Samantha from *Sex in the City*. Being the full package seems like an honor but is more like a prison.

Just when it seems there's enough fear and compliance to last a lifetime, "good" is paired with "real" for the shaming knockout punch. Good men and women die for their country. Good women keep themselves pure. Good moms breastfeed. Good dads spend time with their kids. Good little girls and boys don't cry; they listen quietly and sit still. Good workers arrive early and stay late.

Every faith has its own version of this. You've gotta follow the program if you want to be good and real. If you dance, eat meat, or let out an F-bomb from time to time, you must not be a real Christian/Muslim/Jew. You're not good or real if you don't wear your head scarf, follow the scriptures to the letter of the law, or make your appearance in church every week.

---

1 When I went on NPR, a listener commented that I am a rare, intelligent breed for a woman, one who's actually smart and unusually not full of herself. Thank you for illustrating this point for us.

Sadly, these things send us away from the direction of finding what is real.

The real carrot dangling over our heads, enticing us to keep on turning tricks, is more toxic than we realize. These social definitions allure us into thinking that if we fit this norm we will then be legitimate. It seems contradictory that we achieve our real crown by being fake, but somehow the threat of not being fully accepted can make us do crazy things.

Leading an unexamined life in which you take the map as marching orders from birth and never look back jeopardizes your essence and spiritual wholeness. When you never find out who you are and simply accept the real constructed version that everyone believes you to be, you might be trading immediate comfort for a slow soul bleed-out. It's like hiding all of the footnotes in the margins of our lives, the spaces that we won't let anyone see, the ones we barely acknowledge.[2] We only show our edited versions, relinquishing the lead roles in our own stories. Instead, we send forth our doppelganger, who resembles us to some degree, but is more of a character we've allowed everyone else to construct on our behalf.

> "Your problem is how you are going to spend this one odd and precious life you have been issued. Whether you're going to spend it trying to look good and creating the illusion that you have power over people and circumstances, or whether you are going to taste it, enjoy it, and find out the truth about who you are."
>
> —Anne Lamott

Today's generation is just as frustrated with the matrix as twentieth century philosophers. They make sport out of tackling binary constructions. They often become a cultural punching bag, but they are stronger than they're given credit for. They refuse to put up with things like prior generations. They've got access to new science and are connected as global citizens more than we ever were. They see beyond the matrix, know what's at stake, and want to get real right.

---

2 This is not where your truths belong. They belong up front, integrated within your whole messy and beautiful story.

Deconstruct the Binary

You gotta love the brazen millennials who've pulled their weight to get us unthrown from historic and social tides that project what our behavior should be. They're showing us we don't have to let "What will they think?" hold us by the jugular.

The new generation's blowing of the whistle on the binary has been a major step toward progress. *Binary* means "involving two"; most of us first learned about it in math class. Gender binary has received the most attention recently, mainly because of the transgender bathroom debate, but it's not the only place binaries show up.

In social and historical terms, the binary is used to group people into categories such as woman or man, pretty or ugly, black or white, straight or gay. It's a path that is taught and reinforced repeatedly, requiring careful consideration of why binaries exist and who these constructs actually serve.

Fitting in is overrated.

Binary categories do not serve us well. The expansiveness within our global community allows us to stop subscribing to limiting and narrow boxes that often serve to shame and keep people in their "place." Race, gender, sexual orientation, and other identities have been proven to be socially constructed, not scientifically grounded.

The type of scientific discovery and social progress we've seen means that identifying in nonconventional ways is no longer an automatic conversational rip cord. We don't have to check a certain box to feel good about identity. Despite popular sentiments, self-esteem doesn't rise and fall solely based on our level of confidence or on how good our latest Insta post came out. Sociologist Charles Horton Cooley explains that our identity is created through a process of interactions with people, and our self-reflection about who we think we are according to the exchanges. He calls this the *looking-glass self*, and says that our identity is produced through agreement, disagreement, and negotiation with other people. Our behavior and self-image are both impacted through these interactions and reflections.

If the interactions we have consist of rigid binary codes and shaming techniques, they are knockout punches both to esteem and getting closer to real. So often, we're made to feel we have to hide when we have nothing to hide. There's no room for this anymore.

Get Out of the Closet

There is never enough air to breathe when we are stuck in a closet, afraid to reveal our multidimensional sides.

You can be all and none of the above all at once. Don't feel obliged to check off little boxes for the sake of doing so, especially when they do not allow for realization of the beauty of the human spectrum.

Throughout my study, my students talked and wrote about their binary indoctrination. They'd also been shoved into prescribed either/or roles and categories that were not only bothersome but damaging. Their breakaways were often painful, but vital to their progress. Carlos put it like this:

> *My family should have named me "Tough Guy" because I've always been expected to be stoic, just like all the other men in my family. I've been constantly reminded that "I'm not like everyone else," as if I were committing a crime for not following the same ways of doing things. Whenever I've shown emotion, I've been criticized as "weak." My older brother used to always tell me to "stop being such a girl." It wasn't until I moved away and stopped talking to them for a while that I began to find myself. Now, they're a lot better, and I think they finally got the hint and started to see that I am strong, but don't have to be a tough guy to show that. That honesty and even vulnerability are ways of showing it too.*

Jackie had her own frustrations:

> *I was always called a tomboy growing up. I never went through the Barbie phase and loved hanging out with my brother and his friends. My mom constantly hovered over me, trying to teach me "manners" and how to be "like the other nice girls." My teachers called me "unique," which I think they meant in a good way, but it always made me feel weird and out of place. I got teased all the time. I finally let go of it in high school, and got lucky I was such a good athlete. It's funny how people act differently just because of sports. It was like I proved my worth or something. They finally started to overlook what they saw as my nonconformity,*

because I had become "good enough" in another way. It's all kind of bullshit, because all along I was only trying to be myself—which was exactly what I had always been taught. Growing up, I'd always heard a lot of that from my parents, and teachers: "Be yourself," "Don't copy," but it doesn't seem like they really meant it when I wasn't being what they really wanted me to be.

Beth faced similar issues growing up, but was especially tired of still having to explain herself as an adult:

I've been working in a laboratory as a scientist for years, and I can't tell you how many times people ask me if I am a nurse when I say I work at a hospital. If I had a dollar for every time someone asked me, I'd be rich. People's eyes glaze over quickly when we start talking professional talk, outside of basic things women are "supposed to" talk about. It's like they just can't picture I am capable of anything beyond creating a Pinterest world for everyone around me. It's either that, or they give me the good ol' good-for-you pat, that I am actually a woman who has accomplished something. You can't win.

Camille faced it her whole life, growing up in a primarily white town with little diversity:

You wouldn't believe how many times I've been called "ethnic," or asked if I'm black or white. I'm biracial—my mom is black, and dad is white—so that makes me both. I sometimes felt I didn't fit in to any of my friend groups, and there was always pressure to act more of either category depending on who I was with at the time. Everyone is so obsessed with race—and it is important to me, but it's still only one part of me.

Carlos, Jackie, Beth, and Camille had different circumstances but were struggling with the binary map matrix that didn't recognize their multi-dimensionality. They were tired of the same old questions and reactions simply because of the expectations and roles into which history, society, and family had shoved them. I thought this would make for a good topic in class, so I asked my students what had been thrown upon them because of constructed identity norms.

Me: What's been thrown upon you?

Jenna: I once had a kid throw up on me at the bank.

Pam: My baby throws up on me almost every day.

Me: No, I mean thrown-upon social identities and expectations based on your gender, skin color, social class, birth order, family dynamics, or otherwise. . . .

Ralph: That I have to be the strong one.

Joe: That if I'm an athlete, I'm not likely to be very smart.

Me: What else?

Keisha: That someone is going to expect you to act a certain way, just because of how you look.

Ji-Ho: The idea that I was going to follow in the footsteps of my father, even though he was completely miserable.

Our classroom discussions reminded me of the many patients I've worked with in my therapy room, also trying to untangle themselves from the trappings of the binary. Too much time was spent trying to survive within the closets where they'd been forced. In every instance, it was becoming clear that the less we shove people into these dark spaces, the better for all.

> Stop letting people shove you into the binary. There's not enough room for your soul to fit into the narrow box being forced upon you.

When we waste our whole life working to become what we think we're supposed to be, instead of owning our many sides, it comes at a great cost. We cannot overcome binary indoctrination by constantly trying to become something we're not. Maybe unbecoming is what we need to break out of conformity. Imagine the time and trouble we could save if we were encouraged from day one to discover this.

GET OFF the paved path.
It's way too BASIC for you.
There's AIR to BREATHE.
Oceans to FLOAT in.
Dances to be DANCED.
Songs to SING.
Splendor to BEHOLD.
Stop WAITING for PERMISSION.

Session Twelve Worksheet:
Getting Un-Thrust

Objective:
Unlearn binary indoctrination that breeds conformity.
Pivot toward Real.

Rethink It:
Move from Binary to Real

We're all riders on the storm, thrust into this world with a matrix in our hands. Our identities are complex, but we're heaped into either/or binary categories. We're forced to cram our real selves into the footnotes of our lives, instead of allowing our many dimensions to be integrated fully within our stories. There's little air to breathe in closets, and our best move is to rethink real and break free from forced "becomings" that aren't honest.

Conformity Check

- What has been expected of me just because of social norms?
- What tends to surprise people once they get to know me?
- What aspects of my identity do I want to be recognized?
- What parts of outward appearance frustrate me or create false impressions?
- How much do I conform to social norms and roles?
- What types of positives and negatives result?

Rethink It:
Move from Conformity to Real

Do we really want to live our lives hiding our footnotes in the margins of our lives, instead of allowing us our rightful place to be the main characters in our own stories? Will we spend our time editing ourselves to make for a more polished version of the story, or will we allow ourselves the lead roles in our lives, our full selves, within our rightful places front and center?

Action Steps: Pinpoint Opportunities for
Getting Unthrust and Breaking Out

1. **Begin a new role.** Pretend you just swallowed an honest pill—one that makes you very direct. What would you say to your partner? Your boss? Yourself? Friends? Family? What are your hidden truths? What causes you to keep them in the footnotes of your story, instead of fully stepping into the main character role in your life?

2. **Check out your birthday.** What did your birthday map consist of? What expectations, because of sex, family status, or other circumstances, were thrust upon you? What choices were you given? Since then, what have you held on to, and what have you changed?

3. **Listen.** Play Lady Gaga's "Born This Way." What does it bring to mind? Do you feel the sense of empowerment she emanates? What steps have you taken to embrace your varied sides? What needs to happen next?

4. **Find fellow nonconformists.** Breaking out is hard to do. With whom can you link arms in your journey of unbecoming and finding the real? What people have shown unconditional love and support of your variances, rather than criticizing them? Do you need the anchor of additional people to help you become more unthrust? Text or call someone today to set up a time to unpack some of what you have learned from this session.

Discovering
the Human Museum

Objective:
Unlearn bias that breeds disconnection.
Pivot toward human solidarity.

*Familiarity is the gateway
drug to empathy.*

—iO Tillet Wright

On April 5, 1968, when Steven Armstrong asked his third-grade teacher Jane Elliot why they "shot that King yesterday," she knew it was time to teach he and his classmates a lesson of a lifetime.

The day after Dr. Martin Luther King Jr. was assassinated, Elliot decided to break out the exercise she'd been holding in the wings. She and her students were situated in Riceville, Iowa—a homogeneous town with a population of under 1,000. Elliot felt that the experience of discrimination wouldn't become real without drastic measures.

On day one of what came to be known as the "Blue-Eye Brown-Eye Exercise," she announced that eye color determines intelligence and superiority. She placed collars on all the brown-eyed students, sending them to the back of the classroom. She took away their privileges at recess—since they didn't "deserve" to play with their blue-eyed peers, who were "better, cleaner, and smarter" than them.

Elliot watched her typically thoughtful students turn nasty within minutes. Blue-eyed students became bossy and arrogant. They quickly grabbed hold of their newfound status. The blue-eyed students were clinging to being the "in" social identity group. Years later, one of her students said the exercise made him feel happy, "like I was a king, that I ruled them." The happiness didn't last long.

Social Identity Theory

Academic Definition

Social identity theory, first proposed by British social psychologists Henri Tajifel and John Turner, explains that self-concept relates to the groups we are part of. Our behaviors are directly dictated by expected social behavior within the categories we identify with and associate with. It creates a sense of pride, belonging, and meaning. It can also lead to stereotyping, discrimination, competition, and hostility.

Street Definition

We have hospitality for those we perceive are like us and hostility for those who are not. Some examples of in-groups and out-groups include straight versus LGBTQ, Catholics versus Protestants, Boston Red Sox versus New York Yankees fans, and males versus females. #mypeeps #squad

---

On day two, Elliot reversed the exercise. The brown-eyed students were now on top. The taunting continued, but less intensely. The fresh memories from the previous day seemed to keep the new dominant group from dishing it out as hard as they had taken it. Still, on both days, there was bullying, lower academic performance, and lots of tears. Each time, the superior group of the day got through phonics reading cards faster and performed better in the classroom.

The hate perpetrated by classmates didn't take long to manifest as negative self-dialogue for the out-group. Elliot's students were dealing with what social psychologist Claude Steele, author of *Whistling Vivaldi: How Stereotypes Affect Us and What We Can Do*, calls *stereotype threat*. Besides having to deal with the meanness of their teacher and classmates, they were internalizing damaging stereotypes. They were starting to believe that the horrible things being projected upon them were actually true.

Like Elliot's students, we all have some sort of collar we're assigned that pegs us as being a certain way, based on social identity categories like race, sex, and age. Steele explains that our various identities all come with a set of expectations that we absorb into our consciousness. His research reveals that when we are expected to underperform, we are at risk of doing just that. Steele says that even the threat of stigma can make us more vulnerable to negative outcomes.

Steele cites examples of women underperforming on math tests and black students floundering on tests measuring intellectual abilities. When reminded we're not supposed to perform well, we often don't. Steele worries that these threats permeate US culture, particularly within schools— places where stigma should not have a home.

After two very long and difficult days of Elliot's exercise, her students showed tremendous relief when they were finally allowed to throw their collars into the trash. One student went to great lengths to rip up his collar, piece by piece. When he couldn't shred it by hand, he even started biting chunks out of it. His classmates cheered. Regardless of which side they were on, they didn't want any more part in the exercise either.

Elliot's creation of a microcosm of society right within her own third-grade classroom helps expose how foolish and destructive it is to lump anyone into categories based on arbitrary measures—and how unjust it is to grant or deny privileges based on color, or for any reason. It also shows how quickly we internalize discrimination. Sorting and diminishing collars have been part of our social fabric for so long, they often go unquestioned. We become blind to the fact that they're there. Before we can remove and rip them up, we need to be able to see how and why so many collars have been distributed and unfairly fastened.

Identify Your Blind Spots

In the diversity course that I teach,[1] I bring my students through a set of similarly disruptive and valuable exercises, minus the collars. Everyone starts out fairly sure that they are bias-free. These students are from all over the world, of all ages and walks of life, with friends from all over, who are not just "tolerant" of, but fully embrace, diversity.[2] They think there's *no way* they could be biased. They balk at my hints they might be wrong. They stick to their position—disavowing prejudice and denying culpability with full fervor. *Been there, done that.*

We start by looking closely at the work of Harvard's Mahzarin Banaji and the University of Washington's Anthony Greenwald. They've spent years measuring "implicit cognition"—features of our brains that fall under our conscious radar. This aspect of thinking causes past experience to influence present judgment without us even blinking.

Cognitively, we are wired to put people in categories. Our brains have a natural inclination to group things together. This is the foundation of our out-group social comparison matrix. Once we've completed our sorting, we are likely to (1) overinflate the similarities we share with people in our in-group, and (2) exaggerate the differences between us and the out-group. We then other people. In-groups can form with people from the same family, town, or country, just as much as according to skin color, religious affiliation, and sexual orientation.

In their book *Blindspot: Hidden Biases of Good People*, Banaji and Greenwald show that you aren't necessarily a bad person because of these inclinations. Our brains are mega–sorting machines, churning out automatic, unconscious, and unruly signals. Even with the best of intentions, our minds are susceptible to implicit bias because of "mind bugs"—ingrained habits that lead to errors in how we perceive, remember, reason, and make decisions. This results in blind spots in our thinking and behavior—leaving us prone to stereotypes and prejudice.

---

1 This course is different from the Personal Branding one where I conducted the main grounded theory research study used for this book.

2 "Tolerate" isn't one of my favorite words. I can see it being used for things like headaches, boring lectures, or gas station sushi, but not for how we engage with each other. Differences should be *embraced*, not just "tolerated." Is that too much to ask?

It's not that we have to accept this as fate or use it as an excuse. Together with their colleagues, Greenwald and Banaji built an entire online study known as Project Implicit to help us get to a better place with our behavior. Over 14 million people have taken their Harvard Implicit Attitude Tests to learn about their automatic preferences for everything from sexuality to gender and career, to weight, age, race, skin tone, religion, and more.

For my students, visiting the site is a little like going on Web MD with a medical ailment. You arrive with some concerns but end up leaving pretty unsettled—especially if you weren't expecting to uncover any bias. When you're hit with scientific proof that you do something you don't think you do, or don't want to do, it's a lot worse than learning that the rash on your arm might not go away for a while.

What you don't know can hurt you, and everybody else. Ignoring symptoms doesn't eliminate the problem.

You'd think that once we discover our errors, we'd want to immediately correct them, so things don't escalate. But mind bugs are tricky. Even when we're the ones on the receiving end of bias, we aren't that different than Elliot's students who quickly fell into line. We don't want the worst thing that people could say about us to be true, so we submit to the collar to try and avoid catching even more heat. We give up our own interests to keep peace. It's not that we're all martyrs. Sometimes aligning with the dominant group provides a form of protection from more abuse and scrutiny. And as history has shown, many people have sacrificed their lives, livelihoods, and other sacred things when they've stood up for themselves against power.

One of the more complex and shocking elements of the Project Implicit research findings is that members of certain groups hold many of the same prejudices as outsiders do about their own group. Like Steele's work reveals, we fall for what's being said about us. Maybe that's part of why they say "women eat their own," being harder on each other than males are on women. Project Implicit research shows that most Americans show implicit preferences for whites versus African Americans, which leads to discriminatory treatment and economic, social, and health disparities. Similar associations due to gender bias and ageism have been found.

The data from Project Implicit reveal that we play favorites with our own in-groups. There's not always actual animosity toward other groups, but a natural tendency to favor those with whom we associate. We establish camaraderie over things like being alumni from the same school, fans of the same sports team, residents in the same town, or diehard fans of a band. These connections are often innocent, but when favoritism spills over into racial, class, gender, sexual orientation, age, ability, and religious realms, the consequences are far greater.

With all the unintended results that hidden bias produces, we have our work cut out for us. When we realize how mind bugs can keep us from breaking out of bias, we improve the chances of mitigating their impact on our decision making. Once we've become familiar with our own particular blind spots, we can make our way toward becoming more familiar with the people against whom we discriminate and for whom we hold misconceptions, stereotypes, and prejudices.

Find New Gateways

After the tests, my students were uncomfortable enough to want to start tackling their biases further. We watched iO Tillet Wright deliver his "Fifty Shades of Gay" Ted Talk, highlighting the nuances of the gender and sexual identity spectrum. Wright is an artist, activist, speaker, TV host, and writer who launched his Self-Evident Truths project, with the aim of photographing 10,000 persons who identify as "not one hundred percent straight." His goal: "to show the humanity that exists in every one of us through the simplicity of a face."

With the help of the Human Rights Campaign, Wright is on the cusp of finishing the project for display on the national mall in Washington, DC. He knows that ensuring visibility for anyone identifying on the LGBTQ spectrum is essential for us to make progress. He aims to highlight, not erase, the complexity of identity, saying that until some form of difference pops up in your own backyard, empathy is harder to achieve. He says that "familiarity becomes the gateway drug to empathy."

After watching Wright's online talk, I broke the class into pairs to visit a variation of Martin Rochilin's original heterosexual questionnaire, with questions like,

- What do you think caused your heterosexuality?
- When and how did you first decide you were heterosexual?
- Why do you flaunt your heterosexuality? Can't you just be you and keep it quiet?
- Why are heterosexual people so promiscuous?
- The great majority of child molesters are heterosexual. Do you consider it safe to expose your children to heterosexual teachers?

After the exercise, many of my students who identified as straight were speechless. They had never thought about sexuality like that before. My "out" students—those who openly identified as part of the LGBTQ spectrum —shared their own painful stories of being questioned in ways that belittled them and made them feel like second-class citizens. Between Wright's portraits and the conversations, they were finding new pathways toward empathy. Things were looking up, but we still had a way to go.

Over the weeks we continued to engage with thought-provoking materials. To understand racism, we watched PBS's *Race—The Power of an Illusion*, a scientific rebuttal to our erroneous beliefs about the human species. To unpack sexism, we watched Jennifer Siebel Newsom's award-winning documentary *Miss Representation*, a visceral film that shows how mainstream media and culture undermine women through disparaging portrayals. To deconstruct ableism, we read Jonathan Mooney's *The Short Bus: A Journey Beyond Normal*.

Drawing from the *Class Matters* website, we talked about how classism is often among the most acceptable social prejudices. Many of us agreed that socioeconomic status was the make-or-break factor that either helped mitigate other forms of prejudice or accelerated it. Even if you're in a marginalized group, higher class level and its appearance influence how people perceive and treat us. We also looked at global conditions and studied the If the World Were a Village of 100 research project, one that reveals major disparities across the human spectrum. We searched for familiarity around the world, gaining a lot of perspective along the way.

We spent a lot of time thinking and rethinking. Few stones were left unturned. We tackled endless topics—from fat shaming to slut shaming to mental health stigma. Everyone had their own story of being othered and put down for no good reason. Gateways to empathy were turning up at unique intersections. Most everyone identified with at least one experience of having collars placed on them or those they love. Many could speak of more than one collar.

We kept connecting dots, seeing how *intersectionality* influenced so many facets of finding solidarity. The concept originated with American civil rights activist Kimberlé Williams Crenshaw, who was trying to help explain that social inequities are multilayered. Racism, sexism, classism, ableism, homophobia, transphobia, xenophobia, and other forms of discrimination do not act independently of one another, thus creating complexity and risk for those with intersectional identities. When we have been forced to wear our own collars, we can better recognize and empathize with someone else's plight.

Intersectionality

Academic Definition

The idea that multiple identities intersect or overlap to create a whole that differs from each individual part. These identities include gender, race, social class, ethnicity, nationality, sexual orientation, age, religion, mental ability, physical ability, and beyond.

Street Definition

You may find yourself on the outs in more than one way. You might also be able to identify with the experience of someone who seems very different but has actually experienced similar things as you as because of in- and out-group status. #commonground #sameanddifferent

The further we got into the conversation, the more exhausted and exhilarated we felt. It was heavy. There were plenty of tense, defensive, and awkward moments—but we were managing to stay engaged in a productive conversation. Instead of finger pointing, we were starting to see that it was human tendency to categorize and our difficult social conditioning that were the forces to fight against, not each other. We were not willing to resign ourselves to it. We wanted to be true global thinkers—to break away from the trappings of the mind and society. We were committed to going beyond automatic instincts that were disruptive of the good life we all want.

We wanted to overcome blind spots and free ourselves of stereotypes and all their ugly consequences. Like Wright, we didn't want to erase difference but rather learn to appreciate and embrace the beauty of our complexity. We knew we couldn't just find gateways to empathy, but that we'd have to cross new boundaries and visit new places, too.

Visit the Human Museum

Someone kidnaps you, deprograms your brain of its mind bugs, and brings you to a human museum, with other specimens from around the world. You arrive without blind spots, as if you've never been exposed to the hate and exaggerated difference matrix. You are ready to absorb the full beauty that awaits. Your brain only knows how to register awe, not scrutiny. It's a no-collar zone. You arrive wearing an Everyone Is Fam T-shirt.

There are no dominator curators in sight, deeming which art is worthy or not. Everyone has their place in this museum. The tapestry is breath-taking. No one's covering up under their social-identity Snuggies; instead, they're showing off their distinct features. All the shades are in their full glory; it's safe to be you.

This visit will change you. You have the once-in-a-lifetime opportunity to see something for the very first time: *everyone just as they are*. They are no longer others or "those people," good or bad, right or wrong, in or out, desirable or not. It's magical.

You connect soul to soul with each person you meet, seeing one magnificent work after another. When you see young or old, pretty or ugly, fat or thin, rich or poor, black or white, straight or not, you don't rate or judge. You get curious. Whether close up or from afar, you can really see the gorgeous, rich human spectrum in an unadulterated version. Every wrinkle, bruise, and bump is a gorgeous grit showcase. The traditions,

Look for the beauty in yourself and one another. Even what seem to be smudges are beautiful markings of time and space—not the flaws we've been conditioned to think.

languages, shapes, shades, and fibers of universal essence enthrall you. You behold the human miracle, and it fills your heart with joy.

You wish you had been brought to the museum sooner, especially when you were young, to develop a deep appreciation and knowledge of human art. You fill with awe as your eyes awaken to notice that each of us are inkblots waiting to be deciphered, appreciated, and admired. You start to realize how unwise it would be to allow subjectivity to rule as the guidepost for your own analysis.

Without bias, you're so curious that you revel instead of rumble. You want to keep studying humans out of sheer fascination. Judgment makes way for pure presence, like you're watching your own species on the Discovery Channel, fascinated by mammalian traits. Like an awestruck child, you marvel at the magic, even relishing nuances. Instead of being judgmental, you are nothing but captivated. It's pure harmony, like you're in the middle of an Indigo Girls concert meets Coca-Cola commercial.

What do you see when you see me? My color? My imperfections? My boldness? My impermanence? That I'm too much or not enough of something? My bogus attempts to disguise my fragility and insecurities? Or do you see more? Do you see my strength, my earnestness? My desires? Do you want to know more, or have you already decided that you are emphatically delighted or disgusted? Will you come back and look again and see something different?

Appreciation for one another is the very last thing that dominators want. They want us to judge and not look twice. They do everything they can to keep us from ever setting foot in the human museum. They want to keep us in our place, in a human prison where we are blind to our shared humanity, and instead fight over skin color, political views, religious affiliations, whom we love, or where we live—the kind of hell where there's no time for holding each other up. "You don't deserve that position. Or to love who you love . . . or your own bathroom. Who cares if you have equal pay or equal rights?"

They vandalize our souls, smearing venom all over our human art collection. The more we fight, the less we will challenge who's curating us. This keeps us right where they want us: in primal fear-based instinct mode, so that we go back to our own corners and stop exploring the other wings of the museum. Gotta protect our own works. They don't want us to see our bonds across the collection: that *we are all freakin' masterpieces.*

Made of similar material, we all have shadows and bright spots, fragility and strength. We suffer and rejoice. We yearn for connection and autonomy. We want answers but have a lot more questions. We are paradoxical creatures who differ vastly but also share the desire to live, love, laugh, be free, be safe, and mostly to be seen as the beautiful creatures we are. There's much more cause for solidarity—a sense of unity around a common cause. Imagine what would unfold if we made our mission to get to the good life together?

To keep us from seeing each other's essence, dominators play favorites. They need to keep some of us on their side. Like dysfunctional favoritism within families, societal favoritism is destructive. The favored can be used easily as pawns to fight back against those who haven't been granted special favors; it's a natural tendency to want to keep it that way.

> "Dominator culture has tried to keep us all afraid, to make us choose safely instead of risk, sameness instead of diversity. Moving through that fear, finding out what connects us, reveling in our differences, this is the process that brings us closer, that gives us a world of shared values, of meaningful community."
>
> —*bell hooks*

Return the Favors

Across all societies, men have been granted more favors than women. Same for straight versus LGBTQ persons, mentally healthy versus mentally ill people, and able-bodied versus disabled people. In the United States, whites have been given more favors than people of color. Religion, age, and physical appearance also lead to favors, depending on who the dominator deems in or out. *You're either the featured display or thrown in the basement.*

If you fall into any of the favored categories, it doesn't mean you are a jerk or that you've had everything served to you on a silver platter. Being favored can backfire. Because of the dysfunctional conditions these favors have created, there may be times when all kinds of hate and shade are thrown your way just because you're in one of the favored in-groups, even if you've been awesome to the out-groups and it wasn't your choice to be favored to begin with.

If you're among the favored, it doesn't mean you have failed morally or that you've conspired to get the perks you've been granted. Most favors are distributed right at birth; you didn't have a hand in that. Since they've always been available, you may have never even noticed anything unique about your circumstances compared to people who haven't. No one had ever told you there was a basement at the museum, with people who had been weighed down with collars and thrown away out of sight. No one ever steered you to visit down there to see the realities for yourself.

Just because you have the prize spot in the display case doesn't mean life is perfect for you. You've worked hard and have your own hardships, too. It's frustrating to hear all the gripes laid on you even though you didn't choose the layout of the museum. You resent being broad-brushed as some kind of -ist pig just because you're a guy, or white, or are in another favored group. You hate when unfair assumptions are made about you just because of this. This frustration can become the genesis of dismantling the out-group setup. You get how crappy it feels to be broad-brushed, and you know that it needs to change both ways, that there's room to share space in your prime display case to avoid anyone having to be relegated to substandard basement conditions.

Having privilege doesn't automatically qualify you as being "bad." Our instincts are to defend territory, to deny blame, and—whether we know or like it or not—continue to reinforce destructive human cycles that do none of us any favors. Every person has an opportunity to use that privilege constructively, to speak out and stand up.

Race is an area where obvious favors have been given and withheld. Professor Peggy McIntosh describes her process of shifting away from thinking about racism as acts of individual meanness to seeing them as invisible systems that confer dominance on a group.[3] In an article titled "White Privilege: Unpacking the Invisible Knapsack," she names several aspects of skin-color privilege that she experiences as a white woman. For example, she's able to buy items like dolls and "flesh"-colored Band-Aids that match her skin, and can be in public without fear of being harassed, outnumbered, unheard, distanced, or feared. None of us can be truly free to get to or to enjoy the good life unless we return favors to those who have been denied them.

Dream Bigger

Acknowledging and returning favors is hard business. It can directly threaten pride and identity, and force us to let go of deserving theories. But even if you've worked your tail off, you didn't invent the system in the first place, or if you worry that by sharing your favors, you'll be at a disadvantage, this dysfunctional system will never help us reach the good life together. You don't have to fork over all your goods; it's not always possible. But it is possible to refuse to hoard them like a dominator.

In our dog-eat-dog world, the stakes are high. If you're on the winning side, you own all the properties, and if not, you go directly to jail or the streets. No passing Go, no $200. The Economic Policy Institute reports that the average CEO makes more in one morning than the average minimum wage worker earns in an entire year.

This is a hot-button issue. Many would argue that the CEO has worked hard and "deserves" a personal masseuse and Jimmy Choos. It's a stance common in individualistic cultures, where individual behavior, not social context and structures, are the subject of sharp focus.

We love rags-to-riches stories. They keep us believing in the dream. The you-can-do-anything, try-a-little-harder approach is enticing. Just keep those bootstraps on at all times.

But bootstraps aren't enough. The chances for upward mobility have declined. They've been on the downturn since the late 1970s, but we're highly sentimental creatures. The Dream is a lot more appealing than the wake-up call when we realize sorting begins before we're born. With the

---

3 This is like recognizing that while you didn't pick your place in the museum, you still know it's an unfair setup.

erosion of the middle class and gaping disparities between the haves and have-nots, life paths for many or most of us are cast before we're even able to crawl.

With an 821:1 compensation rate between top dogs versus the bottom 99 percent in the United States, you'd think everyone would be calling bullshit. Who can justify such a split? Still, people take staunch positions on their theories of who is "deserving."

Yes, many wealthy individuals have worked hard, but it's not enough to explain why we accept a society where the most affluent members live the life of Riley, and those with the least resources eat and live under worse conditions than animals in the wild. The Robert Wood Johnson Foundation reports that our zip codes are the number-one factor in determining health outcomes. Those living in poor neighborhoods are much more likely to suffer poor health. How can we accept this?

> "It's called the American Dream because you'd have to be asleep to believe it."
>
> —George Carlin

Theories of deserving don't add up. Over half of wealth is inherited. Who's your daddy? matters. The Century Foundation reported that your father's income and occupation are the greatest predictor of upward mobility. There are always outlier exceptions, but what you start off with has a lot of say.

Then there are the working poor—the over twelve million people in the United States who work at least twenty-seven weeks a year and still fall below the federal poverty level. If you are in this situation and have a family of four, it means you make $24600 or less annually. As commentator Will Rogers expressed, "If there was a correlation between wealth and hard work, we'd see a lot of rich lumberjacks." Same for the working poor.

This isn't a unique problem of today. Caste systems have existed across every society. Bees and ants have them, too. They are a form of categorizing known as "stratification" that organizes people according to socioeconomic status, occupation, income, wealth, and political and social power.

The scramble for status isn't just reserved for social class wars. No matter what the in- or out-group factor involved, we always want to protect ourselves against the perceived and real threats of outsiders. If someone is different, we start throwing all kinds of shade because they're not one of us. Rivals and enemies emerge. Competition and hostility result.

Our tendency to exaggerate common ground within our group leads us to completely overlook similarities across groups. You might think you have more in common with someone you've pegged as same, when there might in fact be more in common with someone you'd pegged as different. Because we're pitted against other groups, we stop looking for the ways we could relate. We keep our swords drawn, instead of confronting the real giants we all face: unchallenged leaders, uncritical thinking, and unjust systems.

> "You do not win by struggling to the top of a caste system. You win by refusing to be trapped within one at all."
>
> —Naomi Wolf

In the same way that intersectionality helps us understand overlapping identities, it can help us see that while we may not relate to being on the outs in one way, we are likely to find ourselves so in other areas. At a minimum, we can likely establish solidarity around being locked in a system that leaves us scrambling for crumbs, and that sets us up to fight, rather than to look for each other's magic.

The University of Wisconsin–Superior has an excellent framework for developing better awareness and skills. They encourage an informed perspective that understands the construction of human categories, along with awareness of key issues and their historical foundations. They emphasize that being a globally aware citizen means we prioritize empathy, engage in effective intergroup communication, and build community across social, cultural, political, environmental, geographic, and economic boundaries.

This new path to conscious global citizenry begins when we buy memberships to the human museum, instead of buying into the caste system. It involves making trips there daily. It means being on the lookout for ways to deconstruct barriers and find intersections in our identities. This approach is part of furthering human solidarity instead of bias—one that dreams bigger and better, rather than succumbing to the chokeholds of collars and systems where most people never have a shot of being displayed the way they deserve to be.

Session Thirteen Worksheet:
Discovering the Human Museum

Objective:
Unlearn bias indoctrination that breeds disconnection.
Pivot toward human solidarity.

Rethink It:
Move from *Bias to Curiosity*

With our tendencies to categorize social identity groups, we fall into the trappings of bias that cause us to judge and degrade instead of lifting each other up. Overcoming mind bugs and blind spots takes work. It starts with identifying our personal tendencies that have been developed in our minds based on our own past experiences.

Connection Check

- What collars have I been assigned?
- When people see me, in what categories do they automatically place me?
- Do I associate with people outside of my in-group(s)?
- What is my usual reaction to difference?
- What's my place in the human museum?
- What are some favors I've been granted that I can return to support the good life for all?
- What's my vision for society? Is it grounded in solidarity or disconnection?

Action Steps:
Move from Disconnection to Solidarity

When we acknowledge our bias, it helps us break out from it and search for familiarity and empathy. Looking for new gateways to appreciating difference, rather than seeing it as a liability or weapon, helps us dream bigger and work on the common cause of getting to the good life without leaving anyone in the basement. Try the following:

1. **Visit Harvard.** Pick a Harvard Implicit Test to test your perceptions of various types of differences. What did you find? How will it impact your behavior moving forward? The tests are located at https://implicit.harvard.edu/implicit/selectatest.html.

2. **Break out the popcorn.** Schedule a movie night and watch the films my students watched to test your assumptions and help you dream bigger. Check out *Miss Representation, Eye of the Storm, A Class Divided,* and

Race—The Power of Illusion. I also recommend Michael Moore's *Sicko*, *Capitalism: A Love Story*, and the rest of his films. You can also look up other documentaries based on the areas you want to unlearn more about. Take note of your reactions. What did you unlearn? What will you do as a result?

3. **Launch your own human behavior experiment.** Dress up or dress down. Do people treat you differently as a result? Spend time outside your typical in-group. What is it like for you? Talk to your friends about their outward appearance and how it affects them.

4. **Interview someone different from you.** Interview someone who identifies with different social identity groups than you. For example, if you are a man, you could choose to speak with a woman. If you are able bodied, speak with someone who is not. If you are Muslim, you could set up a visit with a Christian. Sketch out a few questions in advance to learn more about their experiences based on their group identifications. Reflect on what you learn and identify any intersections in your experience.

5. **Dream bigger.** Embrace your global citizenship. Buy your season pass to the human museum. Visiting often will set your curiosity lens in full force. Be on the lookout for finding ways to snip collars, free people from the human jail, pull people up out of the basement, and create pathways toward solidarity.

SESSION FOURTEEN

Coming Out of Corners

Objective:
Unlearn polarized indoctrination that breeds discord.
Pivot toward common ground thinking.

*Cooperation will become the marching orders of the
human species or we're not going to make it.*

—Tom Shadyac

I t's summer 2016 in Washington, DC. When Arizona congresswoman Kyrsten Sinema takes the stage at the National Association for Social Workers Biennial Conference, the whole room is rocking.

She's like a celebrity to us—not because of her signature swag (although she has been voted best-dressed politician four years straight). Her chic glasses and shoes aren't what's bringing us to our feet. There's so much more.

I'm there with my friend Kathy, going ballistic along with the rest of the audience. We all work on the front lines of social change and services, and we need something to celebrate. Every day, the air we breathe is heavy. We come face-to-face with people who suffer the devastating consequences of our broken sociopolitical system: hunger, homelessness, poverty, abuse, addiction, incarceration, depression, anxiety, and despair. We work in every kind of setting imaginable—from schools to hospitals to clinics and beyond. Whether serving veterans, elders, children, or families, we're deeply committed to reaching and serving vulnerable populations.

When forty-year-old Sinema arrives on the scene, the air turns light and celebratory. She seems as energetic as she was at twenty-eight, when she became Arizona's youngest lawmaker. Everyone is buzzing about her boundless drive and stellar leadership. We hoot and holler in tandem when we learn that Sinema had just been named among the top three most bipartisan congressional leaders.

Sinema spoke about how being a social worker has shaped her path.[1] Our heads are all nodding in sync. She has taken our professional code of ethics to Capitol Hill, and we are elated. The code embodies core values of service, social justice, human dignity and worth, importance of human relationships, integrity, and competence. It's one we'd love to see become maxim everywhere.

It's not only Sinema's noble feats on Capitol Hill that enthrall us. It's her riveting story that explains why she walks her talk so wholeheartedly. At eight, her parents divorced and her father lost his job; she and her siblings became homeless. They took up residence in an abandoned gas station, using a chalkboard as a makeshift wall. There was no running water. No electricity. They wore hand-me-downs and ate powdered eggs. Times were tough.

She worked hard and earned a full scholarship to college, graduating early with honors. Sinema then went on to earn her master's in social work, a law degree, and a PhD. Her own hardships, education, and work within low-income schools drove her to the political arena to bring about sorely needed change.

---

1 Some people hear "social worker" and automatically think you're a child protective services worker who take kids away. They don't always know that the 200,000 of us in the United States trained as clinicians equal more than the number of psychiatrists, psychologists, and psychiatric nurses combined. More than 40 percent of American Red Cross volunteers are social workers. Sinema is joined by hundreds of fellow social workers in national, state, and local elected offices, including US senator Debbie Stabenow and US representatives Barbara Lee, Carol Shea-Porter, Luis Gutierrez, Niki Tsongas, and Susan Davis.

Congresswoman Sinema knows there's no time for wrangling when people's lives are on the line. When we stay in our corners, nothing gets done. She tells us her quest is to always look for shared values that lead to shared solutions. Even at a time of great divide, where hyperpartisanship rules, she's been able to get things done by reaching across the aisle. In her book *Unite and Conquer: How to Build Coalitions That Win and Last*, she says that "unity, alignment, and partnership" are the pathways to bring about needed change.

Sinema says it's vital that we step outside of our comfort zones and extend friendships with those different from us. She worries that the legendary story of Hubert Humphrey and Barry Goldwater, who were said to have been duking it out on the Senate floor by day then leaving to have a drink together at night, have become unlikely occurrences in the face of gridlock and contentious party lines.

She's even leading up a new kind of spin zone for politicians—one that is truly healthy. An avid runner and cyclist, she jumped on the invite to teach a spin class at the Members' gym, spurring on fellow colleagues in Congress to have some fun and start their long days right. The only debate is over song choices; she's been known to jostle Paul Ryan about his musical taste. Besides the bipartisan spin class, she and her colleagues have an entire working group devoted to finding common ground.

Sinema refused to allow the polarization of the DC political swamp to consume her. Instead, she prioritizes the greater good. She's made empathy and finding solutions her signature brand. And if she can do it on Capitol Hill, we can find similar opportunities in our boardrooms, classrooms, living rooms, and communities. Once we see what's possible on our own territory, we realize the chance to bring our positivity and productivity even further. We can become global twenty-first-century citizens, those who can adapt and demonstrate flexibility, empathy, curiosity, and the ability to work across cultures, party lines, professional domains, and other affiliations to bring positive impacts and better outcomes.

Global Twenty-First-Century Citizen

Academic Definition

A person who is committed to adopting a global mind-set, going
beyond traditional boundaries and seeing the interconnectedness of
human beings and phenomena.

Street Definition

You play well with everyone, unafraid to visit different sandboxes
and try new ways of doing things. You'd rather experience life without dirt in your eye from all the mud-slinging that happens. #gobig
#don'tstayhometho

Find Common Ground and Form Brigades

In 2005, Bono pulled on his signature rocker jeans and sunglasses.
He was headed to 1600 Pennsylvania Avenue to meet with the forty-third
president of the United States, the one he'd been bashing publicly during
his concerts. When George W. Bush got wind of it, he invited Bono to the
Oval Office. Bush said he wanted to find out what was behind the accusations, and to see if they could find common ground.

It was an unlikely scene but evolved into a friendship that transcended
Bush's and Bono's personal and political differences. They formed an alliance that went on to help millions of people affected by the AIDS crisis in
Africa. These are the types of hard-to-imagine collaborations that should
be making headlines every day. Instead, we think every inch of the ground
is ablaze, with no space to stop and listen to anyone planted in different
ideological, geographic, or other social identity spaces than us.

The raging wildfire keeps us running scared. We think there are no
safe patches of ground. Instead of using our energy to join forces and form
brigades, so that we can put this fire out together, we fight over who's to
blame. Our only way to go beyond is to hunt for places that offer respite
from the fire, where we can restrategize. It's our only chance for survival.

Like any dangerous fire, it requires the best of our resources to help us rethink Smoky the Bear's "Only *You* Can Prevent Forest Fires," and move to an "Only *We*" way of operating.

Polarization isn't working for any of us, but it's hard to escape with extremes between two-party political systems, rich and poor, young and old, and nations across the world. We are embroiled in inherited battles that encourage us to fight. Everyone is trained to believe that the other side is totally opposite, that there's no common ground to be found. The flames keep getting fanned, instead of finding ways to go beyond.

Our quest to form brigades is disrupted by gasoline dousers,[2] the inflamators out there who love to add fuel to the fire. No matter what side of the spectrum you are on, when you see people on your side doing this, beware. Along the trails, the dousers scream and hold up their "Only Me" signs. There's passion behind the screaming, but the fumes are so toxic that no one can safely get close enough to solve anything. Gasoline dousing is the opposite of conscious global citizenry; with no desire to connect and contribute something, there's no hope that positive and productive change can occur. There's no awareness that going beyond traditional boundaries to see difference and diversity as an asset rather than a deficit could get us to a better place. All inflamators do is get everyone to stay riled up in their corners, thinking caps put away.

Angry, fear-based, oversimplified solutions to problems never take. Life is far too complex to settle upon rote, simple, one-sided answers. The problems we face are too complex and consequential. If we allow our reactions to be based only on what we can see through the smokescreen of someone else's negative behavior, we miss the chance to set the world on fire in a whole new direction.

---

2 Inflamators are not people who peacefully protest, resist, or work to advocate for change. These are the people who are lambasted all over the news, demonstrating extreme behaviors—even violence to make their points known. Gasoline dousers never carry any water—they live to stoke the flames as high as they can go. Unfortunately, they can make the rest of the group they allegedly stand for look just as extreme and irrational. This is why we need rational thinkers to speak up, Sinema-style, to seek shared values, not promote inflammatory behavior.

> ### *Know the Difference Between Advocacy and Antagonism*
>
> *Advocacy* is the act of championing people's rights and well-being. It involves standing up for a social cause, particularly when it affects those who are underserved or marginalized. Advocates seek to raise consciousness on issues, working to mobilize resources for the greater good.
>
> Antagonism is when you treat ideological differences as sport. They see those they disagree with as opponents, and use every trick in the polarized playbook against them. Antagonists' attacks are personal, not policy-directed. They refuse to listen or allow a different side to show up without needling, poking, and ripping it apart. They build walls instead of bridges.

We can't keep getting triggered and miss the chance to see that:

- The people with the crystals in their pockets might not be as different as the ones with the rosary beads in theirs.

- The people wearing jeans have just as important things to say as the ones in suits.

- The people with bindis on their foreheads have something in common with those with ashes on theirs.

- What's "natural" to you isn't the same for everyone.

- First looks don't tell us much at all.

- Where we are born and live doesn't mean we have to stay in our corners forever.

- We want more of the same things than we're taught to realize, but we won't find peace without finding some common ground under our feet.

- We're all lost in our own ways and can't find our way out when we're building walls instead of brigades.

The natural reaction to inflama-tors is to explode—but we need to resist this reaction at all costs. The people who act and think this way need help. We cannot let them speak for the rest of us. They are adored by the media—their provocations sell. They're used to create the illusion of a bigger drama and divide among us. If we really think that people who look, live, love, worship, and engage

Every battle in life comes down to protecting territory. When the ground underneath is on fire, we need to form a brigade, not more firewalls. The only way to stop the destruction is to find common ground, where we can break out of our tendency to fight against each other, not the raging wildfire that needs to be extinguished.

in life differently than us are the extremes of their group's cast stereotype, we've become blinded by the smokescreens that inflamators conjure up.[3] All we can see are our principles that have been drilled into us as "the way," while missing the chance to accomplish better outcomes.

Don't Let Principles Stand in the Way of Outcomes

Hoards of people hold up their signs: "It's a Child, Not a Choice," "We Vote Pro-Life," and "Overturn Roe v. Wade." They hold crosses, each other's hands, and pictures of bloodied fetuses. On the other side of the street, people hold "My Body, My Decision," "Let Women Decide," and "Never Again" signs with coat hangers in tow. This is the scene of one of the most divisive political arguments of our day. The flames burn high on both sides of the street.

Abortion gets people seeing red, and gets them to the voting booths. For pro-life voters, principles don't lead to better outcomes. There is an ironic contradiction at hand for those who think their pro-life stance leads to less abortions. In fact, the abortion rate drops significantly on the watch of pro-choice leaders. During the past three decades, abortion rates have

---

3 A word of caution: you don't necessarily have to be a full-fledged inflamator to fall into this trap from time to time. We can be passionate about principles, but need to remember that we can turn people off instead of being able to effectively convey ideas that contribute toward positive progress. It doesn't mean we give up what we hold true. It means we are able to be nimble enough to negotiate shared desirable outcomes.

remained static or decreased slightly under Republican administrations, versus their counterparts who've seen sharper declines. For example, under President Barack Obama, rates fell from 16 for every 1,000 women (ages 15–44) to 12.5 in 2013. This is the lowest on record since 1971, and half the rate in 1980. For George H. W. Bush, rates remained at 16 between 2001–2008. Similarly, under Bill Clinton's administration, abortion rates fell from 23 to 16.2, while under George W. Bush abortion rates stayed at 16 until the end of this tenure, when it dropped to 15 in 2009.

The U.S. Centers for Disease Control and Prevention report cites increased access to health care, birth control, and other health and social services as far more effective means of reducing abortion than restricting access to it.

This is one of many examples as to why it's necessary to stop, rewind, and look for root issues. Abortion is a loaded debate, packed with moral contingencies galore for each side. But despite venomous disagreement, most would agree that preventing unplanned pregnancies is optimal. Most ideological disagreements keep us tangled over problems without address-ing root causes. We're so busy seeing red, we can't see the greenspaces available to gather and collaborate. This division breeds the type of condi-tion where we become more likely to watch everything go down in flames, rather than form needed brigades to make for a better world.

The "Speak English" debate in schools is another hot-button issue in the United States that leads to poor outcomes and missed opportunities. It's also situated within a larger contentious fight over immigrant access and rights. The mind-set is based on fears that immigrants take some-thing away from America rather than bring gifts to share. In schools, ELL (English Language Learner) students are often seen as draining resources, overlooked for the cultural and linguistic assets they bring to the classroom that help native-born students increase their global capacities.

A 2017 conducted by Maria Arrendono and colleagues actually found that kindergarteners in bilingual classrooms improved significantly on intelligence and attentional control. For those with Speak English bumper stickers affixed on their cars, principles are getting in the way of a better classroom environment for everyone.

Our whole life, we are taught to stick to our principles at all costs. But when principles come at the expense of desired outcomes, we have to think differently. Agility doesn't mean abandoning principles, but it does require us to recognize that what we're fighting for can lead to

Principles that come out of places of territory can leave us backed into corners, fighting like animals instead of seeing more than one side to issues, and seeking common ground.

unintended results. It's all tricky within a world where polarized indoctrination makes us think we have to pick sides and fight aggressively to defend territory. This approach prevents us from finding the common ground that can make us all stand stronger. Society, relationships—anything—will never be perfect, but focusing on desired outcomes is an important start. We don't want to find ourselves in a position when rigid principles cause outcomes that are the opposite of what we were striving for in the first place.

Look for Connections

Another contentious debate around the world relates to how to achieve a more perfect society. Everyone has a different take, and many of our nationalistic beliefs are held accordingly. Like John Lennon, most of us have imagined what society could be like without any war, crime, and inequality. We'd love a land where we didn't need locks or guns. Where trespassing signs are MIA. No killing. No Jerry Springer. No road rage. Where kids aren't left behind. Where black lives matter. No McDonald's for most and Ruth's Chris Steakhouses for a few. Where everyone's needs are met, and there's even time to celebrate our differences. Imagine that.

Most of us wouldn't fight about that kind of vision but would disagree on how to get there. It's the classic battle between individualism and collectivism. In one corner, individualism fights for the needs of the individual. In the other, collectivism fights for the greater good. It's an unnatural separation when we look a little closer—but is seen by many as representing polar opposites. We're taught to think rigidly, in either/or terms instead of both/and. We duke it out in vain—without realizing what we could learn from one other if we stepped out of our staunch ideological corners and started connecting. Neither side is perfect, but we can learn from each other's successes and struggles.

In China, people take care of their elders instead of dumping them in smelly nursing homes the minute they can't remember where they put their reading glasses. There's no *Nineteen and Counting.* Unemployment rates are low. But there's still crime, low fertility, aging population concerns, ethnic tensions, water shortages, and corruption. Many poke holes at democracy, saying that it only gives an illusion of freedom, that we have far less control and freedom than we think.

Both systems have pluses and minuses. You'd think this would make us eager to talk to each other to find out what's working well and what's not. When we travel across borders, we learn valuable information that helps us all get to a better place. For some of us, there may be times when the global terrain can feel like the Wild West—and we revert to thinking we've got to stay in our own spaces. But the opportunity to think globally—in ways that help us form intercultural, interfaith, and interdisciplinary brigades—is one that cannot be underestimated. Our strength is in our shared wisdom and common ground.

It's hard when ideology clamps its teeth down on all of us from an early age. Connection is the only way through. It's where we find our touchpoints for shared interests. If we isolate on polar extremes, we won't be able to work on something positive and productive. Connection doesn't mean that we have to merge our ideas or give up our individual convictions. It does mean taking time to listen to one another across borders, generations, political views, religion affiliations, race, class, gender, sexual orientation, and other affiliations. When we stay stuck in corners trying to prove our points, we give up our ability to be global citizens—those who commit to making life better for everyone, regardless of which team(s) they call their own.

Despite the polarization that permeates our world, every citizen around the globe wants to flourish. No one wants to be controlled by governing systems or other systems that damage our capacity to connect and progress. To varying extents, we are all subject to forms of control, which becomes the birthplace of fear as well as polarized thinking and behavior. This is why we desperately need to work together to forge common bonds so that our ability to set the world on fire in positive ways isn't sabotaged by inflamators.

Widen Your Sandbox

To overcome polarized indoctrination and the resulting disconnection, we need to look for common ground wherever we go. Beyond political terrain, we face polarized thinking that keeps us in silos instead of being able to forge dynamic collaborations. We need a wide sandbox where we can expand and play well together.

Even when you identify with a certain framework, resist the urge to lock it down and never be willing to change. This goes against your efforts to become more agile. Instead, work to fuse perspectives, to keep learning, unlearning, and relearning.

Going beyond toward a global citizen identity isn't just about personal affiliations. Even at work, we are not immune to polarization. It might not be as touchy as hot-button political issues but can silo us nonetheless. Every career has its own form of training in which we are indoctrinated into thinking and doing things certain ways. Instead of combining knowledge and transferring information across disciplines, we often stay insular and cornered off from perspectives that could be very useful.

There's endless learning and unlearning we can accomplish together. Fortunately, there's more attention being given to the critical nature of interdisciplinary bonds that help us make integrated, universal connections.

One way to begin is to take on a What-can-I-learn-from-you? mind-set. This is something schools are doing—adopting the medical rounds model to provide hands-on support for teachers right within the classroom, similar to teaching methods in hospitals when doctors in training watch senior doctors to learn the ropes.

Unlearning polarized indoctrination reaps big benefits. We can enter into meaningful exchanges that enhance our lives personally and professionally. We can discover creative solutions that we wouldn't have considered within the confines of our corners.

We can't keep hanging out in the same tree and expect new fruit to appear.

Branching out to find common ground and new spaces for collaboration can help us stay clear of disconnection that stunts growth and progress. The less divided we are, the more we can harness our collective knowledge and passion to find better outcomes. We can widen our sandbox, allowing room for creative solutions toward common ground.

Interdisciplinary

Academic Definition

Combining two or more academic, scientific, and artistic branches of knowledge. It involves crossing traditional boundaries between schools of thought to respond to new needs within our twenty-first-century global context.

Street Definition

Getting out of your school and work corners to combine knowledge and go beyond unneeded boundaries. Teachers can learn from doctors, scientists from artists. #connectthedots

Session Fourteen Worksheet:
Coming Out of Corners

Objective:
Unlearn polarized indoctrination that breeds disconnection.
Pivot toward common-ground thinking.

Rethink It:
Move from Polarization to Common Ground

With the endless bickering between parties, affiliations, and territories, we are led to believe we have to pick a corner and stay in it, instead of finding common ground. In order to go beyond what is sold to us, we need to venture out and form brigades that helps us become more conscious, global, twenty-first-century citizens.

Common-Ground Check

- In what corners did I start my life?
- Am I still in the corner? What is this like for me?
- Do I spend time with people who see life differently than I do?
- Besides differences, what things do we share in common?
- What principles do I hold dearly? Are there times when they might interfere with outcomes?
- What can I learn from people I'm different from?
- Do I engage in inflammatory actions or associate with those who do? How can I pivot toward more conscious behavior?

Action Steps:
Branch Out and Find Common Ground

Society is filled with inflamators who delight in dumping gasoline on our fires, creating explosions that prevent us from seeing potential common ground. We all stand on different ground for different reasons, but we need to find and use our global lens to help us adopt a universal I-can-learn-from-you mind-set. We might not have a budget to travel the world, but here are some activities to help you cultivate connections that go beyond traditional boundaries:

1. **Pull a Sinema.** Go for a jog, take a spin class, initiate a walk with someone you know has opposite views and perspectives. Practice listening and asking questions, rather than providing your opinion or proving your own point. Try to listen for what made the other people arrive at their positions.

2. **Compare and contrast.** Select principles from a sample of one or two different religious or humanist frameworks, or from one professional domain to the other. How are they similar? In what ways do they differ? What can any of them learn from each other?

3. **Listen.** Play the song "Imagine" by John Lennon. What individual steps can you make toward a better society? What does society need to do more of? Less of? What will be your contribution as a conscious global citizen?

4. **Deconstruct the corners.** To see through religious and political divides, watch the documentary *Seeing Red* by Gerry Corneau and Leah Belsky. What aspects of society do you notice we are being propped up to fight, rather than understand? What will you do as a result?

5. **Bring the world home with you.** Travel everywhere you go with an open heart and mind. The way to the heart is often through the stomach. For starters, learn to expand your palate and try new foods. You can also listen to multicultural/world music, take in performances and art, read books, watch films, and make friendships with people from around the world, or even those who differ in varied ways. Come out of any corners in which you might be situated and give yourself as many opportunities as possible to experience new ways of seeing the world. Form brigades and expand your sandbox.

PART IV

The Going-Beyond Sessions

Find Your Imagineering Lens

Rethink the 4 forms of indoctrination that lead to stagnation:

→ From All-or-Nothing to Fusion Thinking

→ From Always On to Sustainability Thinking

→ From Good Student to Inclusive Thinking

→ From Silo to Integration Thinking

The Going-Beyond sessions will help you unlearn four forms of indoctrination that lead to stagnation. You will pivot toward the glorious dance of becoming more imaginative in your thinking, engineering a life path with social impact, and bringing your imagineering lens to its full splendor. You will say no to paralysis, burnout, shame, cliques, and disintegration, and yes to possibilities most people only dream of. This is our new psychology of thinking: becoming an integrated thinker. *This is the last hurrah, you creative soul. Show us your moves.*

SESSION FIFTEEN

Choosing Your Code

Objective:
Unlearn all-or-nothing indoctrination that breeds paralysis.
Pivot toward fusion.

Imagination creates reality.

—Richard Wagner

When Sheena Iyengar and her research team set up their Wilkin and Sons jam display in an upscale California market, they discovered what happens when we have too many choices. While customers were enticed by the twenty-four jars laid out before them, few purchases were made. They were only one-tenth as likely to buy versus customers who were offered just six jam options. This type of study has been replicated in many ways, leaving decision-making experts like Iyengar to conclude that excessive options can lead to *choice paralysis.*

Barry Schwartz, author of *The Paradox of Choice: Why More Is Less*, agrees. He says that our tendency to hold choice as sacred, as the hallmark of individual freedom and self-determination, might be setting us up for unnecessary anxiety. We lament over decisions before we even make them, hold unrealistically high expectations, then blame ourselves for our perceived failures.

It's one thing when we're trying to decide over cherry or plum jam, or find our way through aisles offering twenty-nine different kinds of chicken soup and fifteen brands of extra virgin olive oil. It's another when we're trying to cook up a code for living—the ethical framework that drives our decisions. Devising one in our anything-goes culture is a lot harder than picking from the fourteen types of Cheerios supposed to help us start our days right.

As difficult as it may be to pinpoint, the last thing we need is to freeze up and experience choice paralysis when it comes to identifying the values that inform how we think and what we do. We need to become imagineers— those who can imagine ways to go beyond and engineer a life that allows us to shine brightest.

Don't Get Lost in the Aisles

When you work in higher education, you see firsthand how the abundance of choices can wreak havoc on students. There are more degree and career tracks than ever before. It's exciting, but it has its downside, too. Limitless can turn out to be limiting. We should never lose sight that choices are a privilege; not everyone has them. But "anything goes" can leave us marinating in worry and angst. "You can do anything" seems a lot better than "You don't have a choice," but in reality, neither extreme is ideal.

Choice paralysis isn't reserved for young people—at every age and life stage, we face confusion over what's right or wrong. Many of my best friends and colleagues in their late fifties, sixties, and seventies are always working on their second-half ambitions. Some have reinvented themselves and started new careers. They've all faced points when life was turned upside down, requiring a complete overhaul of previous assumptions, roles, and identities. Life requires this type of agility and resilience of us at every turn.

Know the Science Behind Choice

In 1935, John Ridley Stroop wanted to find out what would happen if he asked someone to look at words, but instead of reading them, say the color. You can Google it to give it a try.

If you're like most people, you spouted out the words you saw instead of naming the colors. The Stroop test shows we make meaning of words faster than colors. Reading is more automatic for most of us, and color doesn't influence meaning like words do.

When we consider the meaning making required of us in everyday life, it's clear we need to make sure that we're paying attention to more than the automatic impulses of our brains. Think of the mistakes we could be making without a blink.

In *Nudge: Improving Decisions About Health, Wealth and Happiness,* Richard Thalar and Cass Sunstein draw upon behavioral science and economics to explain how and why humans are prone to making mistakes—ranging from consumption to neglect of natural resources to poor investments. Despite popular beliefs, the authors explain that the assumption that we typically make choices in our best interest is false.

Thalar and Sunstein emphasize that we often take the path of least resistance, defaulting to either doing nothing or doing what's fast and automatic. They say we need to learn *choice architecture* to help bring us to better decisions. Thalar and Sunstein emphasize that our choices are not made in a vacuum, and when we don't notice environmental influence, the consequences will be worse than mistaking orange for pink.

At the University of Michigan, Raymond De Young is using Stroop Test research to explore ways we can put choices into perspective, avoiding overconsumption. He calls for an "urgent transition" from the prevailing thinking that choice abundance equals prosperity. He worries that we will continue to experience unwelcome consequences of attempting "limitless growth on a finite planet." De Young suggests that the unfolding resource descent is going to send us into shock, and that learning "behavioral entrepreneurship" is essential for all citizens, so that we can work toward simplicity, frugality, and sustainability.

In my study, my students—who were from twenty to sixty-five years old—repeatedly told me about moments when they felt completely paralyzed by the choices and changes confronting them. There were times when a short span of time would suddenly bring on enormous disruption. This left them in a place where they felt like they were both spinning and stuck all at the same time.

Finding our code to live by can be like trying to find our way through a Cheesecake Factory menu. The revolutionary changes in what we study, what job we pick, who and how we love, where we travel, who we hang with, how we communicate, and how we define our purpose are enough to make us permanently dizzy. Plus, there are always twists in our spirals that we weren't expecting. It can be difficult to know what the good life means, never mind being able to sustain it.

My students told me that they tried going back to what they were first fed, but it wasn't enough protein to keep them going in today's global world. For most of us, the families and communities we originate from were only given one kind of Cheerios to pick from. There weren't as many aisles to go down. Think of the changes we've seen unfold over time:

On resilience:

Boomers (born 1945-1964):
   I had to walk ten miles in the snow to get to school.

Generation X (born 1965-1980):
   I had to wait at the bus stop in the cold.

Millennials (born 1981-1995):
   I didn't always get a turn in the heated front seat on the way to school.

Generation Z (born after 1995):
   They keep calling me special snowflake.

On diversity:

   Boomers: I'm not as bad as Archie Bunker—or my parents, who were openly racist.

Generation X: I didn't get enough exposure until I went to college/work.

   Millennials: 98 percent of my friends are different than me.

Generation Z: Duh. Why do we even need to talk about this?

On relationships:

Boomers: I've been married longer than the sum of all your friends' relationships.

Generation X: My partner and I are consciously uncoupling.

Millennials: Does this seem like an okay first wedding dress?

Generation Z: I much prefer hookups over breakups.

On technology/communication:

Boomers: I wrote letters and used rotary dial phones.

Generation X: I got my first flip phone when I was twenty-five.

Millennials: I was born holding an iPad in my hands, and would rather text than talk.

Generation Z: TTYL . . . I'm on Snapchat.

On finding information:

Boomers: I made regular trips to the library and listened to my teachers.

Generation X: I used Encyclopedia Britannica and read a lot of books.

Millennials: Wikipedia is saved in my Favorites.

Generation Z: My phone tells me everything I need to know, including secrets about my teachers.

On religion:

Boomers: I attended weekly services and gave a lot of time and money to the church.

Generation X: I made obligatory appearances on major holidays.

Millennials: Does yoga count?

Generation Z: We are the religion.

On science:

Boomers: We only talked about it during science class.

Generation X: That Bill Nye guy is entertaining.

Millennials: I hope I can sign up to get myself cloned.

Generation Z: I already have my 23 and Me profile so I know my entire chemical makeup.

On travel:

Boomers: My family drove to the lake every summer.

Generation X: I took my first plane ride on my honeymoon.

Millennials: I've been to eleven different countries.

Generation Z: I get itchy if I'm home for more than a few weeks.

On parenting:

Boomers: Children should be seen and not heard. Or they'll get a slap.

Generation X: We're not your friend, but we will listen.

Millennials: Break out the bubble wrap and helmets.

Generation Z: There are more parenting styles than cereals.

On growing up:

Boomers: I was kicked out of the house at eighteen and went to work.

Generation X: It took me until my thirties, but I survived.

Millennials: I still live at home with my parents.

Generation Z: I'm going to try adulting today.

On school:

Boomers: I got hit with rulers. Most of my friends graduated high school.

Generation X: A lot of my friends went to college. The homework wasn't too bad.

Millennials: They put me on Ritalin in seventh grade. Everyone else was on it, too.

Generation Z: I'll need to know my college choices by kindergarten. I'll finish college in high school and my bachelor's and master's in three years and still won't find a job.

On work:

Boomers: I've stayed at the same company for longer than you've been alive.

Generation X: I only moved a couple times, when there was good reason.

Millennials: I'll stay for no longer than 4.4 years, then start my own company.

Generation Z: I didn't even make it through the job interview. They wanted me to live to work, and I need balance.

The rapid changes in society affect all of us, at every age. It can feel like a free-for-all compared to the way it was. Many of the changing tides reflect incredible advances in travel, communication, science, and technology. Adapting and breaking out from old ways can make us feel like we're spiraling out of control. We know that this kind of monumental change requires us to be agile, but it's a lot to integrate.

When we base our life codes entirely on past thinking, we end up ignoring the reality of our global context. It's not that plain Cheerios don't have redeeming value. But if that's all we eat, metaphorically, we'll miss the chance to activate the agility we need to fuel the kind of vibrant energy we need to make it in the twenty-first century. We can't stay stuck milling in the aisles for long if we want to make progress.

When we're trying to get our footing, messages can still haunt us that our lives have gone totally off the rails because plain Cheerios are no longer a staple. We've been conditioned to think we will go into anaphylactic shock when we venture out and try something different. Simultaneously, today's times tell us we have to indulge in everything to be fulfilled.

Imagineering is a process of imagining and engineering our lives. It doesn't dismiss tradition but instead allows for integrated behavior based on what we have consciously unlearned and relearned. Contrary to what we're often told, we don't

One-size-fits-all options rarely fit anyone. When we try to base our codes for living on what used to work or what's always been done, we miss the chance to develop the kind of vibrant energy we need to think creatively.

have to operate in all-or-nothing terms. We can be grounded while being open-minded and adaptable to new perspectives. We can enjoy choices, but we don't need to be gluttons either. Even when the new global territory feels like the Wild West, we can still find our way through uncharted terrain. There will be times when we don't need to reinvent the wheel, and there will be others when we need a whole new vehicle. It's all part of the adventure.

Fuse Your Code

When I gathered six of my students for our Monday night think-and-do tank meeting, I knew they'd waste no time.[1] I'd just shared with them the findings from my study and wanted to talk with them about how they were imagineering their own codes for living.

They emphasized that they didn't want to get caught up complaining about "problems of privilege," or become like the "worried well," underappreciating their opportunities. They told me they felt lucky that they even had choices. Gratitude was critical. They never wanted to take what they had for granted. They were very aware that few had the luxury of choice.

I rattled off a few intentionally open-ended questions, and everyone started describing how the noise of endless choice affected them. At first, the options were exciting. Then they became distractions from working toward imagineering the kind of life code that allowed them to be the conscious global citizens they wanted to be.

My students told me they wanted a code that was we- not me-focused. Even with good intentions, they still got heat from their families and communities of origin, where agility was interpreted as abandonment. Their families wanted the "we" to mean "them," not a larger global community and perspective. My students come from different countries and contexts, and are all well into their twenties, but all faced generational pressure to stay with the norms their parents and grandparents had followed. It was hard for them to be real when they'd experienced so much change, but the family still pressured them to be earlier versions of themselves.

They were being asked to pull off an epic and contradictory feat— grow, but stay the same. Everyone shot up in their chair when I asked if they've been made to feel they've been disloyal by being told, "You're not the same person" or "You've changed," in a tone clearly not meant as a compliment.

---

1 Meet the team: Liang and Biyu are from China. At the time of our meeting, they had both finished graduate degrees and were deciding their next moves: more school or work. Jessica, from the United States, just finished her master's in social work and was a week away from starting a new job. Amy is from the United States and holds a master's degree in nonprofit management and works at a nonprofit in Boston. Miguel originates from Mexico City, just finished his bachelor's in psychology, and works for a nonprofit. Jenna, from the United States, had just finished her internship and was hired at Massachusetts General Hospital, on her way to becoming a pediatric neurologist.

The accusation of forgetting where we came from stings. We talked about how hard perceived abandonment hits, especially when love for family is unquestionable. Love and loyalty don't cancel out all questions, though. They create temptation to go along to get along. It was hard facing the deep guilt, shame, and isolation that come from choosing a code that doesn't match up perfectly with the people to whom you've been closest—the ones who raised you, whom you respect and love, yet with whom you still have significant differences. The tension was hard to bear.

Miguel said he wanted to get to a place where it didn't feel like such an "identity crisis," but more of a "truth of identity" where sincerity could prevail, and he could be himself with less conflict. He didn't want family to think they were being betrayed, but he

> We're told we "owe" people, but the only thing we owe ourselves, or anyone else, are our unequivocal truths.

knew that his time travelling the globe had changed him. He had expanded his horizons, no longer fitting into the exact space his family had carved out for him.

Integrating one precise "certain" framework—one that you've always known—with the endless sea of choices can make you feel like you're drowning. Going beyond is hard to do, as generational codes are strong undercurrents in all of our lives. Despite the anxiety it provokes to take a stand, maintaining an image based on who people thought we were or needed us to be creates more problems than it solves.

Family tensions are among the hardest to reconcile, but it's usually the first stop necessary to figuring out our codes. None of us wanted to kiss authenticity good-bye, but we didn't want to write off people we love either. Everyone (including myself) agreed that this made us feel like we needed to fuse perspectives together, rather than take an all-or-nothing approach.

> One of life's most epic tensions lies between wanting to be a part and wanting to be apart.

Each generation bases its own codes on the information available, context, and society's progressions (some might argue digressions). They are a lot like fashion trends—what seemed like a good choice in the 1980s becomes laughable, but then manages to resurface.[2] The pendulum is always swinging back and forth—one generation handles things in a certain way with the resources they have available; then the times take a new direction. It's not that one way is good or bad; there are just different approaches in each context. Conflict about what's best—between generations, and even within ourselves—is inevitable. We remain stuck trying to decide what to do, instead of realizing we can fuse something new.

It's not always tensions that get us down. Many of my students talked about having to be "pioneers" in a new global frontier. They didn't have any input from their upbringings—they didn't feel they had much of anything being projected upon them. Although that seemed like a relief to those of us in different situations, it still wasn't easy. My students were forging their way in uncharted territory, which I saw repeatedly in my study and during our meeting. Liang wished for some kind of "basic standards" for global living. She had lived in the United States for a while, her husband was from Israel, and they wished for a more specific guiding frame to follow. She told us:

> *I think there are too many choices. There's like a conflict, because there are no basic standards. Money is like a God, but there's no moral compass. You don't even know what the right way is.*

As we brainstormed possibilities, we kept talking about "basic standards," trying to imagine what a global code of ethics could look like. It's a complicated topic that has created much debate and dissent, but our team loves tackling these kinds of conversations. Many religious groups think they have sole license on universal concepts like love but only sell them within a package that requires conformity to a system filled with contradictions that end up diluting its power. Even the Dalai Lama, in his book *Beyond Religion: Ethics for a Whole World*, advocates against pushing any one paradigm on everyone. He says, "I am a man of religion, but religion alone cannot answer all our problems." He reveres and honors Buddhist

---

2 This is one of the reasons parents are rarely in style. Once they've braved those trends, then realized they're a bit tacky, they don't want to go back again and do that all over again. We will all think Crocs are super weird one day—just ask the Jelly shoes.

teachings and traditions but does not think forcing them upon anyone of a different faith tradition does anyone any good.

Throughout the book, the Dalai Lama emphasizes the progress that's been made in neuroscience, allowing greater understanding of how deliberate cultivation of qualities like compassion, loving-kindness, attention, and a calm mind are beneficial to all. He worries that our focus on the material aspects of life are hampering our instincts for compassion and cultivating moral ethics and inner values. We're living as if stuff will save our souls, and that if someone looks at life through a different lens, we should knock their lights out. Love and light need to be spread, and even if we are drawing on different sources, it doesn't mean we can't find connections to fuse. With 7 billion people on the earth, we will never reach consensus, but we need to start somewhere.

Start with You

Ironically, getting to we first requires us to be self-led. We need to find our own lights and footing on the paths we are trying to navigate. As a team, we kept circling back to our desire to have close relationships with our families, while going beyond traditions that didn't fit with our consciously chosen values. Luckily, Jessica happened to be working toward her internal family systems (IFS) therapy certificate, built on a theory that combines systems thinking with recognizing the multiplicity of the mind.

IFS provides a lens to help us imagineer how to turn our usual habits and behaviors, the ones formed early on as protective mechanisms to keep us functional and safe, into more adaptive behaviors as adults. For example, some of us hate confrontation and will agree to things that go against our grain just to avoid people being upset with us. Some of us struggle with low self-esteem in the context of our families, where we were handed a certain role and struggle to unclamp from it. Some of us were taught hate and fear. Even within a loving kinship nest, there's always going to be some forms of insularity and complicated dynamics that we need to go beyond.

The students on my team and in my study originate from many countries around the world. They felt "totally disrupted" in a new land, trying to make their way. Wherever we're from, when we first leave home, we are forced to become more self-led. My international students dealt with loneliness, identity confusion, and yearning for the familiar. Over time, they began to acclimate into a new rhythm that allowed them to thrive.

IFS offers eight Cs to help us become more self-led when we're trying to make our way in life:

- Calm
- Curious
- Clear
- Compassionate
- Confident
- Creative
- Courageous
- Connected

The eight Cs make a lot of sense. Each trait and behavior lays an excellent foundation for imagineering our codes. Given the complexity of our minds, relationships, and social context, being self-led isn't a me-endeavor; it helps us become better global contributors. This helps us connect, wherever we're situated.

After discussing how IFS applies to transitions from family—whether physical, philosophical, or some combination—Jenna chimed in with some thoughts on how brain science plays a role in our behavior. The reptilian and mammalian parts of our brains influence how we choose to interact and are often at conflict with one another. The reptile in us is led by fear instincts. It can cause us to want to dominate and make quick decisions. It's a bit rough around the edges, but it helps us get out there and do our best to survive.

The mammal side also helps us survive, but through different

Even if we have the most dynamic family in the world, they won't be perfect. No family is. And even if we are enamored with them, we will still have to leave the nest and find our way. It will likely be shockingly painful and disruptive. The resulting growth will make for greater agility.

pathways. It craves attachment, nurturing, and feeding. It prompts us toward community and intimacy. We are contradictory creatures who need Mama's milk, but we can't survive if we're unable to digest solids from the larger terrain. We need to be quick on our feet but grounded in strong connections.

Imagineering our code is necessary but often painful work. We can hand the choice over and let someone else decide, or we can take initiative to lead the way. Choice paralysis can leave us stuck eating plain Cheerios because we're fearful of reactions that may result if we're caught in aisles where we were once forbidden. We might not need to clip our roots altogether. Our fused codes can take the best of what we've learned and unlearned, inviting the reptiles and mammals to travel together. We don't have to throw the milk out with the cereal to design a code that sets us up to soar as conscious global citizens. There's no time for paralysis when the world needs light to pour in from as many sources as possible.

Session Fifteen Worksheet:
Choosing Your Code

Objective:
Unlearn all-or-nothing indoctrination that breeds paralysis.
Pivot toward fusion thinking.

Rethink It:
Move from Paralysis to Fusion

It's easy to get lost in the aisles with the endless choices in living that confront us. Opportunities are exciting, and we never want to complain about privilege, but the rapid changes and possibilities in our world can make us dizzy. We can get stuck in all-or-nothing thinking without realizing that we can fuse ideas together, imagineering a new code for living that allows us to shine the brightest.

All-or-Nothing Check

- How different is my life than that of my parents or grandparents?
- Who are the main influencers in my life? What is their code to live by? What features do I want to see in my own ways of doing things?
- Are there any unnecessary choices I'm spending time on that are taking away from other aspects of my life?
- What five words do I want used to describe me?
- What values would I not compromise, no matter what?
- Do I face tensions or conflict with my family or community of origin to pick sides?
- How can I handle my life in a more imagineering way?

Action Steps:
Go Beyond and Fuse Your Code

The changes we see in society are hard to conceive. The terrain can seem so open that we feel closed in, not knowing which direction to turn. Try some of these steps to help you with your fusion:

1. **Mix up your breakfast.** Plain Cheerios serve a purpose, but be sure to add variety into your routines. Don't glue yourself to one way of doing things; creativity often lets us expand our horizons. We all need some spice of life to keep us energized throughout our long, hard days. Just like we are what we eat, the ideas we consume have a big effect on us. If we only feast on the same old thing, we will stay stagnant.

2. **Set boundaries.** In our sky's-the-limit culture, it's easy to get carried away. As University of Michigan researcher Raymond De Young points out, our

global resources are declining in the face of living beyond sustainable limits. It happens across societies, but also on many levels in our lives. Maybe we choose a job that exhausts us, requiring overwork that can compromise us over the long haul. Maybe we take on too much in our lives. We choose more of what we can realistically handle: too many kids, too big of a house, or too many commitments. We say yes to so much that maintaining it all becomes more complicated than healthy. Even if we're consuming something good, too much of something can overwhelm us. Making simplicity an inherent part of our values system can help. Make choices that sustain you in all areas of your life, considering how a decision at work or with your family affects the other areas.

3. **Compare and contrast.** Select principles from a sample of one or two different religious or humanist frameworks. How are they similar? In what ways do they differ? What can any of them learn from each other? How could these ideas be brought out in your own life?

4. **Listen.** Play "Shake It Out" by Florence and the Machine. What types of devils have you had on your back? What helps you shake them out? In what ways do you need to dance more freely from society's grip without losing your grounding?

5. **Invite people with you on your journey.** Even when there may be resistance from people who eat plain Cheerios, ask them to join you in experiencing something new. Exposure to new ways of engaging in life can be a catalyst for positive growth and change our relationships for the better. If you've been fortunate to sample the tastes of the world, share them. Don't keep your expansion to yourself.

6. **Write out your code.** Take a look at the eight Cs of IFS, the Universal Declaration of Human Rights and, the Social Work Code of Ethics, or a framework you already rely on for moral grounding. Write a one-page code of ethics that you want to live by. Post it in everyday sight to remind yourself and inspire others.

"This is my **SIMPLE RELIGION.**
There is no need for **TEMPLES,** no
need for **COMPLICATED** philosophy.
Our own **BRAIN,** our own
HEART is our **TEMPLE;**
the philosophy is **KINDNESS.**"

—Dalai Lama

SESSION SIXTEEN

Rethinking Work

Objective:
Unlearn always-on work indoctrination that breeds burnout.
Pivot toward sustainability-focused thinking.

*And every day, the world will drag
you by the hand, yelling, "This is important!
And this is important! You need to worry about this!
And this! And This!" And each day, it's up to
you to yank your hand back, put it on your heart,
and say, "No. This is what's important."*

—Iain Thomas

At age twenty-three, Howard Scott Warshaw found himself eye to eye with Steven Spielberg, who was praising the Atari 2600 Indiana Jones video game Warshaw had designed. After its sweeping success, the time had come to take things to another level. Since making a name for himself in Silicon Valley, Warshaw was handpicked for the next big project: creating a game for the 1982 blockbuster movie *E.T.*

When Spielberg told Warshaw his first game made him feel like "he just watched a movie," he says he took it as the "ultimate compliment." As Atari and Spielberg haggled over rights for the game, precious production time was lost. Rather than the nearly full year it took to design the Indiana Jones game, Warshaw was given the task of creating the E.T. game from scratch in just five weeks.

He worked day and night, producing what ended up widely known as the "worst video game of all time." The colossal commercial flop was so bad that game cartridges ended up being dumped into a landfill in New Mexico. The superstar programmer was set up to fail, which he did.

The games have long been buried; fortunately, Warshaw turned his early 1980s downward spiral into momentum. Today, he's known as the "Silicon Valley therapist." His failures—the game, being laid off from Atari, and losing his millionaire status—gave him unique perspective. He now spends his time counseling people in the same types of squeezes that led him to commit to something humanly impossible, then reap crappy results.

The neurochemical rush of being in demand intoxicates us. We relish being touted for what we create. The stimulation leaves us on a constant chase for more, pushing to the point of recklessness. The higher we climb, the harder we fall. The fibers of our initial fixation are thick and hard to untangle, often discovered only once painful lessons have shown up.

We all have our own versions of an E.T. game catastrophe. You go from having a reasonable amount of work and time to complete it to ridiculously insane expectations. This happens when we do well. More is expected. Today's market forces us to rush; quality suffers. The consequences of Warshaw's failure weren't earth-shattering. He floundered for a while, but eventually settled. Not everyone is that lucky.

When Duty Calls, Answer Wisely

David Miller taps me on the shoulder. He had news to deliver. At first, it didn't seem like a big deal, coming out of his usual California-chill tone. Our colleague Rachel, who was to introduce me for the talk I was on deck for, wasn't feeling well; we'd have to improvise. Moments later came the full disclosure.

The news was disturbing. Rachel had had a heart attack in the wee hours that morning. The stress of the job had nearly killed her, but *duty calls*, and she still showed up. "Are you okay?" I asked, realizing the absurdity of the question just as it left my mouth. "No . . . ," she muttered.

You might find this shocking, or chalk it up to stupidity, but Rachel holds a PhD and is cerebral as you can imagine. Always-on work indoctrination had gotten to her—the one that trained her to keep climbing 24/7, at *all* costs.

Like many of us, she was conditioned to stay in permanent overdrive and performance mode. Work indoctrination teaches that we *must* be there, that the show *won't go on* without us. If we take time off, we'll fall *even further* behind. God forbid we let duty's call go to voice mail— we might let someone down. Driven by our ego's desire for validation and recognition, and to be needed, we keep picking up the call of duty. Who else is going to do the work? Plus, we've got bills to pay and a ladder to climb.

For a few seconds, I got self-righteous about Rachel showing up post–heart attack. You may think the same thing. You'd *never* do that. It doesn't mean self-neglect isn't a thing—it might just be less dramatic or look a little different for you. Most of us answer duty's calls, no matter what.

The only true form of work-life balance is that we are expected to do everything in both places. Otherwise, it is elusive and potentially dangerous to believe in. The idea that work-life balance is attainable in our work martyr culture reinforces the idea that work-related stress and illness are individual failings—not organizational and public policy issues that confront people across societies.

Rachel's situation is not an isolated incident. A Yale study published in the *Journal of the American Heart Association* reveals that the very stress that often precipitates a heart attack is also a major hindrance in recovery. The 35,000 young and middle-age women suffering heart attacks every year report trouble finding time to get their bearings because of heaping family and work demands. There is not even time to mend a broken heart.

There's a fine line between caring and caring to the point of self-destruction.

This problem isn't unique to women, or Americans. People are paying the price across the world. The World Health Organization calls today's global work environments "modern hazards." In Japan, the term *karoshi* describes death by overwork, encapsulating the rising number of heart attacks, strokes, and suicides citizens face. A governmental annual report revealed that approximately 21.3 percent of Japanese employees work forty-nine hours weekly. Before her death by suicide, twenty-four-year old Matsuri Takahashi's social media posts lamented on the consequences of her 100-plus hours of monthly overtime: "I want to die" and "I'm physically and mentally shattered."

People are not commodities, but corporate and organizational life tricks us into believing and behaving as if we are.

Always-on work indoctrination is dangerous. A report from Oxford Economics points to a pervasive workaholic paradigm as problematic: "Our 24-7, always on, hard-charging culture has created a nation of work martyrs—the type that take few vacation days, come into the office sick, and pride themselves on being seen at a desk."

It seems absurd, yet we fall for it. You wouldn't accept a lead role in a movie that required you to indefinitely gain fifty pounds, be your own stunt person, and stay on the set day and night, just for the sake of free bagels every Tuesday as consolation. Even if you're raking it in, you'd probably think twice given the risks (unless Jennifer Lawrence was costarring).

But we accept the parts and answer the call of duty since we seem to have no choice. People are depending on us. If we try to modify the script, we pay the price. They'll zing, criticize, look down on, or even fire us. We're scared of hearing, "He's not really a team player, and is just in it for himself," or "She's such a disappointment. She never stays late like the rest of us."

Don't Fry the Motherboard

Even when labor regulations and social policies exist, they are not always held up. Paid vacation time is not a given, either. Making a living in such a competitive, cutthroat market is hard. We get the message that we are dispensable. This is the fallout within societies where achieving status and acquiring money are prioritized over spiritual and community pursuits.

We live with the feeling we're about to fry the motherboard and end up burned out. We've got a headache and a handful of Get Out of Sleep Free cards we're clutching, zooming pass Go week after week, collecting our $200. We hope we're invincible, until sickness comes knocking. I asked my students how their always-on work indoctrination has affected them. Natalie, who'd been at her company twelve years, saw it in full effect:

> *It's Wednesday and I've already worked thirty-eight hours. I'm totally fried but I've learned to keep my head down and mouth shut. My boss is famous for saying once we get done with this project, things will slow down, but there's always another one popping up. When I went to the doctor last week, my blood pressure was high for the first time ever. My friends think I've gone missing. I know I need to change, but last week someone was fired for not staying late when everyone else did. I swear they think we are computers.*

Igor was confronted with strikingly similar conditions, even though he'd only been at work for two years:

> *In theory, I love my work, but in reality, it's super stressful. No matter how much effort I give, it feels like it's never enough. I have a strong work ethic, but it's like we're expected to be five people all at once. Oh— and I want to find a new job, but most of my friends my age are in the same boat. I doubt it's much better anywhere else. The problem is, I can barely sleep. Even when I'm not at work, I'm anxious about it. Three people have gone out on sick leave, but no one talks about it. We just keep going, as if there's not something seriously wrong with the whole situation, like it's totally normal I don't want to be the next one to drop, but it's not looking good.*

The fear of becoming fried was a consistent worry for my students— whether they were in corporate, nonprofit, education, or the private sector. They yearned for purpose and were earnest to do meaningful work, but the situations they were in required them to magically pull rabbits out of their hats. Change seemed to be the only constant. There was little appreciation for the epic stunts being performed. And since we need to preserve the one brain we're given, we started to talk about what they would need to do to prevent the motherboard from billowing with smoke.

Eat Your Soup Now.
There Will Be No Cake Later

Rita worked at a prestigious university for thirty-three years. During her tenure, she secured $15 million in grant funding and was the go-to person for the entire department. She got things done. The classic work martyr, she prided herself on having taken a total of only three sick days in twenty-three years. She's like the growing number of people leaving vacation days unused and skipping lunch to be more productive. No soup for us.

Keeping our heads down and mouths shut isn't the answer. We now have evidence that healthy workers make for healthy organizations. In addition to the moral obligation of leaders, nothing suggests that punitive and exhausting work conditions do anything to help morale, productivity, or the bottom line. In fact, the opposite is true.

When her retirement finally approached, there was no cake. No card. No thank-you gesture—not even a trip over to Panera Bread. It's not that she needed a parade in her honor, but *something* would have been nice.

Unless you're situated in one of those rare organizations where humans are shown they matter, the always-on indoctrination will get you long before there is time to mourn your good-bye cake. The overwork will have already fried your motherboard, corrupting your health, sleep, relationships, and quality of life.

We don't think about this when we're up answering emails and chained to our desks. We think work has our back, that all the overtime we've clocked will be celebrated. But at the end of it all, someone else will come along and sit in our cube and, in time, end up wearing the same "Overworked and Unappreciated" T-shirt. Maybe they'll be lucky enough to find that someone figured out there's a bakery right around the corner when they decide it's their turn to go. *Or not.*

Set Your Own Vault

When work dictates our every move, we can get hurt. The concept of stress originally came from engineers trying to describe how much weight a bridge could bear before collapsing. If we let other people determine how much to pile onto us, we'll start to buckle. We're more apt to come crashing down, like the gymnasts from the summer of 2000 Sydney Olympic Games.

During preliminary rounds, the vaulters sensed something was off, but their concerns were ignored and the competition went on. It wasn't until several of them were injured that the officials finally listened. They discovered the vault was off by five centimeters, a critical variance that explained the gymnasts' uncharacteristic falls. Their dreams were shattered, but nothing could be done.

Moving our bars helps us push back against misguided expectations that cloud our judgment and leave us perpetually discontented. When we refocus our energies, we are better positioned for long-term sustainability. When we break out of always-on indoctrination, we can settle into spaces where we find our own versions of well done, not burnt.

A few centimeters can make or break us, too. Our vaults may be set with terrible imprecision by those in charge. You'd think we'd see through the smoke screens that prevent us from checking the vault. We're too busy replaying our own landings, blaming a shaky performance, not the setup.

Even with steadfast effort and laser focus, we can land flat on our backs when expectations are improperly gauged. Our brains, like bridges, are weight-bearing mechanisms. Like the Sydney gymnasts' knees, they can only handle so much force. We can't leave our fate in the hands of those who carelessly calibrate our expectations for us, without respecting human thresholds. We must first insist that our vaults are set up in a way that showcases our talent without putting us in harm's way. And like gymnasts who follow a careful regimen to prevent injury and keep their career going, we must do the same.

Rescue Your Brain from the Frying Pan

One of the most epic commercial taglines of the 1980s was "This is your brain on drugs"—complete with sizzling pan, two eggs fried to a crisp, and a big dose of fear. Maybe we need a version today that shows our brains as eggs on too little sleep and too much caffeine, and ravaged because of technostress, a fitting new term that illustrates how cooked our brains can become from information overload and constant screen sucking.

According to a *Lancet* 2012 Global Mental Health Report, the pressures of today are most intense between the ages of fifteen and forty-four, when we are trying to establish careers and families and set the foundations for our lives. This is what makes always-on work indoctrination so seductive. We need to earn our degrees, establish independence (if there is such a thing), put food on the table, navigate our relationships, and make our mark on the world.

Always-on work indoctrination within our Age of Anxiety leaves us fragmented, unsettled, and at risk for burnout. It starts early and lasts late into life. The World Health Organization reports that one out of five Americans experience mental health issues, and the National Center for Health Statistics says that 11 percent of us from ages twelve and up are on antidepressants. The Centers for Disease Control and Prevention affirmed in a 2012 study that one out of four US women are on medication for depression or anxiety. Suicide is the tenth leading cause of death in the United States; men are four times more likely to take their lives than women.

Before you check that one last email or wake up in the night sweating over your latest fire at work, remember that none of it is worth frying your brain. No one is going to stand up at your funeral and talk about how fast you got back to them or go on about how stacked your LinkedIn profile was. It's not how you will be remembered.

Look for Sustainability

For short periods of time we can withstand the frying pan, but occupying it indefinitely leads to burnout. Pivoting to sustainability means ending long-term habits of passing Go and collecting $200 until we exhaust ourselves. Instead, we need to end behaviors that leave us at risk.

Some companies are willing to help us. Pedometer programs, free counseling, and coaching sessions are sometimes available to help mitigate intense work conditions. Biogen Idec, a global leader in biotechnology, decided to implement a concierge services program, complete with errand running—as in searching for plumbers, securing pet sitting, and even having shoes repaired for employees. Taking the running around off employees' plates proved valuable, saving them each 12.5 hours per week, on average. As a result, the company saw increased productivity gains, and voluntary departures fell from 14 percent to 5 percent. *Sign me up!*

Unfortunately, few of us can relate to this rare privilege. Chances are you're more likely to say, "That's me!" to one or more of the other examples in this session: whether Warshaw's fast growth trajectory, my colleague Rachel's startling call-of-duty example, or Natalie's or Igor's takes that they should keep their heads down and mouths shut—and that the always-on conditions are inescapable.

Maybe you've had crashes like the Sydney 2000 gymnasts. or you know exactly how Rita felt after putting so many years in without even a crumb of cake to say thanks. Maybe you sense your motherboard is heading in the direction of becoming fried—or that *karoshi*, death by overwork, could happen to you or someone you love.

Sustainability isn't about hiding away or quitting jobs we care about. It's about pacing yourself at a reasonable level, not treating your brain like it's a machine. When duty calls, we can certainly answer, but sometimes we need to turn off our ringers. We need to make sure we are eating our soup—mindfully taking breaks and enjoying life.

Sustainability helps us imagineer our vault to the threshold that inspires soaring without crashing. It's about lifestyle medicine: engaging in activities that nourish through exercise, movement, and rest—ones that keep us from hanging out for extended periods in the frying pan, burning to a crisp. Pivoting toward sustainability means carving out space to invest in things that matter most to you, to help you stop thinking you have five weeks to create an entire masterpiece. None of us want to face seeing ourselves, or our work, buried.

Session Sixteen Worksheet:
Rethinking Work

Objective:
Unlearn always-on work indoctrination that breeds burnout.
Pivot toward building sustainability-focused thinking

Rethink It:
Move from Burnout to Sustainability

Work demands can erode the quality of our lives. We care to the point of destruction. When we don't stop and set boundaries, we can fall to the number-one occupational risk of today: burnout. Set a pace that is focused on longevity and sustainability.

Sustainability Check

- What's my version of an E.T. video game?
- How hot is the frying pan I'm stuck in?
- What do I say to myself during moments when I've experienced failure?
- Even without a concierge, are there steps I can take to make life simpler?
- Have I ever experienced burnout? How did I recover? Am I keeping up with my regiments?
- Of the following, which matter most to me? (Rank them from 1–7.)
  - Relationships
  - Faith/religion
  - Profession/career
  - Education
  - Recreation and leisure
  - Self-improvement/personal development
  - Finances/money

Double-check the rankings. Am I investing in areas that matter the most to me?

Action Steps:
Imagineer Your Work-Life Rhythm to Bring Impact

1. **Take time with your E.T. game.** When you're setting out to do extraordinary things, be sure to budget accordingly. Many times people ask us to operate as robots, forgetting we are human beings. When possible, budget extra time for deadlines, work on teams, delegate, and divide up work.

2. **Trade it in.** Missing sleep or neglecting basic functions like eating and exercising will hurt your health bottom line. Trade in your Get Out of Sleep cards for You've Just Won a Vacation Somewhere. It might cost you some time and money but doesn't have to be elaborate to give you a needed breather.

3. **Listen to your heart.** Know the line between caring and caring to the point of self-destruction. Remember the sage advice of the American Psychological Association, reminding us not to wait until our bodies tell us we're stressed to take care of them. If you are losing hair, sleep, appetite, or energy, take it as a cue to make some changes. We only have one heart and one motherboard—take care of them.

4. **Move through it.** Pick your favorite motivational song to start or end your workday. Keep humming, strumming, and dancing it through your day (even if only in your head). Don't be chained to the rhythm of burnout. Be sure to keep your brain and body tuned through a combo of lifestyle medicine, fun, and a sense of adventure. Nothing is worth getting sick over.

Reimagining School

Objective:
Unlearn good student indoctrination that breeds shame.
Pivot toward inclusive thinking.

*Education is the most powerful weapon, which
you can use to change the world.*

—Nelson Mandela

Jonathan Mooney was twelve years old when he finally learned to read. His journey, which he calls "tortuous," included dropping out of school in sixth grade—then reenrolling, only to be told by high school guidance counselors and teachers that he was destined to end up in jail—or if he was really lucky, flipping burgers.[1] But instead of putting on the orange jumpsuit, or the red polo with Five Guys embroidered on it *(those fries!),* he took a path no one would've guessed.

Against all the odds, and with the help of his mom and sister, Mooney rejected the expectations placed upon him, the ones he'd started to internalize after years of shaming and scolding. He even had his suicide planned

---

[1] Note: Original spelling has been polished up a bit, but the grammar is mostly untouched to keep the full feel and flavor intact.

out. He spent more time in the hallway, hanging out with janitors, than in the classroom. He was on a first-name basis with Shirley, the principal's secretary. He hid in the bathroom, tears streaming down his face, after being humiliated when forced to read aloud to the class.

Mooney was pegged as a screw-up through most of his school years. His behavior was textbook attention-deficit/hyperactivity disorder (ADHD), but until this came to light, he was treated like he didn't belong in school at all. No one would've predicted that the unruly kid squirming at his desk would become the man who would graduate from Brown University with honors in English literature, or go on to become a Truman Scholar. But that's just what he did.

He didn't stop there. Mooney coauthored *Learning Outside the Lines: Two Ivy League Students with Learning Disabilities and ADHD Give You the Tools for Academic Success and Educational Revolution.* Then he hit the road.

Mooney pooled his money and bought an old short school bus, the type used to transport kids to special education classes. He converted it to a makeshift RV, then drove 35,000 miles across forty-five US states in four months. Mooney interviewed people with so-called disabilities, exposing the myths of normalcy and "good student" indoctrination. His second book, *The Short Bus: A Journey Beyond Normal*, tells a very different story than what schools and societies sell: tales of human triumph and resilience, not deficits and disorders. This is imagineering at its finest.

The historic juxtaposition of school has been to clearly see and blatantly ignore the reality right in front of us. We stare students in the eye but somehow don't look at them at all. We tell them to just get back to work, to stop being unreasonable, to ignore their thirst and longings to be seen. They come to realize that this is asking too much, that no matter how much they comply, cry, beg, or act out, they will not be recognized—even in the very place that emphatically purports to do so.

Mooney now calls himself a "thirty-year-old punk," has his own nonprofit, and is one of the great champions of the disability rights movement. He doesn't tiptoe around or mince words. He tells his audiences that "normal people suck"; that human variance should be celebrated, not punished; and that there's no room for school shame and limited definitions of "good" or "smart." Students who think and live differently should not be labeled "those kids," then written off as destined to fail because they aren't like everyone else.

Jonathan Mooney makes it easy to want to jump on the bus with him, chanting "normal sucks." His story is familiar to most of us—whether we have faced screaming teachers and shameful moments because of academic performance, we couldn't sit still, or we weren't cookie-cutter versions of the standards held as acceptable. In the place where we were supposed to be given the chance to flourish, many of us felt like worthless misfits. This is a great tragedy, since we spend all our formative years being indoctrinated that we're not "good" if we don't land at the magical space on the bell curve.

Going on endless rants against schools and raging against the machine are easy. While such action can sometimes feel cathartic, it might not be as productive as we'd hope. Broadening our definitions of *normal* and *good* takes brave voices, like Mooney's, to help redefine *normal*. It takes collective action and community to reimagineer.

> "Education is one of the most beautiful and liberating things we can pursue in our lives, but too often it is approached as a restrictive, punitive, linear, and moralistic act."
>
> —Jonathan Mooney

Stop the Crash and Burn

When education is what it can be, it transforms lives. At its best, education embodies Horace Mann's description as "the great equalizer," spurring on imagination, creativity, and conscious citizenry. When this happens, it's pure gold, like Andrea Bocelli's voice. *Grazie.*

Schools can also traumatize, holding people in psychological prison and even becoming pipelines to physical prison. Schools mistake brilliant people like Jonathan Mooney for being abnormal. When this happens, it is nothing short of catastrophic. His own turn of events is rare. Too often "those kids" do end up in jail, underachieving, and even dead. *As Lost at*

School author Ross Greene put it, "The wasted human potential is tragic." School trauma, where "good" student indoctrination blasts the repeated message that you have to be one way or you're unworthy, leads to serious problems.

School Trauma

Academic Definition

School trauma is the experience and aftermath of having at least one and often a series of deeply distressing instances of powerlessness and shame perpetrated by teachers, administrators, or peers.

Street Definition

Those moments in school that left serious scars. You got put down by people who were supposed to care, leaving you feeling broken. #doomed #scarred4life

---

Students are not the only ones traumatized by the systems. We need to reimagine schools as places where students and teachers could trade in their "Get Me Out of Here" signs for ones that read, "I Matter." Let's make schools places where students can tear off the "lazy," "difficult," and "stupid" labels that were hastily affixed on them and replace with "creative," "insightful," and "rising leader" ones. It's the twenty-first century, right? We're ready for this.

We have a lot of signs and labels to swap out. The problems and opportunities are too big to go solo. Money needs to be put where mouths are. In theory, everyone *loves* schools, students, and teachers—*until* it's time to pay up.

Schools are busy trying to fix a plane while it's already in flight, as Harvard's Richard Elmore puts it. We can't keep blaming planes crashing on pilots, crew, and passengers and not the people in charge of ensuring there's enough money to pay for fuel and rules are in place to ensure mechanical equipment is functioning properly. We need an army of policymakers, politicians, and businesses side by side with teachers, students, and families—with everyone at the table, as if people's lives depend on it—because they do. Our whole future does. It's not just individual students getting left behind. It's entire communities, and droves of teachers and administrators, dropping like flies.

It's time to start treating teachers like the dignitaries they are.[2] We can't keep disparaging them and wonder why 50 percent of them leave because of burnout, most within the first three years on the job.

> **There has never been a group so simultaneously vilified and revered as teachers.**

And it's not purely stress symptoms causing the mass exodus. Many teachers find themselves in an ethical pickle once they've arrived on the scene to do a job, where they find their hands tied from carrying out the actions they know would make a difference.

As education leader Doris Santoro points out, burnout is pervasive, but there's something more going on. What we often mistake as burnout is actually a case of demoralization—low morale associated with a system filled with obstacles. After repeatedly hitting walls, teachers can't find the intrinsic moral rewards that brought them to teaching in the first place. They can't find that needle in the educational haystack.

Santoro's research reveals that we often misinterpret the reasons teachers leave as signs of weakness—that they are quitters who can't take the heat. Sometimes the opposite turns out to be true. Teachers can start to feel like they are joining the side of the Dark Army by staying. It's *Lord Voldermortish*; they morally cannot be death eaters. They leave because they can no longer justify participating in a system seeming to do more harm than good.

What's good for our students is good for our teachers and administrators, too. We can't keep using them as landing pads for our pointing fingers; instead we need to acknowledge the traumatic and complex circumstances they are trying their best to navigate. The crash and burn needs to stop. It starts with a whole new lineup of programming that makes sure that the planes are fueled and equipment is working to show we actually care about what happens to all the people on the planet.

---

2 Not drill sergeants wannabes. If you're acting like you hate students—screaming at them incessantly or being a hard ass just because you feel like it—*please* pick a different path. *Liking people is a prerequisite to working with them.*

Students are not commodities. They are not consumers or game show contestants, or empty buckets to be dumped into. They are not our pet projects, blank slates waiting for wisdom to be imparted. They arrive already creative, curious, barely able to sit still. Then we train them. We systematically suck every last drop of joy out, and then we called them "disengaged" and "unruly." This isn't just a classroom situation gone wrong, but a pervasive historic tide that has destroyed us for far too long—the kind of injustice that penetrates our collective consciousness and to which we must never resign ourselves.

Change the Channel

Teachers and students will remain on the side of losing if the current educational system stays as is. At present, it seems that a game-show type of programming prevails—the kind that puts the entire jackpot of human sustainability at risk, with only a few winners. We can't keep rolling the dice; change needs to happen. For starters, here are the shows that need to be taken off air permanently.

Who Wants to Be a Millionaire?

In this commodity mind-set, people and education are characterized as goods, cheapening their true value. Neither should be lumped as such, but *that's the M.O.* of the popular show that puts dollar signs in our eyes. The questions and answers are predictable:

Which of the following best characterizes $ucce$$

A. Money.
B. Getting in to your dream college so that you can make money.
C. Getting your dream job so that you can make money.
D. All of the above.

Even phone-a-friend lifelines won't help us escape the $ucce$$-is-spelled-with-dollar-signs indoctrination. It's waved in front of us across every step of our education: our value in society rests on how much bacon we bring home. It conditions us to think $ucce$$ can only be measured in six-figure increments, that the value of education is only in the type of job it lands you, not that it actually helps you think or become a better person.

One of the underlying problems within our hypercompetitive market is that education has moved away from a human development model to a business model. Institutions are groveling for dollars behind the scenes just as much as students are. Money muddies the educational waters. When we put such a huge price tag on learning, it gets in the way of basing decisions according to human flourishing —the *real good life* that can come out of education, the kind when everyone stops salivating over dollars and sees the greater rewards in positioning human beings to reach their fullest potential.

We need to stop promising money as the answer and instead tell students the truth: that no matter how much money they earn, they will spend what they make on stuff that won't last, and it still won't make them any happier. Money is usually *the factor* that holds people hostage in toxic relationships, breaks up families, and is all forked over to the nursing home anyway.

The economic realities of today are intense, and budgets have to reconcile to keep things afloat. But when we treat education as a commodity, the whole system shifts behaviorally; the intentions fundamentally change. We land in a space of measuring value according to dollars, not human progress.

Survivor

Schools should be the safest islands of all; instead there are countless castaways from education. The challenges given at every turn for students and teachers create unnecessary danger and shame. We need to stop voting them off the island after they've been starved—whether of basic needs, rights, and dignities, or of intellectual, social, emotional, and spiritual protein. Everyone deserves immunity from elimination. We can't celebrate the emergence of a sole survivor but need to create alliances among our tribes to move from thinking we have to outwit, outlast, and outplay each other, and instead turn attention on creating a new tribal council that wants everyone not just to survive, but to thrive.

We tell students that they matter, to relax, to enjoy the sweetness of their years—the "best" time of their lives. But the tacit expectations we place upon them speak louder. They are cheered on from an early age to perform; the more they do, the more rewards the system delivers. Sit them still, work them from morning to night, give them little prizes, keep them hungry for As and 100s. Remind them that if they want to be "successful," they need to start early, jumping through hoops propped out for them for as long as they can hold up—and then some. This mentality lasts well beyond childhood. It's not much different, and even worse later on, whether in college or on the job, when stakes and pressures reach an elevation that becomes compromising and disparaging. The elusive ceiling leaves us flailing and untethered, and then we come crashing down.

The Gong Show

We can't keep propping students, teachers, and administrators up on stage, expecting them to deliver a show of a lifetime, then after a few minutes whack the mallet and laugh in their faces. When we define talent in narrow and limiting ways, celebrating only a handful of acts, we diminish the rest. The constant audition is a huge distraction and waste of energy. Plus, the prizes for Best Student and Best Teacher of the Week pale in comparison to not having been pressured and humiliated onto the stage in the first place.

Wheel of Fortune

Some students spin the wheel and get lucky; others go bankrupt. Affluent schools and their privileged constituents are given all the vowels and consonants they need, while the wheels of poor schools are rigged to land on bankruptcy.

They become places where, as Jonathan Kozol, author of *Savage Inequalities: Children in America's Schools*, describes, we ask individuals, especially those most marginalized among us, to "break down doors that have been chained and bolted" in advance of their arrival. Resources cannot be left up to chance. The puzzle isn't as difficult to solve as we make it, but it requires the best of our collective will to stop the show that favors the few and leaves it up to chance for the many.

Family Feud

Schools and families need to be in partnership, not in a face-off against each other. We quickly judge each's motivations rather than engage in ways that help us understand. When we ignore family context, including assets and barriers—keys to effective dialogue—we miss the chance to get a fuller picture. We can't ask families to conform to so-called norms that are not inclusive and do not represent the full body of perspectives at hand.

American Gladiators

While the strength and agility that hard-core competition and team pride can foster are impressive, it can come at a cost. When we're so nationalistic we become centric, our tendency cranks up to want to dominate and bash anyone not on our team. It's exhilarating to have a sense of belonging, but it becomes dangerous when we put ourselves in a permanent position of defending territory rather than building alliances and seeing our shared humanity.

They arrive curious and willing global citizens, capable of speaking any language, loving any person, entertaining any possibility, wired and ready for endless connections. Then we insulate them, convince them to join one team, to only recognize one way as "right," and to brutalize anyone in the arena who doesn't think, worship, look, or love like them. Then we think violence is about music, video games, or other cultural artifacts. We don't recognize it as internalized and misdirected anger bred from indoctrination that strips us of our capacities to be open and directs us instead to defend turf and fight back at all costs.

Add a New Lineup

It's time to discontinue shows that put their participants in harm's way. We have the opportunity to promote inclusivity, where everyone—teachers and educators alike—gets the resources they need to truly thrive. When you cheapen students and their teachers to being like contestants on a game show, even though the game is rigged, viewer discretion won't be enough. The shows need to be cancelled, even if it's mid-season. Clearly, we need new shows to help us go beyond school trauma and shame. Here are some immediate replacements:

The Price Is Right

The value of education is priceless, but the price tag has become ridiculous. Spending belts need to be tightened in other areas to make room for the most important investment of all. We can't keep gypping students. Money needs to be poured in from policymakers and those who can to make sure students and their families who are struggling already don't fall further behind. The price needs to be right for teachers and educational professionals, too. They shouldn't be making peanuts for the prestigious work that they do. We need to take a cue from places like Finland to make sure better bids are available to all.

Double Dare

If you're going to put people on a human hamster wheel, at least make it worthwhile. We need to air the ultimate show that allows for messiness, embraces creativity, and encourages people to take some risks while having fun. We need the kind of show that throws a little slime around without being too toxic. The dares and challenges should allow for practice with stunts that will equip for the bigger obstacle course to come. When education doesn't leave room for play or offer experiences that connect with the real world, it's not doing its job. We need to allow opportunities to "dare greatly."

> **"Who at the best knows in the end the triumph of high achievement, and who at the worst, if he fails, at least fails while daring greatly, so that his place shall never be with those cold and timid souls who neither know victory nor defeat."**
>
> —*Teddy Roosevelt*

Name That Tune

When schools become deprived of the arts, everyone suffers. We need music, along with all forms of art in heaping doses, to replenish the heart and souls of our schools. Arts and aesthetics are just as important as mathematics. Music and science pair better than we'd first think. The arts should be integrated across everything we do to keep creativity and beauty alive and well. *On the other hand, school concerts featuring screeching*

recorders or talent shows with repeated renditions of Meghan Trainor and
Justin Bieber—someone needs to put an end to that kind of madness.

Are You Smarter Than a Kindergartener?

We need to start with basic manners of life and foundations of learning;
even fifth grade might be too ambitious. We can take a cue from Robert
Fulghum's 1990s bestseller *All I Really Need to Know I Learned in Kinder-*
garten. And not the new-school versions where kids discuss their college
ambitions at circle time. Rather, we should invoke the old-school kind of
kindergarten, complete with cookies and milk (gluten-free and soy are
fine when necessary), afternoon naps, and cleaning up our own messes.
We should live Fulghum's message in full force: share everything, play
fair, don't hit people, and say you're sorry. We draw, paint, sing, dance,
and work some each day, and hold hands and stick together, stay aware of
wonder, and remember that, like goldfish, hamsters, white mice, and seeds
in Styrofoam cups, we all die. We also need to remember the first word we
learn in Dick-and-Jane books—*look*—
and that basic sanitation, the Golden
Rule, love, equality, and sane living are
what we should strive toward every day.

> It is impossible for our hands to be simultaneously in the position of holding hands and pointing fingers. When we learn to face off against the roots of our problems and not each other, we begin to reclaim some of the magic of our unadulterated selves.

Amazing Race

Much of our education in life comes
outside the classroom. Interactions with
people and terrain first unfamiliar to us
are like gold. Travel to and communication with other lands not only serve as
great adventure but give us perspective that a textbook can't. We have
unprecedented opportunities to send students outside their bounds—to
explore, discover, and experience life through endless lenses. Sending
them on their own version of an amazing race allows them to use deductive
reasoning to figure out clues, navigate foreign territory, interact with people
across the globe, and perform various challenges that help them develop
into thriving, conscious, twenty-first-century global citizens.

* * * *

We are all affected by what happens in schools. Like Jonathan Mooney, many of us have endured trauma from the current education-is-a-game-show mind-set that prioritizes money and performance over people. We need to stop the crash and burn and instead find new inclusive programming that helps everyone's potential for limitless growth and impact. We cannot subscribe that only one type of student is "good," shaming and excluding the rest. We need to pivot toward inclusive thinking, where all students and educators know that they matter.

Session Seventeen Worksheet:
Reimagining School

Objective:
Unlearn good-student indoctrination that breeds shame.
Pivot toward inclusive thinking.

Rethink It:
Move from Trauma to Inclusivity

Schools can be places where we flourish or flounder. Each of us have unique experiences that have left their marks, for good or bad. Every experience teaches us something. It is important to reflect on what you have learned in order to know what you might need to unlearn about yourself. School trauma is hard to shed and can make us think we are defective, instead of realizing that normal sucks and "good student" is a form of indoctrination to be unlearned.

School Shame Check

- What kind of game show was my school experience like?
- What positive messages did I receive?
- What types of negative ones did I receive?
- Who are my positive role models and influencers?
- How can I move beyond any negative experiences to embrace a new learning mind-set and to do my part in making education better?

Action Steps:
Imagineer Inclusive Ways of Seeing

1. **Forget normal.** Most of us have quirks, and areas where we struggle or fall in the fringes of the bell curve. Instead of shame being a default, embrace your underdog identity—there's gumption that comes with it. People who have experienced shame are more likely to be empathic. Refuse to let myopic constructions corrupt the human spirit. Embrace difference, and work hard to mine for strengths.

2. **Go beyond the plane.** Education can be an amazing journey, but sometimes it causes crashes. If you were relegated to feeling you are bad or abnormal, understand that some mechanical problems need fixing. There are many pathways to learning outside the classroom. Adopt a forever-learner mind-set as discussed in session 7.

3. **Change the channel.** Human beings are not commodities. If you are caught in a situation when the game-show mind-set is prevailing, find ways to reframe what is being sold to you. Only participate in shows

where creativity reigns. It's okay to be messy and more fun when everyone is included.

4. **Stop, look, and listen.** Listen to "Another Brick in the Wall" by Pink Floyd. Watch *Waiting for Superman* or *Freedom Writers*. Good teaching and schools are worth their weight in gold. Reflect on what you've seen and heard. How can you take your frustrations and use them to become a more conscious global citizen who helps make education a better experience? Consider volunteering at a school, doing something nice for a student or teacher you love, or donating time or money to help support education. Contact your legislators and ask them to fight hard for our schools. Schools need all of us to help them reimagineer.

Maintaining Your Mentalligence

Objective:
Unlearn silo indoctrination that breeds darkness.
Pivot toward integration.

*The only way to make sense out of change
is to plunge into it, move with it,
and join the dance.*

—Alan Watts

When I first set out on my grounded research study with my graduate students, trying to understand what contributed to their identity and resilience, I had no idea that I was about to open Pandora's box, wrapped in dynamite. I've always had an aversion for me-search, work that is directed by personal interests, versus proper scholarly methods. At the beginning, I brought my game face, planning to stay safely within the intellectual lane. Then came the swerving.

It seemed innocent enough at the time. My student's stories had been inspiring me for years. I was so set on helping them find their way that my own need for detoxification was totally out of focus. Who knows how long I would've avoided it if it weren't for them, and Lyla, the wonder therapist. When I started to wake up and tune in, the spiral I was engulfed in gave me no choice but to face my own disintegration. The mound of data collected over five years buried me, but ended up leading to a full-fledged soul excavation.

Things were dark for a while.

When I first broke out of the church, I'd thought I'd found *the light.* I went all-or-nothing; education was my new form of being born again. It seemed like the place to be, with no Kool-Aid in sight at first. I bathed in the certainty of science and peer-reviewed methods.[1] No more of "God said it, that settles it." I clung to evidence like it was the cross. I wanted to bypass messiness; the last thing I wanted was to keep holding onto the fears I've always carried. I lived in my headspace, doing everything I could to avoid my emotional and spiritual sides and needs. I thought I'd cracked the code and set myself free. But then my students—and the universe— showed me something different.

The other side of the fence wasn't all roses. Even though there were a lot more lenses available, there were still strong whiffs of insularity. Insularity becomes the birthplace of hate. Instead of looking for ways to join hands, we point fingers. We don't see that, in many ways, we're after the same things, and we're under the same rule of forces beyond our comprehension. We're being asked to continue a fight that we didn't start in the first place. We can't stay stuck in junior high school behavior if we want to be adults who contribute as global citizens.

As I straddled the fence, I watched a lot of bickering go back and forth between religion and science, and conservatives and liberals. I saw the one thing we all have in common: FEAR. We spend all our energy defending territory, blind to what we could accomplish if we went beyond it. Fear is darkness. The resulting silos it breeds are dangerous. We need more light.

---

1 *Peer-reviewed* means that the research being published, typically in a journal, has undergone a process of examination by other scholars who affirm that it meets criteria for proper research methodology.

Know That Light Is Light

We can't shut each other out entirely and expect to overcome darkness. Light is light, even though we all see it through different lenses. It doesn't mean there aren't sharp contrasts across domains, but there's still room to shine brighter together.

The word on the street is different. You hear how dark the other is. All you hear about are the horrible things people do in the name of religion. There's little talk about how it influences people to do miraculously loving and extraordinary things. Many leaders of our time have pointed to their faith as informing good deeds like feeding the hungry, clothing the poor, and building hospitals, schools, and nonprofits.

Academics and scientists do magnificent things, too. Research has pioneered breakthroughs that touch every one of us to the betterment of humankind. Investigation sheds light on complicated problems and brings advances that make the impossible possible. People in academia and science teach us how to learn, live, and connect better. Without this type of knowledge, we would still be in the dark ages.

Evidence is critical, but our minds do not have the capacity to explain everything. There's room for mystery and discovery. We don't have to agree or even like each other, but we should recognize together that silos only breed darkness. Luckily, divisions between science and the spiritual are blurring. Intersections are being found. Faith is showing up on the evidence-based radar, nudging academics to recognize it as a protective factor in resilience. Quantum physics and string theories in science are showing that light is vibrating within each of us; that we're all connected by a universal energy that's always moving. Forces cause this connection that we don't fully comprehend.

Scientific and religious realms aren't the only silos. Plenty that's *unmeasurable* goes down outside the ivory tower also, worthy of recognition than it's given. While academia's process of determining credibility is solid, artists and musicians also undergo their own form of peer review, too. We often leave art, music, the visual and performing arts, and spirituality on the fringes, even though all are critical sources of light. They are forces that can break through deep divides, bringing people together and helping us make meaning of life. We need to listen to what Drake songs are telling us about our culture as much as we need to do a deep reading of stellar literature. It's not one or another. Both can teach us a lot.

In this kind of integration, we need to allow for lights from every side to emit as brightly as they can. When we fight, we're covering up sources that we desperately need. At a time when old and disintegrated institutions are collapsing, we need to take a good look at the rubble to understand what went wrong and how to repeat it from happening. We need light to help us rebuild new spaces that welcome everyone. When all voices are raised, we reach our highest collective light. We need artists, poets, spiritualists, academics, scientists, and religious folk to find spaces to dance together.

Fear, not each other, is our enemy. But we're too busy yelling to hear the whispers of our hearts that would tell us otherwise.

My own light had grown dim in the face of my own disintegration. When I took on my full-time role in academia, I swung from one clique to the next, so set on evidence that I thought I could operate from the neck up forever. But the universe has its own way of teaching us things. Without my consent or collusion, I was handed a stick of dynamite that I needed to handle with care.

Get Closer to Fine

It's 8:30 on a Tuesday morning, and I'm pulling my usual fumble through the underground garage at my office, where I'm always greeted by a pitch-perfect "Goood mooorning" from Randy, my favorite garage attendant. I echo back with the full enthusiasm he deserves for his consistency with cheerful greetings. It helps my mood. I'm a little tired after a weekend of presenting at a women's leadership conference where everyone was talking a good game about supporting each other, then pushing each other in the hallways, competing to sell books and services and one-up each other.

Once I swiped my badge, I planned to head straight upstairs, to my full day of meetings ahead. But then I heard, "I like your voice," which would generally be a creepy thing, especially in Boston where people tend to pride themselves on being stoic and even a little grumpy (except for Randy, who makes up for the rest of us). I'd never seen the voice-liker before, but he drew me in.

We locked eyes; his were beautifully blue against the backdrop of his dark skin—a rare Vanessa Williams combination that I'm a sucker for. His head tilted, and it started to feel like I was in a scene from Harry Potter. There was no *stranger danger*, though—I was at ease as he spoke like he was in a whole different dimension. It felt like I had known him for a thousand years, so the code he was talking in made sense.[2]

He told me that I had an important message to deliver, that I was going to help change the world and there would be a lot of work to do. He kept telling me the world needed healing, that what was ahead would require a lot from me, that I'd need help. He kept saying not to worry, that "people" were already looking out for me, that I wasn't alone. "You know what I'm saying, right?" he asked me over and over. I knew. It was like a chapter from *The Alchemist*, where I was learning about my personal legend. I thanked him and nodded, not out of politeness, but sincere appreciation. From a rational level, it was a bizarre encounter. I thought about what all the domains would have to say about this:

Science: You just experienced "confirmation bias"—believing evidence you'd already formed conclusions about. It was just brain pattern recognition, nothing more than a coincidence.

Church: God is speaking to you. He has a plan for your life and wants you to do His will.

New Age: The universe is watching out for you. Your vibration is strong. There's good energy today—the moon must be full. Maybe he's from a past life.

Psychiatry: Maybe the two of you are a little bit delusional. You might want to look into some Abilify or at least take a few days off. Don't repeat the story out loud.

Indigo Girls: There's more than one answer to these questions pointing me in a crooked line. And the less I seek my source for some definitive, the closer I am to fine.

---

2 At the end of the conversation, he told me to look up "Huna," a theory of metaphysics and shared consciousness founded by Max Freedom Long. No wonder it felt like he was reading my mind. His studying had clearly paid off.

As I rode up to my floor, I flashed back again to the conference a couple of days earlier, where I had a similar experience with Julia, an intuitive woman who happened to attend my presentation. When she hugged me after, it felt like the love of a million grandmothers—or to be more specific, my own late grandmothers, aunts, and childhood best friend, Margo. It was epically comforting and odd, prompting me to blurt out, "I love you," to her, which was totally out of behavioral bounds at a professional conference.[3] But I had never felt that much love in a hug before; something spoke to me at a soul level. Julia later told me that a lot of people she's been close with have died, and that she often had people come through her. She matter-of-factly told me that those I'd lost were trying to send some love my way. I was a little spooked, but mostly appreciative.

When I arrived at my desk, I was ready to shift from all things paranormal to answering emails and writing reports. I'd had my fill of bizarre for the week. Then, I noticed on my desk a small white Dixie cup filled with Andes mints and Kit Kats and a handwritten smiley face on it. My late Grandma Jennie, who lived to be 103, loaded me up with Andes whenever I visited. It was her signature hostess candy when she had her bridge group over. And Kit Kats were *the* very candy that my late Auntie Jackie and Auntie Terry[4] always pulled out of their kitchen drawers when we visited. Had these powerhouse women in my life, the ones whom I had felt with me the entire time I'd been soul detoxing, stopped in to leave a treat?

I'll leave it up for you to decide. I honestly don't think they sent an express care package from the cosmos. It was probably one of my nice colleagues spreading a little springtime cheer. I can't make full sense of the interaction, but I do find myself getting goose bumps every time I relive it. It doesn't make complete sense, but for once, instead of having to settle what was precisely "right," I knew I had to keep an open heart and mind. The words of my favorite Indigo Girls song were nudging me to stop looking for definitive and get closer to fine.

---

3 Usually, you're lucky to get a stiff handshake and a half smile, especially on the East Coast. The most excitement is coming home with a handful of business cards and a free coffee mug.

4 My two aunts were awesome, badass, no-frills lesbians of the 1980s who didn't take any BS from anybody but would give you the shirts off their backs.

My openness allowed me to set aside my bitterness about brownie points and let the light pour back in. When I first was handed the dynamite at the beginning of this whole brain and soul expedition, I faced hard choices. At first, it felt like I was going to blow everything up and start over, but then I realized I might destroy myself and others in the process. The stick was too dangerous to bury. The flame was white hot, and I couldn't simply hand it off. I had to figure out what to do with it. I decided to chuck it at the places that perpetuate indoctrination, being careful not to hurt the people who were held hostage by it just as much as I'd been.

My new pilgrimage helped me handle the dynamite as best I could and start integrating. I realized that the Beatitudes and lessons about being "salt and light" were the foundations that later became the intentions I set on my yoga mat. The command to love my neighbor was the premise of my entire professional code. They were the same essence, described in different terms. I listened to Alanis, danced to Tracy Chapman, and put crystals in my pocket. I reread Danielle LaPorte, Paulo Coelho, and Marianne Williamson. I walked labyrinths, visited wise healers, and read psalms. I studied spirals and wrote poems. I got out of my head and into my heart. I traveled to Santa Fe and lit candles for my loved ones, and went to Colorado and cried on top of the Rocky Mountains. I wasn't on science sabbatical by any stretch. I still went to work, read Kahneman and peer-reviewed studies, and taught rational and critical thinking skills to students.

I was cracked wide open but started feeling whole again.

It helped me remember all the times that love enveloped me in my home and at church. My parents especially modeled kindness—their old hippie ways that prompted them to convert were a big part of their nonjudgmental spirit. I used to listen in on all my mama's calls. She was the go-to person for our entire church community. When someone was struggling, the phone rang. I never got any juicy details on what exactly people were dealing with, but I knew it was serious. Mama did a lot more listening than talking. She was a safe, powerful healing light—and I doubt at the time she knew I was watching so intently or that I would go on to choose a professional path that so closely mirrored what she was doing with no recognition, compensation, or late-night Twitter shout-outs.

Even though light and darkness coexist, there's light to be found when we look for it. Signs are everywhere. We can find light in the sound of a voice, a piece of old-fashioned candy, a loving embrace, and a two-hour phone call. We can find it in science's particle theories and hallelujah songs and mystics working to raise the vibration. We can find it in concerts and art museums and on the back of motorcycles. We don't have to have precision about its best forms and sources, sometimes it arrives in unexpected places, getting us a little closer to fine.

We all say we want the truth to be told, but then hide from it when it presents. The truth is that everything is chaotic and complicated, that we can speak from both sides of our mouths and be telling the truth, that life is one giant contradiction. When we get more comfortable with discomfort, we make way for integration to happen.

Spiral On

When my students first started to talk about their transitions from darkness and disintegration to upward spirals, I was impressed by their insightfulness and their agility. Time after time, they revealed that their capacity to work their way upward relied on unlearning and pivoting. This was the inception of the UP acronym.

My students have given us a lot of gems. The key finding in my research was that fusion is the gateway to *collective efficacy*: the idea that we do well when we all do well. There's no time to waste bickering about who's the boss. We need to find spaces where we can all dance. Cliques, silos, and the ignorance they breed bring us all down.

You can dance in these ways, too. If becoming more agile has become your new mission, then you've realized the kind of rethinking it takes. It's a tall order, one that relies on the best of your curiosity and sense of adventure. You know that BS societal rules only bring us down:

- Storms automatically equal ruin.
- Normal is real.
- Authoritarian control is optimal. Nice finishes last.
- There's one set life formula: Science + art + culture + spiritual don't mix well.
- Success and failure are separate entities.

- Everywhere you go, you need to show up as the airbrushed you, filters in full force.
- If you just jump through this one more hoop, you can rest. Numbing out is the only relief. Mindlessness is inevitable.
- All you need are your bootstraps, a stiff upper lip, and your Suck It Up T-shirt.
- Chaos automatically equals a downward spiral.

You now realize that plot twists can be fun. Moreover, binary categories never capture our true essence, there are multiple contingencies, staying woke to human multidimensionality is lifeblood, and global citizenry is *amazing*. There's a way to disrupt myopic constructions, get unstuck, and spiral up.

You've become a master rethinker, pockets filled to the brim with a massive collection of lenses that help you see beyond and expose the insidious blind spots our human fam faces. You're more curious than George and nimbler than Jack. You fuse science, art, culture, and spiritual forces. You have *way* more questions than answers. You're not afraid to breathe in impermanence. You approach attachment with caution. You embrace the spectrum of energy swirling about, always on the lookout for new possibilities. You're obsessed with novelty and variety. You're always thirsty for more.

Your behavior will continue to take form, and you reflect the kind of creative vibrancy that's gone AWOL in society. People notice you're not basic meat and potatoes. You're a new kind of conscious badass. You're a little quirky, but endearing nonetheless. You quit hustling for acceptance. Stop handing your soul over. Reject the matrix of the past. Tell conformity to eff off once and for all. Harness chaotic energy for good.

And the best part: it's not about you or just for you. It's for everyone's sake. Work, school, and relationships take on a whole new meaning. Everything changes. Your essence will shine, and you'll pivot like never before, flipping chaos on its head—the only way to see beyond, redefine success, remain skeptimistic, and create a conscious DIT (do-it-together) life. You now have your own signature spiral—chaos and all—to integrate. You're ready to do your thing and dance your way to the good life.

Session Eighteen Worksheet:
Maintaining Your Mentalligence

Objective:
Unlearn silo indoctrination that breeds darkness.
Pivot toward integration.

Rethink It:
Move from Silo to Integration

Everything is cult when we stay in silos. Opening our hearts and minds to varied perspectives can help us harness energy and move in a positive and productive direction. We can find and use our imagineering lens to shine our lights bright, to their highest potential, inching a little closer to fine.

Mentalligence Check

- Am I committed to becoming more agile, conscious, and connected as a global thinker?
- Am I showing up as an airbrushed version of myself, instead of being real?
- Do I feel undo pressure to choose a side of myself and stick to it?
- What aspects of myself do I need to integrate?
- How will I keep moving my spiral in an upward direction?

Action Steps: Use Your Resources to
Maintain your Mentalligence

1. **Review your mentalligence journey.** Revisit your quiz results, notes, and anything else that documents your progress along the way. How has the process changed you? What will your next moves be?

2. **Form dynamic circles.** Reach out and find fellow conscious global citizens to connect with. Engage a wide variety of people and learn together in community.

3. **Do some kidulting.** Don't be all kid or all adult—integrate them both. Approach life with the wonder of a child, allowing curiosity and creativity to reign with the maturity and depth of an adult who wants to take responsibility to make positive contributions to our world.

4. **Vibrate on high.** Let your light source guide you and allow you to vibrate with love and positive energy. Even when life drags you down, or people go low, go high. Positivity is contagious.

5. **Live and let live with love.** Let curiosity, not judgment reign. Don't try to police everyone else. Instead, work to understand how indoctrination traps all of us and set a positive and productive example.

Draw upon your own code of ethics to work toward a do-it-together good life.

6. **Dance with all your heart and mind.** It happens now. Claim your birthright to dance freely. Don't abandon head for heart or heart for head. Look for wholeness, not happy-talk superficiality. Stay agile, and keep spiraling UP.

Everything is CULT.
We say OUR vows and ritualize
everything as a means of SAFETY and
SECURITY, albeit a FALSE sense.
We're on a perpetual pilgrimage to
SATISFY our SOULS, to find some
inspiration that DOESN'T exist
in the places we're searching.
We hunt for something that will
SET US FREE, and when we think we've
found the HOLY grail—immortality;
happiness; easy, healthy, fun; or so-called
success—we become OBSESSED,
which ironically makes us more bound
than ever. Maybe happiness
INSTEAD comes from our imperfections,
from brokenness, from not knowing.
Maybe DEPROGRAMMING comes
through this kind of disruptive process—
the one that bids us to ENTERTAIN
ambiguity. The process prompts us to get
MESSY as we cobble together new
framings that are CONTRADICTORY
and IMPRECISE, but HONEST
and VALIANT.

SPIRAL PLAYLIST

The sacred musicians who have been on my playlist loop while I wrote, and through many years of spiraling:

Alicia Keys

Andrea Bocelli

Beyoncé

Chris Cornell

Drake

Eddie Vedder / Pearl Jam

Enya

Florence and the Machine

Glen Phillips / Toad the Wet Sprocket

Indigo Girls

Joan Baez

John Denver

Katy Perry

Lady Gaga

R.E.M.

Tracy Chapman

DISCLAIMER

There are contradictions in this book. Even having poured over the literature, there will be contradictions. By the time the book has gone to print, there will be new knowledge that expands on my present understanding. I'm not Noam Chomsky, but one thing that he did, besides writing hundreds of books and articles, was admit when his original thinking was misguided. He revoked an entire theory, in fact. You will find inconsistencies within the pages, and while that sometimes frightens me, it also excites me. I'm an early career researcher, and this is the biggest study I've taken on to date—the mother methodology—known as *grounded theory*. It's ambitious (and a bit nuts) to try coming up with a theory of mind, and then having it cross over to one of soul, too. It's been a tall order, but the emergence of collective efficacy has been an epic process to behold.

If you are a skeptic like I hope you will be, you will find things in here with which you vehemently disagree. Don't hide your dismay. Stand up and offer your versions, your truths, your breakthroughs, your unique ways of integrating. We are about building a true community of mentalligent travelers—those who are all about the pivot, who not only enjoy listening to opposing viewpoints but are always prepared to eat some serious humble pie. Bon appétit!

MANIFESTO OF THE MENTALLIGENT

There is no greater gift we can give to ourselves and
one another than to open our minds to rethink and unlearn
what we've been sold And instead see beyond.

We may be weary, but we're awake.
Our eyes are open; we refuse to stumble around the dark.
We seek the light, even when it exposes us,
searing away all we've known.
We reject oversimplified explanations of complexity.
We consciously choose awareness
over blind comfort and compliance.
Our Reflective Lens helps us see in new ways.
We think sleepwalking through life is a waste.

We are not held hostage by the beckoning call
of our phones, bosses, partners, parents, or children.
We relish presence, not frenetic mode.
We don't let ideals of *perfect* sabotage *good enough*.
We don't confuse *doing* with *being*.
We know lamenting about the past and ruminating
about the future are traps of the mind.
Even in the midst of chaos, we breathe in impermanence, using our
mindful lens to stay focused and accepting.
We think jumping through all the hoops set out for us is dangerous.

We see beyond our narrow selves, seeking
ways to be global contributors.
We know *self-efficacy* is good, *collective efficacy* is better.
We don't need prescriptive or patriarchal
formulas to govern our lives.
We refuse to politely comply with indoctrination
that squashes our truths,
or limits the lifeblood of human growth and
potential at any time or place.
We are unbound, wielding our universal lens
to break free from centric,
and open up to shared possibilities.
We think ignorance sucks.

We don't need to constantly fix ourselves.
We're already magical in raw form.
We need honest voices, collaboration, global spaces.
Where science + art + culture + spiritual epically fuse—
Instead of bickering about who's the boss. . . .
Places where we can let our hair down, check pretenses at the door, be
as real as humanly possible, roll sleeves up,
strip down, and rebuild.
Where chronological, linear, and fixed give way
to fluidity and curiosity.
Where *the way we've always done things* vanishes,
giving rise to new horizons.
We are agile thinkers, using our imagineering lens
to overturn stagnation and go beyond.
We think basic is boring.

We're okay with getting a little roughed up.
Messy and raw give us needed experience.
Our wrinkles, bruises, and bumps show off our grit.
We breathe impermanence. Suffering and joy are life's air—
We take turns inhaling and exhaling them both.

We don't insulate ourselves, or those we love, in bubble wrap—
Instead, we lean in to the possible lessons of each moment.
We walk barefoot and brave—
Our feet anchor earth, but our souls cannot be tethered.
We think falling down hurts, but we don't hermit
away from life because of it.

Waking up *is our strength.*
Tuning in *is our way back to center.*
Breaking free *is our birthright.*
Going beyond *is our dance.*

We think *outside the box, and within the*
endless twists of our life spiral.
We're not airbrushed, contrived, or scripted.
We are messy, raw ruminators, rebels, renegades, skeptics,
underdogs, misfits, and recovering try-too-hards who
make learning self-compassion a daily lesson.

We're made of steel and stardust; salt and bone
(not sugar, spice, everything nice, snakes, snails, or
puppy dog tails—or any broad-brush imposition recipes
for thinking or behaving).

We think we owe it to ourselves, and one another,
to embrace multiple lenses
and move beyond myopic constructions
that corrupt the human spirit.
We link arms in solidarity, looking for gateways to
finding the good life together.

We're not strong or certain every second.
Sometimes we're scared and wobbly—
But we're always *moving*, always *agile*, always *mentalligent.*

ACKNOWLEDGMENTS

I am writing this in the spirit of embracing chaos—because no matter how hard you try, you will somehow leave someone out and regret it for years, or at least until the next reprint. So, *sorry and thank you* to everyone.

Modeling agility requires some dismantling of behavioral patterns—the kind that compel me to want to write an entire book of acknowledgments, praising and touting everyone, including my mail person for all they have delivered to me. I'll start with that—it's all true. There have been epic deliverers at every turn. But if I rant too long, it will diminish those of you I held on to the tightest and longest during all my storms. Still, thank you, universe and all its inhabitants. Even you, Coconut the dog. Seriously. If I know you, you have touched me—whether you are Randy the doorman greeting me on my way in the office, Jim who makes my favorite kale juice, or you're right up there on my iPhone Favorites with your own special ring tone, *I love you.* We are all connected. For real.

Since I'm trying to apply the wisdom of four years of therapy with my trusted Lyla, who helped me recognize my shame-fueled tendency to default into perfectionism mode, I am remembering *my therapeutic homework right now.* That even if I hurt someone's feelings, reparations can be made, and I don't need to make a lifelong penance for it. It's not gonna kill any of us. Whew. Thank you, Lyla. Your clinical magic is working. #recoveringperfectionist #codependencywasmydrug.

Thank you, teachers and students who are teachers.

Noam Chomsky, I admit to stalking you. You say not to search for heroes, but you are one of mine. Sorry not sorry.

Deborah Hermann, Nancy Biren Castino, and Gina Despres: The three of you are my teenage idols. Writing teachers are goddesses; you are that to me.

Even though my math anxiety still lives on, Bill Hebert came closest to setting me free. Thank you to you and Kris for introducing me to theatre, basketball and New York city.

Vance, the universe could not have delivered you at a more perfect time. You are a force of nature. Your capacity to navigate research and conviction for the work impresses me.

My graduate students who survived my Personal Branding class who were willing to get real and deconstruct authenticity with me. We all feel wobbly, but are stronger together as we've emerged out of hiding. Thank you for teaching me the lessons of integration in such compelling ways.

My undergraduate and doctoral students, even Where's-the-Professor Guy, who showed me that at every level we continue to rumble with school shame, but that it doesn't have to win.

So many of you lit up my life from day one, and continue to do so: Wonman, MJ, Nicolette, Shelby, Brittany, John, Andrea, Tom, Katy, Danielle, Stephen, April, and Curtis—you are luminaries.

To Scout Design Studio at Northeastern—Alexa, Christina, Jena, Joe, Kevin, Molly, Brennan, and Nick for your extraordinary partnership.

To the Dream Team—Joy, Thor, Kim, Rebecca, and Abbé. Each of you have been my eyes, hands, and legs. Your mission minds will continue to take you far, and I believe in your infinite potential. I cherish every conversation and minute spent with each of you. We have accomplished everything we set out to, yet we've only just begun.

Thank you, dear colleagues and dynamic circles.

To those who have bravely come to see me for therapy. I hold your stories with me in my heart, ee cummings style. You are beautiful Inkblots to behold. Thank you for your trust and gumption.

Linda Elder, for your steadfast work to spread critical thinking. When you shared your art of Richard with me, I was at a loss for words, and still am. You epitomize intellectual agility and humility.

Susan David, for being such a champion of agility. You mesmerize.

Amy Morin, whose extraordinary strength has inspired the world.

Robert Brooks, for staying on the phone longer with me than you had time for, and modeling the virtues I aspire to.

Allen Frances, for covering more ground with me in fifteen minutes than most can in that many years. Your rebellion sparked one in me.

Douglas Bernstein, Doris, and the incredible folks at NITOP and VIC-TOP, including Steve. I've never squeezed onto such a small balcony with so many kindred souls. Best fireworks ever.

My incredible colleagues at Northeastern. This is where I could get carried away and ramble on for ten pages. *All* of you mean something distinct and special to me: Jane, Sara, Carol, Tova, Chris, Gail, Joe M., Joe V., Michael, Camelia, Ellen, Julie, Ian, Francesca, Stephanie, Patty, Carl, Earlene, Francesca, Siu Ming, Fred, Lynda, Ian, Liz, Astrid, Kemi, Mike, Art, Tammy, Leah, Neenah, Kathy, Kristen, Nick, Laura, Chuck, Jacob, Lisa, Catherine, Teresa, Amy, Georgia, Carolyn, Janice, Peter, John, Emily, and Peggy—you've all managed to trigger my appreciation button repeatedly. Your thought partnership and friendship mean everything.

To my friends at TedX Ocala for helping me tell this complicated story, and Taipei American School, especially Dan Long, Catriona Moran and the wellness committee—you are all the ultimate conscious global citizens.

Tara, Christina, Camilla, Tom, and the entire Worcester State University community. Thanks for not kicking me out then and for embracing me so wholeheartedly now.

My friends at NAMI—the Chicken Car crew—Patrick, Alex, and Nate; Fred Frese, Rudy Caseres, Howard Trachtman, and the gorgeous gritty souls at GBCAN—I feel safer and more at home with you than I do most.

Mentalligent people I haven't met but want to be like when I grow up: Jane Elliot, Jonathan Mooney, Lynne Twist, Elizabeth Gilbert, Rob Bell, Donald Miller, Anne Lamott, Glennon Doyle, Brené Brown, Mary Williamson, Danielle LaPorte, and Oprah Winfrey.

Scott T, for the reminders of the trade-offs for evil, and for seeing me before I could see myself.

Julia, for hugging me like the grandmother incarnate you are.

Sisters of Perpetual Indulgence and my LGBTQ friends, especially Sister X, who saw my sadness and intervened.

Agapi, you've helped unbind my heart with your enormous heart and helped me look for synchronicity everywhere. Your happy dances fill me up.

Gary, you filled in missing pieces to my puzzle and gave me a map worth using—one without judgment or prescription, and by and for which I am awestruck and grateful.

Allison Janse, Kim Weiss, Bob Land, Lawna Oldfield, and the entire team at HCI, for your excellent thought partnership and commitment to promoting healthy living. Marilyn, for not running away when I told you I was going to be next, and for being the stellar global thinker you are. For surviving my Elaine Benes–style work-it proposals and pushing me where you knew I needed to go.

Thank you, family of origin, and of divine intervention.

To Red, Michele, Mel, Laura, Jess, and my long-last Chap-Aid. You've given me some of the best memories of my life.

Karenporter, thank you for always mashing up my name, and for being real enough to make every human and animal in your presence 100 percent at ease. I miss your face.

Evangeline, our Boston walk talks and your hospitality have meant everything. You are that character in my novel who always manages to dance. We will return to Santa Fe.

Cameron, for teaching me what it means to be a Holder of the Frequency, and about unconditional human regard, metaphysics, and still water.

Ana, Eduardo, Liz, Joe, Odete, Gilbert, Uncle John, Uncle Joe, Nellie, Nathan, Elaine, and the hundreds of aunts, uncles, cousins, friends of bakers, hairdressers and factory owners who have adopted me even though I'm neither Portuguese nor Catholic. Beijinhos to all.

Lenny, Amanda, Kate, Elle, Jane, Nancy, Stacy, Matt, Hayden, and Harrison, spaghetti and Camp Costa are always on.

Karyne, Becky, Shelly, my three Lisa's, Jerry, Jacqueline, Beth, Naz, Jean, Ken B, Pam, Ken, Michael, and Adam, for your new and enduring friendships. Even when I am in my writer's cave or melancholic hiatus, you are with me the whole time.

Paul, your timing is impeccable—chartering a trip around the world at the precise time I endeavored to undertake this kind of project. Thanks for taking me along on the train and for your stellar insights and solidarity from our MH days.

Elizabeth—Thank you for *everything*, especially helping me reclaim inner Alanis. You've kept me from letting my brain swallow me whole more than once. I always know it's you when the phone chirps five times in three seconds. It's your turn.

Carol, the mother mentor, you are a model of mindfulness and intellectual humility. Plus, you are more fun to hang out with than teenagers on Red Bull. Thank you for yanking me out of my room and reminding me to breathe instead of working until my eyes start seeing white dots. You make me smile every time.

Karen, we haven't had any fun yet. Your ability to laugh and love keeps me going.

Kathy, the queen of generosity. You have more stories than Forrest Gump but manage to keep your poker face. You're the testament of human resilience. How you were able to hang through my chaos may be one of your most epic feats to date. You have breathed so much air into mentalligence, all while embodying it.

Heidi—You were the first I wrote to, and one who has put up with my spiral antics the longest. Don't lose your Question Authority button. Thanks for the interpretative dances.

Ken, for answering a high percentage of my texts and for traveling this journey with me in your own unique way. I've always seen you, and that your brilliant art is only one small representation of your fabric.

Harry, Maura, Dana, Barbara, K, and Warren, and my huge squad of nieces and nephews. Thanksgivings can be uncomfortable sometimes, but

I love you all. We've all got more unlearning to do; at least we've had some fun along the way.

To Mama and Papa, you are *the foundation* for my values, longings, and *deep love* for my neighbor. That's the love I have for you, too, my bears. 143 forever.

Ryan, I know it's redundant—you've heard me say it a thousand times and then some—but thank you for inspiring *every page*. This book is your book. I believe in your song.

Tori, I marvel at your tenacity and depth. You are a Boss. Always have, always will. And never a lunk. I miss you, yet you're with me every second. There's no one like you. Costa gang sign to you.

Scott, your gorgeous soul makes me smile. Thank you for being brave and real, and for spiraling with me for so long. You are a giant sparkler in my life.

To the ones I continue to offer much grief and praise for: Grandpa Fran, Margo, Grandma J, Nana Lee, Grandpa Lee, Grandpa Al, Maria, John, Auntie Jackie, Auntie Terry, Anna, and Lucy. Thank you for staying with me the whole time and for sending those Andes mints and Kit Kats to spook and stoke me, and for keeping watch during all those event–full moon fests.

Thank you, Divine Universe.

For all the spirals that have been and yet to come. I've traveled so far; the circles are endless.

NOTES

Stuck

ix *Virginia Wolf quote:* Wolf (2015). *A Room of One's Own* reprint edition. Hackney: Albatross Publishers.

The Waking Up Sessions

2 *Agility definition:* Dictionary.com, http://www.dictionary.com/browse/agility.

2 *Indoctrination definition:* Dictionary.com, http://www.dictionary.com/browse/indoctrinate.

Session One—The Physics of Mentalligence

3 *The quality of your life depends on:* Elder, L., Paul, R. (2013). *30 Days to Better Thinking and Better Living Through Critical Thinking.* New Jersey: Pearson.

4 *narrow prescriptions of success:* Nash, L., Stevenson, H. (2004, February). Success That Lasts. *Harvard Business Review,* https://hbr .org/2004/02/success-that-lasts. See also Effing, M. (2009). The Origin and Development of Self-help Literature in the United States: The Concept of Success and Happiness, an Overview. *Atlantis,* 31(2), 125–141.

4 *We expend a lot of time and energy covering up:* Uncovering Talent A new Model of Inclusion, Deloitte University Leadership Center for Inclusion, https://www2.deloitte.com/content/dam/Deloitte/us/Documents/about-deloitte/us-inclusion-uncovering-talent-paper.pdf. See also Savitsky, K., Epley, N., & Gilovich, T. (2001). Do others judge us as harshly as we think? Overestimating the impact of our failures, shortcomings, and mishaps. *Journal of Personality and Social Psychology,* 81 (1), 44–56.

4 *We put it all out there:* Bazarova, N., Choi, Y. (2014). Self-Disclosure in Social Media: Extending the Functional Approach to Disclosure Motivations and Characteristics on Social Network Sites. *Journal of Communication,* Cornell University, Ithaca, NY. See also Varnali, K., & Toker, A. (2015). Self-Disclosure on Social Networking Sites. *Social Behavior and Personality,* 43(1), 1–13.

4 *It's a popular buzzword:* Our Biases Undermine Our Colleagues' Attempts to Be Authentic. Opie, T., Freeman, E. (2017). *Harvard Business Review,* https://hbr.org/2017/07/our-biases-undermine-our-colleagues-attempts-to-be-authentic. Also see Mumford & Sons and the Worst Marketing Buzzword of 2013, https://www.inc.com/adam-vaccaro/thats-just-about-enough-talk-about-authenticity.html.

4 *Who we think we're supposed to be:* Sheldon, K. M., Ryan, R. M., Rawsthorne, L. J., & Ilardi, B. (1997). Trait self and true self: Cross-role variation in the Big-Five personality traits and its relations with psychological authenticity and subjective well-being. *Journal of Personality and Social Psychology,* 73(6), 1380–1393.

5 *Hans Christian Andersen tale:* Andersen, H. C., Burton, V. L., & Houghton Mifflin Company. (1949). *The Emperor's New Clothes.* Boston: Houghton Mifflin Co.

6 Emotional intelligence, *coined by Daniel Goleman:* Goleman, D. (1995). *Emotional Intelligence: Why it Can Matter More Than IQ.* New Your: Bantam Books.

6 *Forever learner (benefits):* Laal, M. (2012). Benefits of Lifelong Learning. Procedia–*Social and Behavioral Sciences,* 46, 4268–4272. See also Coleman, J. (2017). Lifelong Learning Is Good for Your Health, Your Wallet, and Your Social Life. *Harvard Business Review,* https://hbr.org/2017/02/lifelong-learning-is-good-for-your-health-your-wallet-and-your-social-life.

7 *Agility is what really matters:* David, S. (2016). *Emotional Agility: Get Unstuck, Embrace Change, and Thrive in Work and Life.* New York: Avery.

7 *Change as life's only constant:* Heath, C. Heath D. (2010). *Switch: How to Change Things When Change Is Hard.* New York: Random House. See also Burke, W. (2011). *Organizational Change, Theory and Practice.* Thousand Oaks: Sage Publications.

7 *Ethics of reciprocity:* New World Encyclopedia. http://www.newworldencyclopedia.org/entry/Golden_Rule.

7 *Impact-driven living:* Steger, M. F. (2009). Meaning in life. In S. J. Lopez (Ed.), Oxford *handbook* of positive psychology (2nd ed., pp. 679–687). Oxford, UK: Oxford University Press. See also Ryff, C.D. (1989). Happiness is everything, or is it? Exploration on the meaning of psychological well-being. *Journal of Personality and Social Psychology,* 57, 1069–1081.

8 *Fall prey to* imposter syndrome: Corkindale, G. (2008) Overcoming Imposter Syndrome. *Harvard Business Review*, https://hbr.org/2008/05/overcoming-imposter-syndrome.

8 *Perfectionistic thoughts . . . are the birthplace of self-loathing:* Brown G. P., Beck A. T. (2002). Dysfunctional attitudes, perfectionism, and models of vulnerability to depression. In Flett G. L., Hewitt P. L. (Eds.), *Perfectionism: Theory, research, and treatment* (pp. 231–251). Washington, DC: American Psychological Association.

8 *Self-compassion needs to be a daily practice:* Neff, K. (2012) *The science of self-compassion.* In: Germer C, Siegel R (eds) *Compassion and Wisdom in Psychotherapy.* New York: Guilford Press, pp. 79–92.

8 *Integrated view of ourselves based on mindful presence, not a performance:* Evans, Baer, & Segerstrom. (2009). The effects of mindfulness and self-consciousness on persistence. *Personality and Individual Differences,* 47(4), 379–382.

8 *When we avoid succumbing to blind spots that impede our ability:* Banaji, M., Greenwald, A. (2013). *Blindspot: Hidden Biases of Good People.* New York: Bantam Books.

8 *Centric beliefs and behavior hinder progress:* Elder, L., Paul, R. (2013). *30 Days to Better Thinking and Better Living Through Critical Thinking.* New Jersey: Pearson.

9 *We build meta-awareness, the capacity to think about thinking:* Flavell, J.H. (1979). Metacognition and Cognitive Monitoring: A New Area of Cognitive-Developmental Inquiry. *American Psychologist.* Vol. 34, No. 10, 906–911.

Session Two—Changing Directions

13 *The way you live your days:* Dillard, A. (1989). *The Writing Life.* New York: Harper Collins.

15 *The drill-and-kill academic treadmill:* Long, C. (2013). 'Drill and Kill' Testing Scrutinized at 2013 Education Nation Summit. National Education Association, http://neatoday.org/2013/10/07/drill-and-kill-testing-scrutinized-at-2013-education-nation-summit-2/.

16 *Learning can help us become conscious citizens:* Gardner, H. (2006). Five Minds for the Future. Boston: Harvard Business School Publishing. See also Smith, H. (2010). Future Minds: Interview with Harvard Professor Howard Gardner. Super Consciousness: The Voice for Human Potential: http://superconsciousness.com/topics/society/future-minds-interview-harvard-professor-howard-gardner. See also Gardner, H. (2015). Beyond Wit and Grit: Rethinking the Keys to Success. TedX Talk, https://www.youtube.com/watch?v=lfzrN2yMBaQ.

17 *Positive psychology is the scientific study of what makes life worth living:* Seligman, M. E. P., Steen, T. A., Park, N., & Peterson C. (2005). Positive psychology in progress. Empirical validation of interventions. *American Psychologist,* 60, 410–421. See also Friedman, H.S., Kern, M.L., Hampson, S.E., & Duckworth, A.L. (2014). A New Lifespan Approach to Conscientiousness and Health: Combining the pieces of the causal puzzle. *Developmental Psychology,* 50(5), 1377–1389.

17 *Psychological science and practice call us to rethink our typical ways of framing life:* Peterson, C. (2013). *Pursuing the Good Life: 101 Reflections on Positive Psychology.* New York: Oxford University Press.

18 *"Eudaimonia" or "human flourishing" can be fostered:* Seligman, M. (2011). *Flourish: A Visionary Understanding of Happiness.* New York: Simon and Schuster.

18 *Scholars like Paul Woodruff and Luc Ferry call the good life:* Schuler, D. (2008). *Liberating Voices: A Pattern Language for Communication Revolution.* Boston: MIT Press.

18 *Gary Chapman . . . calls it "living the change you want":* Chapman, G. (2000). The Good Life. Public Sphere Project, http://www.publicsphereproject.org/content/good-life.

18 *Gets drowned out in the face of school climates that push for individual and institutional advancement:* Brown, P.M., & Elias, M.J. (2012). Prosocial education: Weaving a tapestry to support policy and practice. In P.M. Brown, M.W. Corrigan & A. Higgins D-Alessandro (Eds.), *The handbook of prosocial education* (pp. 767–800). Blue Ridge Summit, PA: Rowman and Littlefield Publishing Group. See also National School Climate Center: http://www.schoolclimate.org/.

20 *Albert Bandura's theory of self-efficacy:* Bandura, A. (1977). Self-efficacy: Toward a unifying theory of behavioral change. *Psychological Review,* 84(2), 191–215.

20 *Most people in leadership, business . . . can recite the short list of skills:* Ovans, A. (2015) How Emotional Intelligence Became a Key Leadership Skill. *Harvard Business Review,* https://hbr.org/2015/04/how-emotional-intelligence-became-a-key-leadership-skill. See also Goleman, D. (2011). They've Taken Emotional Intelligence Too Far. *Time Magazine,* http://ideas.time.com/2011/11/01/theyve-taken-emotional-intelligence-too-far/.

20 *EI doesn't resonate across cultures, especially those that are collectivist:* Emmerling, R., Shanwal, V., & Mandal, M. (Eds.) (2008). *Emotional intelligence: Theoretical and Cultural Perspectives.* New York: Nova Science Publishers.

21 *Carl Rogers quote:* Rogers, C. (1961). *On Becoming a Person: A Therapist's View of Psychotherapy.* New York: Houghton Mifflin.

21 *Bandura's theory of self-efficacy helps us set and reach goals:* Bandura, A. (1997). *Self-Efficacy: The Exercise of Control.* New York: Freeman and Company.

21 *An injury to one is an injury to all.* Bedolia, L. (2007). Intersections of Inequality: Understanding marginalization and privilege in the post-civil rights era. *American Political Science Association,* 3, 232–248.

22 *The lens of "success" often propagated in individualistic frameworks:* Carducci, B. (2012). Expressions of the self in individualistic vs. collectivist cultures: A cross-cultural perspective teaching model. *Psychology Learning and Teaching,* 11 (3), 413–17.

23 *The difference between empathy and sympathy:* Wispé, L. (1986). The distinction between sympathy and empathy: To call forth a concept, a word is needed. *Journal of Personality and Social Psychology, 50*(2), 314–321.

24 *Ethics of Reciprocity Academic Definition:* New World Encyclopedia. http://www.newworldencyclopedia.org/entry/Golden_Rule. (see prior note)

24 *(IRB) application:* See https://www.hhs.gov/ohrp/irbs-and-assurances.html.

24 *What researchers like to call* thick data: Maxwell, J. (2005). *Qualitative Research Design.* Thousand Oaks: Sage Publications.

25 *Coding all the data:* Locke, L., Silverman, S., & Spirduso, W. (2010). *Reading and Understanding Research.* Thousand Oaks: Sage Publications.

25 *When we hide truths, we resort to maladaptive ways of coping:* Von Hippel, W. & Trivers, R. (2011). The evolution and psychology of self-deception. *Behavioral and Brain Sciences,* 34(1), 1–16.

26 *Paradigms have existed that interfere with human progress and potential:* Freire, P. (1996). *Pedagogy of the Oppressed.* New York: Bloomsbury.

26 *Unconditional positive regard:* Rogers, C. (1956). *Client-Centered Therapy (3 ed.).* Boston: Houghton Mifflin.

28 *Values in Action (VIA) Inventory:* See https://www.viacharacter.org

Session Three—Cutting Strings

31 *Alvin Toffler quote:* Toffler, A. (1971). *Future Shock.* New York: Bantam Books.

31 *Sociallyinferior:* Socialanxietysupport.com. http://www.socialanxietysupport.com/forum/f26/my-life-is-going-taking-a-downward-spiral-98275/.

32 *Would call underfunctioners:* Lerner, H. (2014). *The Dance of Anger: A Woman's Guide to Changing.* New York: HarperCollins.

33 *Even super-achievers can end up with the same level of doubt:* Mossakowski, K. (2011). Unfulfilled expectations and symptoms of depression. *Social Science & Medicine,* 73(5), 729–736. See also Burt, R. S. (1992). *Structural holes: The social structure of competition.* Cambridge: Harvard University Press. See also Suniya, L., Barkin, S., Crossman, E., & Cicchetti, D. (2013). I can, therefore I must: Fragility in the upper-middle classes. *Development and Psychopathology,* 2(4), 1529–1549.

33 *They catch us by surprise:* Lempert, K. M., & Phelps, E. A. (2014): "Neuroeconomics of Emotion and Decision Making", in Glimcher and Fehr, eds., Neuroeconomics: Decision Making and the Brain, Elsevier, 2nd ed., ch. 12. See also Livet, P. (2010): Rational Choice, Neuroeconomy, and Mixed Emotions, *Philosophical Transactions of the Royal Society,* 36(138), 29–269. See also Swinkerls, A., & Giuliano, T.A. (1995). The measurement and conceptualization of mood awareness: Monitoring and labeling one's mood states. *Personality and Social Psychology Bulletin,* 21, 934–949.

34 *Errors in judgement known as* confirmation bias: Klayman, J. (1995). Varieties of Confirmation Bias. *Psychology of Learning and Motivation,* 32, 385–418. See also Science of Us (2017), http://nymag.com/scienceofus/2017/01/kahneman-biases-act-like-optical-illusions.html.

34 *The amygdala, a small structure in the brain that regulars fear responses:* Science Daily, https://www.sciencedaily.com/terms/amygdala.htm.

34 *Kahneman relates much of our levels of awareness to brain functions he calls System 1 and System 2:* Kahneman (2011). *Thinking, Fast and Slow.* New York: Farner, Straus and Giroux. See also Kahneman, D. & Tversky, A. (1973). Availability: A heuristic for judging frequency and probability. *Cognitive Psychology.* 5(2), 207–232.

35 *Metacognition Academic Definition:* Flavell, J. H. (1979). Metacognition and cognitive monitoring: A new area of cognitive–developmental inquiry. *American Psychologist, 34*(10), 906–911. See also Kuhn, D. & Dean, D. (2004). A bridge between cognitive psychology and educational practice. *Theory into Practice,* 43(4), 268–273.

35 *Downward Spiral Thinking Types:* Adapted from Centre for Clinical Interventions Unhelpful Thinking Styles, http://www.cci.health.wa.gov.au/resources/docs/Info-UT%20Unhelpful%20thinking.pdf. See also the work of Aaron T. Beck, MD, https://aaronbeckcenter.org/beck/ and Burns, D. (2008). *Feeling Good, The New Mood Therapy.* New York: Harper.

37 *Know the Difference Between Metacognition and Rumination:* Nolen-Hoeksema, S., Wisco, B. & Lyubomirsky, S. (1991). Rethinking rumination. *Perspectives on Psychological Science.* 3(5), 400–424. See also Koriat, A., Ma-ayan, H., & Nussinson, R. (2006). The intricate relationships between monitoring and control in metacognition: Lessons for the cause-and-effect relation between subjective experience and behavior. *Journal of Experimental Psychology: General,* 135(1), 36–69.

38 *Adrienne Rich quote:* Rich, A. (1977). "Claiming an Education" speech delivered as the convocation of Douglass College.

40 *Imposter Syndrome Academic Definition:* Clance, P.R. & Imes, S.A. (1978). The imposter phenomenon in high achieving women: Dynamics and therapeutic intervention. *Psychotherapy: Theory, Research and Practice.* 15(3): 241–247. See also: McElwee, Rory O'Brien; Yurak, Tricia J. (2010). The Phenomenology of The Impostor Phenomenon. *Individual Differences Research.* H.W. Wilson. 8(3): 184–197.

41 *Our salaries, hips and lips are never big enough:* American Society of Plastic Surgeons (2016). 2016 Plastic Surgery Statistics, https://www.plasticsurgery.org/documents/News/Statistics/2016/plastic-surgery-statistics-full-report-2016.pdf. See also International Society of Aesthetic Plastic Surgery, https://www.isaps.org/news/isaps-global-statistics.

44 *Work toward transfer:* Perkins, D. N., & Salomon, G. (2012). Knowledge to go: A motivational and dispositional view of transfer. *Educational Psychologist,* 47(3), 248–258.

Session Four—Popping Bubbles

47 *Rumi quote:* Rumi, J. (1995). *The Essential Rumi.* New York: HarperCollins.

47 *It's the generation of coddling:* Twenge, J. (2014). *Generation Me: Why Today's Young Americans are More Confident, Assertive, Entitled and More Miserable Than Ever Before.* New York: Atria.

48 *What sociologists Susan Douglas and Meredith Michaels call the "new momism":* Douglas, S. & Michaels, M. (2005). *The Mommy Myth: The Idealization of Motherhood and How It Has Undermined all Women.* New York: Free Press.

48 *Brigid Schulte, award-winning Washington Post reporter and New America Fellow, calls "stupid days":* Schulte, B. (2014). *Overwhelmed: Work, Love and Play When No One Has the Time.* New York: Sarah Crichton Books.

50 *Gold-plating grit:* Brown, B. (2015). *Rising Strong.* New York: Penguin Random House.

50 *Emotional granularity:* Feldman Barret, L. (2006). Solving the Emotion Paraox: Categorization and the Experience of Emotion. *Personality and Social Psychology Review.* 10(1), 20–46. See also Feldman Barret, L., Mesquita, B., Ochsner, K. & Gross, J. (2007). The Experience of Emotion. *Annual Review of Psychology,* 58: 373–403. See also Feldman Barret, L. (2016). Are You in Despair? That's Good. *New York Times,* https://www.nytimes.com/2016/06/05/opinion/sunday/are-you-in-despair-thats-good.html.

51 *Know the Science Behind Feeling and Healing:* Lieberman, M., Eisenberger, N., Crockett, M., Tom, S., Pfeifer, J. & Way, B (2007). *Psychological Science* 18(5), 421–428.

54 *Eckhart Tolle quote:* Tolle, E. (1999). *The Power of Now: A Guide to Spiritual Enlightenment.* Vancouver: Namaste Publishing.

57 *Create a shadow resume:* Looser, D. (2015). Me and My Shadow CV. The Chronicle of Higher Education, http://www.chronicle.com/article/MeMy-Shadow-CV/233801.

58 *John Dewey quote:* Dewey, J. (1985). *How we think.* Lexington: DC Heath & Co.

Session Five—Waking the Sleepwalker

61 *Evidence definition,* Dictionary.com, http://www.dictionary.com/browse/evidence.

61 *Aldous Huxley quote:* Huxley, A. (1949). *The Art of Seeing.* 6th impression edition. London: Chatto & Widus.

63 *Mike Birbiglia:* Birbiglia, M. (2010). *Sleepwalk with Me and Other Painfully True Stories.* New York: Simon and Schuster. See also Finn, R. (2011). From Sleeping Bag to Starbucks. *New York Times,* http://www.nytimes.com/2011/02/27/nyregion/27routine.html.

64 *Consciousness academic definition:* Dictionary.com, http://www.dictionary.com/browse/consciousness. See also: Ornstein, R. E. (1972). *The psychology of consciousness.* Oxford, England: Penguin. See also obert van Gulick (2004). "Consciousness." Stanford Encyclopedia of Philosophy; and Mead, G. H. (1910). Social consciousness and the consciousness of meaning. *Psychological Bulletin,* 7(12), 397–405.

64 *Sapient beings . . . possess a high capacity for thinking skills:* Elder, L., Paul, R. (2013). *30 Days to Better Thinking and Better Living Through Critical Thinking.* New Jersey: Pearson.

67 *In lockstep with the American Psychological Association:* American Psychological Association (2013). APA Guidelines for the Undergraduate Psychology Major, http://www.apa.org/ed/precollege/about/undergraduate-major.aspx.

67 *A big no-no in interpreting scientific research:* Babbie, E. (2014). The Practice of Social Research (14th ed). Belmont: Thomson Wadsworth.

67 *Know the Difference Between Self-Help Fads and Scientific Evidence:* American Psychological Association, Presidential Task Force on Evidence-Based Practice. (2006). Evidence-based practice in psychology. *American Psychologist, 61*(4), 271–285. See also: American Psychological Association. Tackling student skepticism of psychology: Recommendations for instructors. Psychology Teacher Network, http://www.apa.org/ed/precollege/ptn/2012/08/student-skepticism.aspx.

68 *Move beyond WEIRD:* Henrich, J., Heine, S. & Norenzayan, A. (2010). The Weirdest People in the World? *Behavioral Brain Science,* 33 (2–3), 61–83. See also: American Psychological Association (2010). Are your findings WEIRD? *APA Monitor,* 41(5), 11.

69 *Salovey and Mayer didn't intend for their paper to travel that far:* Bronson, P. (2009). Daniel Goleman Defends Emotional Intelligence. *Newsweek* http://www.newsweek.com/daniel-goleman-defends-emotional-intelligence-223456. See also Yale Center for Emotional Intelligence, http://ei.yale.edu/who-we-are/history/.

69 *The way Goleman packaged it that makes some scientists shake their heads:* Joseph, D. L., & Newman, D. A. (2010). Emotional intelligence: An integrative meta-analysis and cascading model. *Journal of Applied Psychology, 95*(1), 54–78. See also Murphy, K. (2006). *A Critique of Emotional Intelligence: What are the Problems and How Can They Be Fixed?* New York: Lawrence Erlbaum Associates.

69 *One criticism of EI is that it doesn't translate well across cultures and varied populations:* Grant, A. (2014). The Dark Side of Emotional Intelligence. *The Atlantic,* https://www.theatlantic.com/health/archive/2014/01/the-dark-side-of-emotional-intelligence/282720/.

71 *Oreos, even though they are allegedly as addictive as crack:* Pappas, S. (2013). Oreos As Addictive As Cocaine. *Live Science,* https://www.livescience.com/40488-oreos-addictive-cocaine.html.

72 *We will inevitably have "muddy points" when we're trying to learn:* Mostelle, F. (1989). The Muddiest Point in the Lecture as a Feedback Device in On Teaching and Learning: *Journal of the Harvard-Danford Center,* 3, 10–21.

Session Six—Flipping Couches

77 *Sherman quote:* Alan Sherman. Goodreads.com, https://www.goodreads.com/quotes/97959-a-normal-person-is-the-sort-of-person-that-might.

77 *Swiss psychologist Hermann Rorscharch…made them famous in 1921:* Famous Scientists. https://www.famousscientists.org/hermann-rorschach/. See also: Akavia, R. (2013). *Subjectivity in Motion: Life, Art, and Movement in the Work of Hermann Rorscharch.* New York: Routledge.

81 *A social work practice theory founded by Bertha Capen Reynolds in the early 1900s:* Reynolds, B. (1985). *Learning and Teaching in the Practice of Social Work.* Washington DC: National Association of Social Workers Press.

81 *Dr. Martin Seligman pointed to the merit of strengths-based thinking:* Seligman (1998). The President's Address (Annual Report). *American Psychologist,* 1999, 54, 559–562.

82 *Frederickson…explains how negative emotions narrow* thought-action repertoires: Frederickson, B., & Joiner, T. (2002). Positive emotions trigger upward spirals toward emotional well-being. *Psychological Science,* 13(2): 172–175.

83 *Dr. Allen Frances . . . blew the whistle on psychiatry:* Frances, A. (2014). *Saving Normal: An Insider's Revolt Against Out-of-Control Psychiatric Diagnosis, DSM-5, Big Pharma, and the Medicalization of Normal.* New York: HarperCollins.

83 *Of the 2.8 billion drugs ordered, antidepressants were in the most frequently prescribed category:* Center for Disease Control website (2015). https://www.cdc.gov/nchs/data/databriefs/db283.pdf. See also: Kantor, E.D., Rehm, C.D., Haas, J.S., Chan A.T., & Giovannucci, E.L. (2015). Trend in Prescription Drug Use Among Adults in the United Statistics from 1999–2011. JAMA, 31 4(17), 1818–1831.

84 *Big Pharma, which has been called "America's New Mafia":* Drake, D. (2015). Big Pharma is America's New Mafia. The Daily Beast website. https://www.thedailybeast.com/big-pharma-is-americas-new-mafia.

86 *Depression…Global Crisis, estimating its effect on 350 million people worldwide:* World Health Organization (2012). http://www.who.int/mediacentre/news/notes/2012/mental_health_day_20121009/en/.

86 *A first-of-its-kind longitudinal study:* Milkie, M., Nomaguchi, K. & Denny, K. (2015). Does the amount of time mothers spend with children or adolescents matter? *Journal of Marriage and Family,* 77 2), *355–372.*

Session Seven—Embracing Your Spiral

90 *Spiral definition:* Dictionary.com, http://www.dictionary.com/browse/spiral.

91 *Friedrich Nietzsche quote:* Nietzsche, F. (1999). *Thus Spake Zarathustra,* Thomas Common translation. New York: Dover Publications.

91 *Some resilience researchers worry:* Shaw, J., McLean, K. C., Taylor, B., Swartout, K., & Querna, K. (2016). Beyond resilience: Why we need to look at systems too. *Psychology of Violence,* 6(1), 34–41.

93 *Early-twentieth-century physicist Henry Poincare called this* dynamical instability: Holmes, P. (2007). History of dynamical systems. Scholarpedia.com, http://www.scholarpedia.org/article/History_of_dynamical_systems.

93 *His "butterfly effect" theory explains how the timing of the flap of a butterfly's wings:* Dizikes, P. (2011). When the Butterfly Effect Took Flight. *MIT Technology Review.* Technologyreview.com, https://www.technologyreview.com/s/422809/when-the-butterfly-effect-took-flight/.

95 *Role Conflict Academic Definition:* Fisher, C. D., & Gitelson, R. (1983). A meta-analysis of the correlates of role conflict and ambiguity. *Journal of Applied Psychology,* 68(2), 320–333.

95 *There are more ways of communicating, work options, gender identities, relationship arrangements, and family structures:* World at Work (2015): Trends in Workplace Flexibility. World at Work website, https://www.worldatwork.org/adimLink?id=79123. See also Steinmetz, L. (2017). Beyond "He" or "She": The Changing Meaning of Gender and Sexuality. *Time Magazine,* http://time.com/4703309/gender-sexuality-changing/. See also Finkel, E. (2014). The All-or-Nothing-Marriage. *New York Times,* https://www.nytimes.com/2014/02/15/opinion/sunday/the-all-or-nothing-marriage.html. See also: Pew Research Center (2015). The American Family Today. Pew Social Trends website, http://www.pewsocialtrends.org/2015/12/17/1-the-american-family-today/. See also: Social Trends Institute (2017). Mapping Family Change and Child Well-Being Outcomes. World Family Map website, https://worldfamilymap.ifstudies.org/2017/files/WFM-2017-Full Report.pdf.

97 *In many cultures, spirals are associated with the divine feminine, the womb, and goddesses:* Beyer, C. (2017). Spirals. ThoughtCo website, https://www.thoughtco.com/spirals-95990.

103 *Paulo Coelho quote:* Coelho, P. (1993). *The Alchemist, 25th anniversary ed.* New York: HarperCollins.

103 *Carl Jung quote:* Jung, C. (1925). Marriage as a psychological relationship. Jungcurrents website, http://jungcurrents.com/jung-consciousness-pain.

Session Eight—Unfriending Chicken Little

115 *Critical Thinking Academic Definition:* See Elder and Paul session one note.

107 *Daniel Kahneman quote:* See Kahneman session three note.

108 *Taking in the equivalent of 174 newspapers a day:* Levitin, D. (2014). Hit the Reset Button in Your Brain. New York Times, https://www.nytimes.com/2014/08/10/opinion/sunday/hit-the-reset-button-in-your-brain.html.

108 *The March 2017 cover of TIME magazine jostles us:* Time Magazine (2017). Mindfulness: The New Science of Health and Happiness.

108 *Miller worries that this misconception prevents us from even* looking *for the truth:* Miller, M. (1988). *Boxed In: The Culture of TV.* Chicago: Northwestern University Press.

108 *Today, six companies…have it wrapped up:* Lutz, A. (2012). These six corporations control 90% of the media in America. Business Insider website, http://www.businessinsider.com/these-6-corporations-control-90-of-the-media-in-america-2012-6.

109 *The* Washington Post *called the 2016 campaign a "gusher":* Farhi, P. (2016). One billion dollars profit. The Washington Post, https://www.washingtonpost.com/lifestyle/style/one-billion-dollars-profit-yes-the-campaign-has-been-a-gusher-for-cnn/2016/10/27/1fc879e6-9c6f-11e6-9980-50913d68eacb_story.html?utm_term=.971b74888cc7.

110 *Know the Science and Roots Behind Mass Hysteria:* Schneier, B. (2003). *Beyond Fear: Thinking Sensibly About Security in an Uncertain World.* New York: Copernicus Books.

110 *We live in the most peaceful and prosperous time in history:* Roser (2017). Our World in Data website, https://ourworldindata.org/.

111 *Public health experts…report that zip codes predict health outcomes:* Robert Wood Johnson Foundation website, https://www.rwjf.org/en/library/collections/better-data-for-better-health.html.

111 *By 2030, the World Health Organization says stress-related, noncontagious illness will be our prime concern:* World Health Organization (2014). Global status report on noncommunicable disease.

112 *Noam Chomsky quote:* David Cogwell website, *http://www.davidcogwell.com/Political/Chomsky_Interview_93.htm.*

113 *JFK quote:* John F. Kennedy (1962). Commencement address at Yale University.

114 *Demagogue Academic Definition:* http://www.dictionary.com/browse/demagogue.

115 *They found that getting to the pop's center took 252 licks:* Heid, C. (2013), Tootsie Pops: How many licks to the chocolate? *Significance,* 10: 47–48.

116 *Know the Essential Intellectual Virtues:* Critical Thinking Foundation website, http://www.criticalthinking.org/pages/valuable-intellectual-traits/528.

117 *Laura Bynum quote:* Good Reads website, https://www.goodreads.com/author/quotes/3069952.Laura_Bynum.

Session Nine—Waiting for Marshmallows

121 *George Carlin quote:* I am awake website, http://www.iamawake.co/14-of-the-best-george-carlin-quotes/.

122 *They rake in billions of dollars from jolly new playmates every year:* Stephens, D.L., Hill, R.P.,& Bergman, K. (1996). Enhancing the consumer-product relationship: Lessons from the QVC shopping channel. *Journal of Business Research,* 37(3), 193-2000. See also: Statista.com, https://www.statista.com/statistics/536530/qvc-revenue/.

123 *His now famous Stanford marshmallow test:* Mischel, Walter; Ebbesen, Ebbe B.; Raskoff Zeiss, Antonette (1972). "Cognitive and attentional mechanisms in delay of gratification." *Journal of Personality and Social Psychology.* 21(2): 204–218.

123 *In 2011, Mischel and colleagues tracked down fifty-nine of the original subjects:* Casey, B. J., et al. (2011). Behavioral and neural correlates of delay of gratification 40 years later. *Proceedings of the National Academy of Sciences,* 108(36), 14998–15003.

124 *Know the Science Behind Buying:* Nobel, C. (2012). What neuroscience tells us about consumer desire. Harvard Business School, http://hbswk.hbs.edu/item/what-neuroscience-tells-us-about-consumer-desire.

124 *Our tendency to compare ourselves becomes "grotesquely exploited":* Speth (2013). *America the Possible: Manifesto for a New Economy.* New Haven: Yale University Press.

124 *Count on us to support 70 percent of the gross domestic project:* Toosi, M. (2002). Consumer spending: an engine for U.S. job growth. *Monthly Labor Review, https://www.bls.gov/opub/mlr/2002/11/art2full.pdf.*

124 *Ninety percent of what we buy goes to the trash within six months:* Zero Waste International Alliance website, http://zwia.org/.

125 *Our departure from a time when we used to make things to one in which the primary objective is to consume them leads us to trouble:* Bauman, Z. (2011). *Consuming Life.* Cambridge: Polity Press. See also Definition of Consumerist Culture. ThoughtCo website, https://www.thoughtco.com/consumerist-culture-3026120.

126 *Happiness has a set point:* Lyubomirsky, S., King, L., & Diener, E. (2005). The Benefits of Frequent Positive Affect: Does Happiness Lead to Success? *Psychological Bulletin,* 131(6), 803-855. See also: Lyubomirsky, S. (2007). *The How of Happiness: A New Approach to Getting the Life You Want.* New York: Penguin.

126 *Our merry and bright grow dim in the face of social comparison:* Suls, J., & Wills, T. A. (Eds.). (1991). *Social comparison: Contemporary theory and research.* Hillsdale: Lawrence Erlbaum Associates.

127 *C. JoyBell C. quote:* Good Reads website, https://www.goodreads.com/quotes/392300-the-unhappiest-people-in-this-world-are-those-who-care.

128 *Putting time between the impulse and action helps prevent unnecessary indulgences:* Benson, A. (2017). Stopping Overshopping website, https://www.shopaholicnomore.com/category/proven-strategies/.

130 *Emmons asked one group of participants:* Emmons, R.A. & McCullough, M.E. (2005). Counting blessings versus burdens: An experimental investigation of gratitude and subjective well-being in daily life. *Journal of Personality and Social Psychology,* 84; 377–389. See also: Emmons, R. (2008). *Thanks! How Practicing Gratitude Can Make You Happier.* New York: Houghton Mifflin.

130 *Sonja Lyubomirsky found similar results in her lab:* Lyubomirsky, S., King, L., & Diener, E. (2005). The benefits of frequent positive affect. Does happiness lead to success? *Psychological Bulletin* 131: 803–855. See also Lyubomirsky, S. (2007). *The How of Happiness: A New Approach to Getting the Life You Want.* New York: Penguin.

131 *Liz Dunn reported that:* Dunn, Elizabeth W., Lara B. Aknin, and Michael I. Norton. "Prosocial Spending and Happiness: Using Money to Benefit Others Pays Off." Current Directions in Psychological Science. Harvard Business School Digital Access website, https://dash.harvard.edu/handle/1/11189976. See also: Nicholson, C. (2010) Generosity might keep us healthy. Scientific American website, https://www.scientificamerican.com/podcast/episode/generosity-might-keep-us-healthy-10-10-26/.

131 *Giving is another pathway to the good life:* Twist, L. & Barker, T. (2006). *The Soul of Money: Reclaiming the Wealth of Our Inner Resources.* New York: W. W. Norton. See also: Post, S. (2011). *The Hidden Gifts of Helping: How the Power of Giving, Compassion, and Hope Can Get Us Through Hard Times.* San Francisco: Jossey-Bass.

131 *Volunteering is another way to boost individual and collective resilience:* Jenkinson, C., Dickens, A., Jones, K., Thompson-Coon, J., Taylor, R., Rogers, M., Bambra, C., Lang, I., & Richards. S. (2013). Is volunteering a public health intervention? A systematic review and meta-analysis of the health and survival of volunteers. *BMC Public Health,* 13(773).

Session Ten—Embracing Impermanence

137 *W. Somerset Maugham quote:* Maugham, W.S. (1944). *The Razor's Edge.* New York: Vintage International.

138 *Jon-Kabat-Zinn introduced it in the late 1970s:* Zinn, K.Z. Guided Mindfulness Practices with Jon Kabat-Zinn. Mindfulness CDS website, https://www.mindfulnesscds.com/.

138 *Mindfulness Academic Definition:* Khoury, B., Lecomte, T., Fortin, G., Masse, M., Therien, P., Bouchard, V., Chapleau, M., Paquin, K., & Hofmann, S. (2013). Mindfulness-based therapy: A comprehensive meta-analysis. *Clinical Psychology Review,* 33(6). 763–771.

139 *Entrepreneurs are experimenting with mindfulness as a success hack:* Gupta, P. (2014). 9 Mindfulness hacks to help you succeed. Forbes.com website, https://www.forbes.com/sites/yec/2014/10/07/9-mindfulness-hacks-to-help-you-succeed/#5d67e9d163f4.

139 *Companies…are paying a fortune to…teach employees:* Wieczner, J. (2016). Meditation has become a billion-dollar business. Fortune.com website, http://fortune.com/2016/03/12/meditation-mindfulness-apps/. See also Chen, A. (2015). Why companies are promoting mindfulness at the office. The Wall Street Journal website, https://blogs.wsj.com/atwork/2015/03/16/why-companies-are-promoting-mindfulness-at-the-office/.

140 *Know the Science Behind Mindfulness:* Chambers, R., Yee Lo, B.C., Allen, N.B. (2008). *Cognitive Therapy and Research.* 32(3), 302–322. See also: Hassed, C. & Chambers, R. (2014). *Mindful Learning: Mindfulness-Based Techniques for Educators and Parents to Help Students.* Boston: Shambhala Publications.

142 *Humor and motivation help us through dark moments:* Overholser, J. (1992). Sense of humor when coping with life stress. *Personality and Individual Differences,* 13(7), 799–804.

142 *Calls life "brutiful":* Doyle, G. (2014). *Carry On, Warrior: The Power of Embracing Your Messy, Beautiful Life.* New York: Scribner.

142 *Calls grief the "art behind all real art":* Pretchel, M. (2015). *The Smell of Rain on Dust: Grief and Praise.* Berkeley: North Atlantic Books.

143 *American musician Glen Phillips, who was mourning the loss:* Demaria, R. (2016). A Deep Conversation with Glen Phillips. Indpendent.com website, http://www.independent.com/news/2016/apr/25/deep-conversation-glen-phillips/.

147 *Robert Frost quote:* Poets.org website, https://www.poets.org/poetsorg/poem/nothing-gold-can-stay.

148 *M. Scott Peck quote:* Peck, M.S. (2003). *The Road Less Traveled, Timeless Edition: A New Psychology of Love, Traditional Values, and Spiritual Growth.* New York: Touchstone.

Session Eleven—Purging Kool-Aid

152 *Global definition:* Dictionary.com, http://www.dictionary.com/browse/global.

153 *Noam Chomsky quote:* Good Reads website, https://www.goodreads.com/quotes/34766-either-you-repeat-the-same-conventional-doctrines-everybody-is-saying.

153 *In the fall of 1978, cult leader Jim Jones did just that:* Guinn, J. (2017). *The Road to Jonestown: Jim Jones and Peoples Temple.* New York: Simon & Schuster.

155 *Groupthink Academic Definition:* Janis, I. L. (1972). Victims of groupthink: A psychological study of foreign-policy decisions and fiascoes. Oxford, England: Houghton Mifflin. See also: Wetherell, Margaret (1996). Constructing identities: the individual/social binary in Henri Tajfel's social psychology. In: Robinson, Peter W. ed. *Social Groups and Identities: Developing the Legacy of Henri Tajfel. Social Psychology Series.* Oxford, U.K.: Butterworth-Heinemann, pp. 269–284.

157 *The word* scapegoat *is based on biblical lore:* Dictionary.com, http://www.dictionary.com/browse/scapegoat.

165 *"Please Understand Me":* Keirsey, D., & Bates, M. (1984). *Please Understand Me: Character and Temperament Types.* Carlsbad: Prometheus Nemesis Books. See also Abel Zoe's adaption Poemhunter.com, https://www.poemhunter.com/poem/please-understand-me-4/.

Session Twelve—Getting Un-Thrust

167 *Adrienne Rich quote:* Brainyquote.com, https://www.brainyquote.com/quotes/quotes/a/adrienneri163809.html.

171 *The hotter their partner, the realer they become:* Kling, K. C., Hyde, J. S., Showers, C. J., & Buswell, B. N. (1999). Gender differences in self-esteem: A meta-analysis. *Psychological Bulletin,* 125(4), 470–500.

171 *Not caring has become a cultural badge:* Manson, M. (2016). *The Subtle Art of Not Giving a Fuck.* New York: HarperCollins.

171 *Real women aren't too bossy, aggressive, or domineering:* Snyder, B. (2015). Can women be strong leaders without being labeled "bossy?" Stanford Graduate School of Business website, https://www.gsb.stanford.edu/insights/can-women-be-strong-leaders-without-being-labeled-bossy. See also: Eagly, A., & Blair, T. (1990). Gender and leadership style: A meta-analysis. *Psychological Bulletin,* 108(2), 233–256. See also: Cuddy, A.J.C., & Fiske, S. T., & Glick, P. (2004). When professionals become mothers, warmth doesn't cut the ice. *Journal of Social Issues,* 60(4), 701–718.

173 *They make sport out of tackling binary constructions:* Giang, V. (2015). Transgender is yesterday's news: How companies are grappling with the 'no gender' society. Fortune website, http://fortune.com/2015/06/29/gender-fluid-binary-companies/.

174 *Have been proven to be socially constructed, not scientifically grounded:* Goodman, A.H., Moses, Y.T., & Jones, J.L. (2012). *Race: Are We So Different?* Wiley Online: *American Anthropological Association.* See also: Gannon, M. (2016). Race is a social construct, scientists argue. LiveScience website, https://www.livescience.com/53613-race-is-social-construct-not-scientific.html . See also: Risman, B. (2004). Gender as a social structure: Theory wrestling with activism. *Gender & Society,* 18(4), 429–450.

174 *Sociologist Charles Horton Cooley explains:* Cooley (1902). *Human Nature and the Social Order.* New York: Scribner's.

Session Thirteen—Discovering the Human Museum

181 *iO Tillet Wright quote:* Tillet, iO (2012). Fifty Shades of Gay. TEDx Women event. Ted.com website, https://www.ted.com/talks/io_tillett _wright_fifty_shades_of_gay. See also: Self-Evident Truths Project website, http://www.selfevidentproject.com/.

181 *When Steven Armstrong asked his third-grade teacher Jane Elliot why they "shot that King yesterday":* Elliot, J. (2016). *A Collar in My Pocket: Blue Eyes/Brown Eyes Exercise.* CreateSpace Independent Publishing. See also: Bloom, S. (2005). Lesson of a lifetime. Smithsonian website, https://www.smithsonianmag.com/science-nature/lesson-of-a-lifetime-72754306/.

182 *Social Identity Theory Academic Definition:* Tajfel, H., & Turner, J. C. (1979). 'An integrative theory of intergroup conflict'. In: AustinW. G. and Worchel, S.(eds.) *The Social Psychology of Intergroup Relations,* Monterey: Brooks/Cole.

183 *Elliot's students where dealing with…stereotype threat:* Steele, C. (2014). *Whistling Vivaldi: How Stereotypes Affect Us.* New York: W.W. Norton & Company.

184 *They've spent years measuring "implicit cognition":* See previous note on Banaji and Greenwald.

186 *We watched iO Tillet Wright:* See previous note on Wright.

187 *Martin Rochilin's original heterosexual questionnaire:* Rochilins, (1972). Heterosexual Questionnaire. The University of Texas at Austin. UWGB.edu website, https://www.uwgb.edu/pride-center/files/pdfs/Heterosexual_Questionnaire.pdf.

187 *We watched PBS's Race*—The Power of an Illusion: PBS.org website, http://www.pbs.org/race/001_WhatIsRace/001_00-home.htm.

187 *We watched Jennifer Siebel Newsom's award-winning documentary* Miss Representation: TheRepresentationproject.org website, http:// therepresentationproject.org/film/miss-representation/.

187 *We read Jonathan Mooney's* The Short Bus. See previous note on Mooney.

187 *Drawing from the* Class Matters *website:* Classmatters.org website, http://classmatters.org/.

187 *Studied the If World Were a Village of 100 research project:* 1oopeople.org website, http://www.100people.org/statistics_100stats. php.

188 *The concept originated with American civil rights activist:* Crenshaw, K. (2010). Mapping the margins: Intersectionality, identify politics, and violence against women of color. *Stanford Law Review,* 43(6), 1241–1299. See also: Crenshaw, K. (2016). The urgency of intersectionality. TEDWomen. Ted.com website, https://www.ted.com/talks/kimberle_crenshaw_the_urgency_of_intersectionality.

188 *Intersectionality Academic Definition:* See previous note.

191 *bell hooks quote:* hooks, b. (2003). *Teaching Community: A Pedagogy of Hope.* New York: Routledge.

193 *Professor Peggy McIntosh describes her process of shifting away from thinking of racism as acts of individual meanness:* McIntosh, P. (1988). White privilege: Unpacking the invisible knapsack. Working paper for the Wellesley College Center for Research on Women.

193 *The Economic Policy Institute reports that the average CEO makes more in one morning than the average minimum wage worker:* Michel, L. & Schnieder, J. (2017). CEO pay remains high relative to the pay of typical workers and high-wage earners. Economicpolicyinstitute.org website, http://www.epi.org/publication/ceo-pay-remains-high-relative-to-the-pay-of-typical-workers-and-high-wage-earners/. See also Hodgson, P. (2015). Top CEO's make more than 300 times the average worker. Fortune.com website, http://fortune.com/2015/06/22/ ceo-vs-worker-pay/.

193 *They've been on the downturn since the late 1970s (chance for upward mobility).* Kraus, M.W., & Tan, J. (2015). Americans over-estimate social class mobility. *Journal of Experimental Psychology,* 58, 101–111. See also: Clemens, A. (2016). New analysis shows it is more difficult for workers to move up the income ladder. Washington Center for Equitable Growth website, http://equitablegrowth.org /research-analysis/carr-wiemers-interactive-piece/.

194 *George Carlin quote:* See session nine note.

194 *The over twelve million people in the United States who work at least twenty-seven weeks a year:* United States Department of Labor (2015). Bureau of Labor Statistics website, https://www.bls.gov/opub/reports/working-poor/2015/home.htm. See also: Center for Poverty Research website, https://poverty.ucdavis.edu/faq/who-are-working-poor-america.

195 *Naomi Wolf quote:* Wolf, N. (2002). *The Beauty Myth: How Images of Beauty Are Used Against Women.* New York: HarperCollins.

195 *The University of Wisconsin–Superior has an excellent framework for developing better awareness and skills (global aware):* website, University of Wisconsin-Superior website, https://www.uwsuper.edu/globalawareness/getting-started/index.cfm#_1_1995949. See also Association of American Colleges and Universities Global Learning: Key to Making Excellence Inclusive. AACU website, https://www.aacu .org/liberaleducation/2015/summer/whitehead.

Session Fourteen—Coming Out of Corners

199 *Tom Shadyac quote:* Shadyac, T. (2014). *Life's Operating Manual: With the Fear and Truth Dialogues.* Carlsbad: Hay House.

199 *When Arizona Congresswoman Kyrsten Sinema takes the stage: NASW conference:* (2016). Socialworkers.org website, https://www .socialworkers.org/Events/NASW-Conferences/2016-NASW-National-Conference/Speakers.aspx.

200 *It's her riveting story that explains why she walks her talk so wholeheartedly:* Sinema, K. (2009). *Unite and Conquer: How to Build Coalitions That Win and Last.* San Francisco. Berrett-Kohler. Roig-Franzia, M. (2013). Kyrsten Sinema: A success story like nobody else's. The Washington Post website, https://www.washingtonpost.com/lifestyle/style/kyrsten-sinema-a-success-story-like-nobody-elses/2013/01/02/ d31fadaa-5382-11e2-a613-ec8d394535c6_story.html?utm_term=.8daOeeb2760e.

201 *She's even leading up a new kind of no spin zone for politicians:* Collins, E. (2017). Taking a spin class? A congresswoman could teach you. USAToday.com website, https://www.usatoday.com/story/news/politics/2017/01/17/kyrsten-sinema-arizona-congresswoman -spin-class/96501634/.

202 *When George W. Bush got wind of it, he invited Bono to the Oval Office:* Associated press (2005). Today.com website, http://www.today .com/id/9755936/ns/today-today_entertainment/t/bono-visits-bush-white-house/#.WdzvAhNSzUo.

205 *The abortion rate drops significantly on the watch of pro-choice leaders:* Bagri, N. (2016). The sharpest drops in abortion rates in America have been under Democratic presidents. Quartzmedia.com website, https://qz.com/857273/the-sharpest-drops-in-abortion -rates-in-america-have-been-under-democratic-presidents/.

206 *Far more effective means of reducing abortion than restricting access:* Center for Disease Control and Prevention (2013). CDCs Abortion Surveillance System FAQ's. CDC website, https://www.cdc.gov/reproductivehealth/data_stats/abortion.htm.

206 *ELL (English Language Learner) students are often seen as draining resources:* Tse, L. (2001). *Why Don't They Learn English? Separating Fact from Fallacy in the U.S. Language Debate.* New York: Teachers College Press.

210 *Interdisciplinary Academic Definition:* Dictionary.com website, http://www.dictionary.com/browse/interdisciplinary.

Session Fifteen—Choosing your Code

215 *Robert Wagner quote:* GoodReads.com website, https://www.goodreads.com/quotes/1056017-imagination-creates-reality.

215 *They discovered what happens when we have too many choices:* Iyengar, S. S., & Lepper, M. R. (2000). When choice is demotivating: Can one desire too much of a good thing? *Journal of Personality and Social Psychology, 79*(6), 995–1006. See also: Iyengar, S. (2011). *The Art of Choosing.* New York: Hachette Book Group. See also: Tugend, A. (2010). Too many choices: A problem that can paralyze. New York Times website, http://www.nytimes.com/2010/02/27/your-money/27shortcuts.html.

215 *Our tendency to hold choice as sacred…might be setting us up:* Schwartz, B. (2016). *The Paradox of Choice: Why More is Less.* New York: HarperCollins.

217 *Know the Science Behind Choice:* MacLeod, C. M. (1991). John Ridley Stroop: Creator of a landmark cognitive task. *Canadian Psychology, 32*(3), 521–524.

217 *The authors explain that the assumption that we typically make choices in our best interest is false:* Sunstein, C., & Thaler, R. (2009). *Nudge: Improving Decisions About Health, Wealth, and Happiness.* New York: Penguin.

217 *He calls for an "urgent transition" from the prevailing thinking that choice abundance equals prosperity:* De Young, R. (2104). Using the Stroop effect to test our capacity to direct attention. Seas Umich website, http://seas.umich.edu/eplab/demos/st0/stroopdesc.html.

225 *Does not think forcing them upon anyone of a different faith tradition:* Lama, D. (2011). *Beyond Religion: Ethics for New World.* New York: Houghton Mifflin Harcourt Publishing.

226 *The reptilian and mammalian parts of our brains influence how we choose to interact and are often at conflict with one another:* Northcutt R.G. (2012). Variation in reptilian brains and cognition. *Brain Behavior Evolution,* 82:45–54. See also: Puelles L., Harrison M., Paxinos G., Watson C. (2013). A developmental ontology for the mammalian brain based on the prosomeric model. *Trends Neuroscience.* 36:570–578. See also: Baer, D. (2013). How to know if you're working with mammals or reptiles (And why it matters to your creativity). Fastcompany.com website, https://www.fastcompany.com/1682363/how-to-know-if-youre-working-with-mammals-or-reptiles-and-why-it-matters-to-your-creativity.

226 *IFS offers eight C':* Anderson, F., Sweezy, M., & Schwartz, R. (2017). *Internal Family Systems Skills Training Manual: Trauma-Informed Treatment for Anxiety, Depression, PTSD & Substance Abuse.* Eau Claire: PESI Publishing.

Session Sixteen—Rethinking Work

231 *Iain Thomas quote:* GoodReads website, https://www.goodreads.com/quotes/997789-and-every-day-the-world-will-drag-you-by-the.

231 *At age twenty-three, Howard Scott Warshaw found himself eye to eye with Steven Spielberg:* NPR.org website, http://www.npr.org/2017 /05/31/530235165/total-failure-the-worlds-worst-video-game.

233 *The very stress that often precipitates a heart attack is also a major hindrance in recovery:* Dreyer, R.P., Dharmarajan, K., Hsieh, A.F., Qin, L., & Krumholz, H.M. (2017). Sex differences in trajectories of risk after rehabilitation for heart failure, acute myocardial infarction, or pneumonia. *Circ. Cardiovascular Qualitative Outcomes,*10 (5).

234 *A governmental annual report revealed that approximately 21.3 percent of Japanese employees work forty-nine hours weekly:* McCurry, J. (2015). Clocking off: Japan calls time on long-hours work culture. TheGuardian.com website, https://www.theguardian.com/world/2015 /feb/22/japan-long-hours-work-culture-overwork-paid-holiday-law.

234 *A report from Oxford Economics points to a pervasive workaholic paradigm as problematic:* Projecttimeoff.com website: https://www .projecttimeoff.com/.

237 *The concept of stress originally came from engineers trying to describe how much weight a bridge could bear before collapsing:* Lazarus, R., & Folkman, S. (1984). *Stress, Appraisal, and Coping.* New York: Springer Publishing.

237 *During preliminary rounds, the vaulters sensed something was off, but their concerns were ignored and the competition went on:* ABC newsgo.com website: http://abcnews.go.com/Sports/story?id=100494&page=1.

238 *The pressures of today are most intense between the ages of fifteen and forty-four:* Raviola, G. et al. (2011). A global scope for global health—including mental health. *The Lancet,* 378(9803), 1613–1615.

238 *Suicide is the tenth leading cause of death in the United States:* National Institute of Mental Health website, https://www.nimh.nih.gov/
      health/statistics/suicide/index.shtml.

238 *Remember the sage advice of the American Psychological Association:* American Psychological Association (2012). Stress in America:
      Our Health at Risk. APA.org website, https://www.apa.org/news/press/releases/stress/2011/final-2011.pdf.

Session Seventeen—Reimagining School

243 *Nelson Mandela quote:* The Washington Post website, https://www.washingtonpost.com/news/answer-sheet/wp/2013/12/05/nelson
      -mandelas-famous-quote-on-education/?utm_term=.ecd7058cf843.

243 *Jonathan Mooney was twelve years old when he finally learned to read:* Mooney, J. (2007). *The Short Bus: A Journey Beyond Normal.*
      New York: Henry Holt. See also Cole, D., Mooney, J. (2000). *Learning Outside the Lines: Two Ivy League Students with Learning Disabilities
      and ADHD Give You the Tools for Academic Success and Educational Revolution.* New York: Fireside.

245 *When education is what it can be, it transforms lives:* Freire, P. (2013). *Education for Critical Consciousness.* New York: Bloomsbury
      Academic. See also Learning as Transformation: Critical Perspectives on a Theory in Progress. *The Jossey-Bass Higher and Adult Education
      Series.* Eric website, https://eric.ed.gov/?id=ED448301.

246 *As Lost at School author:* Greene, R. (2014). *Lost at School: Why Our Kids with Behavioral Challenges are Falling Through the Cracks
      and How We Can Help Them.* New York: Simon & Schuster.

246 *Schools are busy trying to fix a plane while it's already in flight:* Elmore, R. (2004). *School Reform From the Inside Out.* Cambridge:
      Harvard University Press.

247 *We can't keep disparaging them and wonder why 50 percent of them leave because of burnout:* Friedman, I (2000). Burnout in teachers:
      shattered dreams of impeccable professional performance. *Journal of Clinical Psychology,* 220(5), *595–606.* See also: Phillips, O. (2015).
      Revolving door of teachers cost schools billions every year. NPR.org website, http://www.npr.org/sections/ed/2015/03/30/395322012/
      the-hidden-costs-of-teacher-turnover.

247 *Burnout is pervasive, but there's something more going on:* Santoro, D.A. (2011). Good teaching in difficult times: Demoralization in the
      pursuit of good work. *American Journal of Education,* 118(1), 1–23.

249 *There are countless castaways from education:* ACLU.org website, https://www.aclu.org/issues/juvenile-justice/school-prison-pipeline.
      See also: PBS.org website, http://www.pbs.org/wnet/tavissmiley/tsr/education-under-arrest/school-to-prison-pipeline-fact-sheet/.

252 *The value of education is priceless, but the price tag has become ridiculous:* National Center for Education Statistics. NCES.ed.gov website,
      https://nces.ed.gov/fastfacts/display.asp?id=76.

252 *Teddy Roosevelt…quote:* Roosevelt, T. (1910). "Citizenship in a Republic" speech at the Sorbonne, Paris, April 23, 1910. http://www
      .theodore-roosevelt.com/trsorbonnespeech.html.

253 *We can take a cue from Robert Fulghum's 1990s bestseller:* Fulghum, R. (1988). *All I Really Need to Know I Learned in Kindergarten.*
      New York: Ballantine Books.

Session Eighteen—Maintaining Your Mentalligence

257 *Alan Watts quote:* Goodreads website, https://www.goodreads.com/quotes/200854-the-only-way-to-make-sense-out-of-change-is.

259 *Quantum physics and string theories in science are showing that light is vibrating within each of us:* The Nature of Reality. PBS.org website,
      http://www.pbs.org/wgbh/nova/blogs/physics/2013/08/the-good-vibrations-of-quantum-field-theories/.

ABOUT THE AUTHOR

Dr. Kristen Lee, Ed.D., LICSW, known as "Dr. Kris," is a recovering perfectionist, proud Mama, and an internationally recognized award-winning author, clinician, researcher, educator, speaker, and activist with over twenty years of experience. As lead faculty for Behavioral Science at Northeastern University in Boston, her research and teaching interests include individual and organizational well-being and resilience, particularly for marginalized and underserved populations. She is the author of *Reset: Make the Most of Your Stress,* Winner of the Next Generation Indie Book Awards Motivational Book 2015. She is a regular contributor to the *Huffington Post* and *Psychology Today.* Dr. Kris's work has been featured on NPR and CPS radio.

Her signature ability to engage with a diverse range of audiences has led her to be invited to speak nationally and internationally to students, educators, health and mental health professionals, business leaders, and general audiences. Some of the venues she speaks at include Harvard University, Ted X, Virgin Pulse, and Johnson & Johnson. In her spare time, she can be found out on the running trails, attempting tricky yoga poses, eating peanut butter cups, and drinking kale juice—but not all at once.

Connect with her at: www.kristenlee.com or @TheRealDrKris.

INDEX